"A devotional in the most all-encompassing sense, *Seasons of Wonder* sets readers on a path that leads to a year filled with more hope, more sweetness, more grace, and more love. Light shines from this book like a star lamp. Like the very stars."

—MARGARET RENKL, author of *Late Migrations* and PEN Award winner

"Some devotional efforts heap contempt on human bodies and speak of the natural world as a disposable ladder to heaven. Bonnie Smith Whitehouse goes in the opposite direction. Reading *Seasons of Wonder* and following its instructions is an immersion in lived righteousness. Getting saved, in Professor Whitehouse's vision, is becoming more whole and less divided in our affections. She invites us to drop the psychic burden of dualistic thinking and to become more attuned to our own resources, whether it's the Bible, Alanis Morissette, the Tao Te Ching, or an inquisitive child in *Star Wars* pajamas. Receive her eloquent witness. It is a gift."

–DAVID DARK, author of *Life's Too Short to Pretend You're Not Religious*

"At a time when it has been increasingly difficult to comfortably show up as a lover of the Lord and an unapologetic Black woman, I found solace in *Seasons of Wonder*. By removing the oft-imagined barrier between the sacred and the secular, Whitehouse suggests that we can find faith work everywhere. It slipped its way into my heart and has been awarded a place on my list of most beloved titles."

—AMBER O'NEAL JOHNSTON, author of *A Place to Belong*

"In an age of disruption, we are scrambling to find meaningful ways to connect. *Seasons of Wonder* is a necessary and timeless gift—a wise, big-hearted, practical invitation to carve out time for holy gatherings with the people we love."

—IAN MORGAN CRON, author of *The Story of You*

"For all of us still trying to know God, Bonnie Smith Whitehouse has created this accessible, delightful, educational companion guide. The opposite of didactic, *Seasons of Wonder* proceeds from a premise we all need in our fractured world: that the spiritual life is not about dogmatic belief but curiosity and wonder. This book honors the mystic and the child of wonderment in each of us."

—HEATHER LANIER, author of *Raising a Rare Girl*

"Bonnie Smith Whitehouse offers a joyful gift to Christians and seekers in this practical and poetic devotional. This handbook for prayer and life feels like a chat with your wisest friend, and includes suggestions for all ages and stages of life."

—REV. CLAIRE BROWN, co-author of *New Directions for Holy Questions: Progressive Christian Theology for Families*

"In this lovely volume, Bonnie Smith Whitehouse amplifies the value and beauty of the liturgical calendar for families. This treasure trove of activities, crafts, recipes, and spiritual practices is tailored to each month of the year. *Seasons of Wonder* gives families the incentive to gather, wonder, reflect, and honor their Christian faith together, vibrantly."

—JULIE BOGART, author of *The Brave Learner* and *Raising Critical Thinkers* and founder of Brave Writer

"Bonnie Smith Whitehouse is a master at metaphor, prose, and possibility. To read her book, even if you can't always do the daily practices, is a gift that will open wonder and joy into your day."

—REV. DR. BECCA STEVENS, founder and president of Thistle Farms

SEASONS

OF

WONDER

SEASONS

OF

WONDER

MAKING THE ORDINARY SACRED
THROUGH PROJECTS, PRAYERS,
REFLECTIONS, AND RITUALS

BONNIE SMITH WHITEHOUSE

CONVERGENT

NEW YORK

Published in the United States by Convergent Books, an imprint of Random House, a division of Penguin Random House LLC, New York.

CONVERGENT BOOKS is a registered trademark and its C colophon is a trademark of Penguin Random House LLC.

Grateful acknowledgment is made to the following for permission to reprint previously published materials:
The Brothers of the Society of Saint John the Evangelist: "Altar Bread Recipe and Text of Advice," www.ssje.org/2017/07/31/altar-bread. Used by permission of the Brothers of the Society of Saint John the Evangelist. Friends United Press: "The Work of Christmas," poem excerpted from The Mood of Christmas and Other Celebrations by Howard Thurman, copyright © 1973 by Howard Thurman. Used by permission of Friends United Press. All rights reserved. Hope Publishing Company: "Lord of the Dance," words by Sydney Carter, copyright © 1963 by Stainer & Bell Ltd. (Admin. Hope Publishing Company, www.hopepublishing.com). Used by permission of Hope Publishing Company. All rights reserved. Margaret P. Jones: "God Is a Surprise," written by Harry H. Pritchett, Jr. Reprinted by permission of Margaret P. Jones. Sister Ruth Fox, OSB: "A Blessing for Righteous Indignation" by Sister Ruth Fox, OSB. Reprinted by permission of the author. Holly Tosco: "The Liturgical Colors Song" by Holly Tosco. Reprinted by permission of the composer.

LIBRARY OF CONGRESS CATALOGING-IN-PUBLICATION DATA
Names: Smith Whitehouse, Bonnie, author.
Title: Seasons of wonder / Bonnie Smith Whitehouse.
Description: New York: Convergent, [2022] | Includes bibliographical references.
Identifiers: LCCN 2022026365 (print) | LCCN 2022026366 (ebook) |
ISBN 9780593443316 (hardcover) | ISBN 9780593443323 (ebook)
Subjects: LCSH: Catholic families—Religious life—Miscellanea.
Classification: LCC BX2351 .S625 2022 (print) | LCC BX2351 (ebook) |
DDC 248.4/82—dc23/eng/20220720
LC record available at https://lccn.loc.gov/2022026365
LC ebook record available at https://lccn.loc.gov/2022026366

Printed in the United States of America on acid-free paper

crownpublishing.com

2 4 6 8 9 7 5 3

First Edition

Book design by Caroline Cunningham

FOR BEN, HENRY, AND PETER,

MY TRUE HOME AND THE LOVES OF MY LIFE,

AND FOR TALLU,

MY OLD SOUL SISTER

The Word is living, being, spirit, all verdant greening, all creativity. This Word manifests itself in every creature.
—HILDEGARD OF BINGEN (1098–1179)

Our goal should be to live life in radical amazement, [to] get up in the morning and look at the world in a way that takes nothing for granted. Everything is phenomenal; everything is incredible; never treat life casually. To be spiritual is to be amazed.
—ABRAHAM JOSHUA HESCHEL (1907–72)

CONTENTS

MARCH: EMBRACE MYSTERY   57

APRIL: WELCOME INCARNATION   93

MAY: ADORE CREATION   117

JUNE: COME ALIVE   137

INTRODUCTION

The world is charged with the grandeur of God.
—GERARD MANLEY HOPKINS

Not so long ago, I walked out barefoot into the night. Dewy blades of grass grazed my ankles, and the ground squelched a little with each step I took. A swath of stars shone overhead. Anchored to Mother Earth by the soles of my feet, I knew at once that I *was*, that I *am*, and that I *will be* of this vast creation. I'm downright *creaturely*. Holy ground is right here beneath these forty-something-year-old feet of mine. I closed my eyes and really noticed the atmosphere travel through my lungs' corridors, and I allowed myself to be shocked: to take in a breath, to stand barefoot on the ground, and to breathe in this glorious universe we share—it felt like a marvel.

I yearn for the shocking but joyful little moments like this, the wisps of awe that fill me with nothing but wonder at the simple awareness of my existence as a human creature in this glorious, gob-smacking universe of ours. To me, these shocking little moments are prayers, alleluias, and canticles of praise all rolled into one. As a mother, a professor, and a grown-up going about my day, I often long to return to what I would call these "wonder moments." Marveling at the intricate geometry of a dandelion while sitting in the front yard of my childhood. Marveling as I feel my own blood coursing through my body after swimming in a cold river. Marveling at the tenderness that wells up in my throat as a perfect stranger washes my feet as part of a Maundy Thursday ritual.

I believe these little startling moments of marvel to be manifestations of the divine, and I want to help you and the people you love hunt down, discover, and savor them together. This book is aimed at reminding you and your family (and by "family" I mean the people you love—your children, your spouse, your parents, your friends, your roommates, or your family of choice) that we are part of the wondrous, grand spirit of the universe.

Seasons of Wonder can easily be read and applied in solitude or in community. This book is designed to be a guide that helps you set aside a little time every week of the year to broaden your understanding of divinity, specifically the radical idea that everything is sacred. The birthplace of faith is not dogma, creed, or doctrine; faith emerges from awe, wonder, and joy. Just to be alive in creation is holy.

Month by month, week by week, *Seasons of Wonder* invites you and the people you hold dear to dwell in a universe charged with and animated by God's divine presence. In the following chapters, you will find a theme for each month. The monthly themes are linked to both the Earth's seasons and the liturgical seasons, which are an ancient way Christians have marked holy time. Each month invites us to think about an action. In January, our theme will be the ambitious but attainable idea that we might "transcend dualities." During the following month, February, we will "encounter contemplation." The month of March will be a time to "embrace mysteries," and then in April, we will "welcome incarnation." In May, we will "adore creation." June is a time to ponder what it means to "come alive," and in July, we will "cultivate resilience." August is a time devoted to savoring and cherishing "the holy pause," and throughout September, we will find ways to "gather courage." October is a month to "light a fire." Through November, we will "point to love," and as the calendar year closes, we will "look for the light" in December. Then, the circle begins again, and we shall seek to transcend dualities once again as a new calendar year begins in January. Each month's themes are carefully designed to link what is happening on the Earth to what is happening on the Christian calendar. Furthermore, each month will introduce new things to discover as a family, such as:

- liturgical seasons
- special days in the life of the Christian church
- simple but meaningful actions, recipes, or crafts that are fitting to the season.

HOW TO USE THIS BOOK

THE WEEKLY RITUAL: REFLECT, WONDER, TRY

At a brief but special time each week, you and your family will gather together simply and comfortably. Mealtimes are a natural way to gather, or you might choose a time for a family meeting (perhaps with a special treat). Each month includes opportunities to discover something new together about the story of God's love or God's creation. And each month offers simple recipes or crafts connected to the month's theme or the liturgical season. Within each month, four weeks focus on a simple action—like stargazing, birdwatching, breathing, or dreaming. These actions are deceptively simple superpowers! Each week will offer an opportunity to *reflect* on that action. Then, I will invite you to *wonder* (as a verb) about questions and varied *wonders* (as a noun) together; the question will gesture to something we can discover about love, the sacred, or creation. Finally, I will invite your family to *try* a simple action aimed at connecting you to each other and to the divine presence. And because moments that will shape your family life can occur throughout the year, I've included four additional weeks of activities that you can insert whenever they arise, such as opportunities to celebrate birthdays, recover from a sick day, travel together, and bless our homes.

SURPRISE, SURPRISE, GOD IS A SURPRISE

As an English professor, I've taught my students about metaphors for many years. Metaphors use comparison to help us imagine concepts that are difficult to grasp. We can't help but want to know what God is like, so we use metaphors and our holy imaginations to get closer to God. Some metaphors found in the Bible to help us imagine what God is like include: God as Mother Hen. God as Still Small Voice. God as Fountain. God as Potter (and humans as clay). God as Bread. God as Mother Bear. God as Light. God as King. God as Father. God as Eagle. God as Sun. God as Lamb. God as Vine. God as Woman in Labor. God as Midwife. The psalmist-poet-king David describes God as Shepherd, Rock, Fortress, Shield, Horn, and High Tower. Contemplating the varied ways humans have used what they've encountered in the world to imagine the divine makes me feel grateful and wistful.

I'd like to introduce you to a metaphor for God that may be new to you—one that has stayed with me since I was a little girl. At my Episcopal summer camp on a mountain in Tennessee, I learned a catchy, cheeky song written by the Very Rev. Harry Pritchett called "God Is a Surprise." Imagine counselors playing guitars under the trees, wearing tie-dyed T-shirts, and leading eighty kids making hand motions and dancing like wildlings. The chorus of that song remains instructive to my middle-aged self who is still trying to know God, and its words are:

> Surprise, surprise,
> God is a surprise, right before your eyes.
> It's baffling to the wise.
> Surprise, surprise, God is a surprise.
> Open up your eyes and see.

To consider God as *Surprise* is to have your expectations upended and transformed. Wonder is a stance of radical amazement, a posture, an overall disposition of being open in body, in mind, and in soul. Wonder is being willing to empty yourself, to release your preconceived notions so that you can be surprised by new information, whether that information be sensory, emotional, or intellectual. Wonder is therefore a state of vulnerability that we can work to cultivate in ourselves and in others. It seems to me that the foundation of a faithful life is not a set of rules and certainties. The foundation of a faithful life is living with awe, wonder, and astonishment. When the lenses through which you see the world are awe and wonder, you find yourself looking for God as Surprise all the time. Surprise can come when you're listening to a friend tell a story about her life before you knew her, studying microbiology, singing in a grand cathedral, encountering a conversation online, harvesting tomatoes, or taking a walk through a bustling city. When you live with tender, vulnerable, openhearted, awe-filled faith, you're always on the lookout for opportunities to connect the divine and the ordinary.

For more than twenty years, I have been a professor who teaches students about reading, writing, and ways of knowing. As I reflect on what I have learned, I believe the most important takeaway from my professional experiences is this: There's nothing more valuable than curiosity, than a student who is willing to have their mind changed, and thus is open to the world. So many of us walk into experiences, conversations, and situations bringing the knowledge we have memorized from the past. In our minds, we rehearse what we are going to say next before *actually experiencing* what is being said by others. We walk through our lives often overestimating how others are perceiving what we say, how we look, or what we do. And so, we may miss what glorious things may be happening before our very eyes. But, when you consider God as *Surprise,* you walk into the world with a hand stretched open wide and a big, vulnerable heart. When you consider God as *Surprise,* you're always on the hunt for people, places, and moments that illuminate that ultimate illusion: the illusion that we are separate from God.

THE WORLD AS GOD'S BODY

I am a follower of Jesus—a Christian—and I have been an active member of the Episcopal Church throughout my entire life. I am a member of what's called the *laity*, which means I have not taken holy orders, but I take my ministry as a baptized Christian seriously, particularly when it comes to prayer, worship, theological thinking and study, and discerning my calling as a child of God and, thus, a part of God's creation. Recently, a friend told me that she didn't think of me as a "person of the church" but that she saw me more as a "person of the Earth." My immediate response to that comment was this: "But, the church *is* the whole of creation!"

Many people think of "church" only as a building or an institution. One of the main aspirations of this book is to help us envision "church" and "God" using our holy imaginations. To think bigger. To "think" with our bodies. What if, for example, we regard the Earth not as a collection of rocks, trees, seas, and creatures, but as the *body of God*? How might this change every step we make? How might regarding the Earth as God's body affect every nickel we spend? The votes we cast? The words we say to ourselves and to others? The idea of God enfleshed in the world is ancient and faithful.

Richard Rohr, a Franciscan priest and writer, has helped people rediscover something important about Jesus, and that is the often-overlooked fact that Christ is not Jesus' last name! Rather, *Christ* is Jesus' historical and cosmic *purpose*. Rohr explains that in Jesus, the formless (God) takes on a form (human being), thus making God easier to love. *Christ* is *not* a surname but an old idea—an idea much older and bigger than Jesus of Nazareth or the Christian religion. *Christ* means "the anointed one," "the Body of God," or "God made flesh in the world." Jesus of Nazareth is the embodied, incarnate version of that Spirit, a presence with whom Rohr says we can "fall in love."

If we take this idea seriously—and believe me, I do!—then we can fall in love with those elements of "the Body of God" day after day, month after month, season after season, year after year. If we take this idea seriously, then all of us are infused with the divine. This is what the radical, life-altering concept of incarnation is all about, and it can and should change everything about how we see ourselves, our friends and families, our planet and the creatures and flora on it, and the strangers we encounter on the sidewalk or online. Consider that these little shocking moments of wonder are charged manifestations of the grand presence of Christ in me, in you, and in this dazzling, vast—and imperiled—blue planet we call our beloved home.

EQUIPMENT

The earliest Christians gathered in homes—not in grand cathedrals. They sat around tables sharing simple meals. They warmed their hands by hearth fires. Worshipping at home in small communities can be a beautiful way to dwell in wonder with your loved ones, and the equipment you'll need is simple and inexpensive. Some suggested items to have on hand include:

+ A singing bowl or bell, to call your people together
+ A Bible (NRSV with Apocrypha or another modern translation), *The Book of Common Prayer,* and *A New Zealand Book of Common Prayer,* if you can get one. Two other suggested titles are *Common Prayer: A Liturgy for Ordinary Radicals* by Shane Claiborne and *New Directions for Holy Questions* by Claire Brown and Anita Peebles.
+ Candles
+ A special oil for anointing. I like to use fresh olive oil infused with a few drops of lavender essential oil, but any plant-based carrier oil you have on hand will do.
+ A rosary or chain of beads for prayer (see more on page 72)
+ A special bowl or container for gathering prayers on little slips of paper
+ Consider together: What are some simple pieces of artwork your family holds sacred? Perhaps a photograph of a cherished person or meaningful place, a statue of St. Francis, a painting of Mary, or a drawing made by a child or a loved one.

CREATE YOUR OWN CHRONICLE OF WONDER

To my great surprise, one of my favorite courses in graduate school was on a method of qualitative analysis called narrative inquiry. Narrative inquiry asks: How do we make meaning together? How do the stories we have inherited and the stories we tell help us understand the world and our place in it? Narrative inquiry forms the foundation of the questions, conversations, and endeavors I encourage you and your loved ones to employ throughout the seasons. As you wonder together, you are learning how to know and love one another through that richest and most ancient form of data collection: telling, hearing, and collecting stories. I urge you to appoint someone to log notes throughout the year; believe me when I say you will treasure looking back on a record of your gatherings!

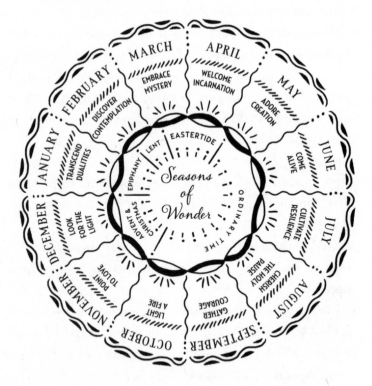

THE SOLAR CALENDAR AND THE LITURGICAL CALENDAR

Imagine time not as a long straight line but as wheels within wheels. *Seasons of Wonder* draws from two sources of organizing time: the solar calendar and the liturgical calendar. The solar calendar is composed of twelve months made up of 365 days per year, roughly the amount of time it takes for the Earth to revolve around our sun. From January to December, we organize time around days, weeks, months, rites of passage, holidays, weather, and so on.

But another way to order time is the Christian liturgical calendar, which is part of life in Catholic, Episcopal, Anglican, Orthodox, Lutheran, Presbyterian, and Methodist churches, as well as many other denominations. The liturgical seasons are: Advent, Christmas, Epiphany, Lent, Easter, Pentecost, and Ordinary Time (or the green season). Each of these seasons has particular moods, feelings, prayers, and practices. Each season is even associated with a particular color! The liturgical calendar implores us to consider all time as sacred: It reflects the life of the Church; the life, teachings, death, and resurrection of Jesus, as well as patterns we find in the natural world—planting, harvesting, and coming back to life.

GATHERING AS A CIRCLE

> It is all a circle, the ancestors said—an endless circle within a circle. The drum is a circle. The dance ground is a circle. The Earth is a circle. There is no us or them, no top or bottom, no beginning or end, no lines of division—only a seamless embrace. The answer is within. It has existed since long before time began, and it will be there long after the last campfire fades. For even if we are not there to see it, the stars will make their great circle of the heavens to mark their way home.
> —STEVEN CHARLESTON, *Ladder to the Light*[2]

When we come together each week, we are like the earliest followers of Jesus' way. When we gather around a table in a circle, we make everyone's faces, expressions, and responses visible to one another. We are not gathering as a line with one person in charge and others following. When we gather in circles with our family and friends, we link arms (sometimes literally and often figuratively), strengthen our connections and bonds, and even allow new rituals and traditions to emerge. When we gather as a circle season after season, we participate in the eternal, since, like circles, the seasons form cycles of birth, death, and rebirth.

USING LANGUAGE TO EXPRESS THE DIVINE

There are so many ways to speak of the divine presence, and generally, I will follow people from different religious traditions both within Christianity and throughout the world's religions in using the words *Spirit, God, Creator,* and *Love.* My faith has been enriched by Buddhist teachings on meditation, peace, mindfulness, and suffering. As I have learned about the Great Spirit of Native wisdom, my understanding of courage, resilience, hope, and prayer has deepened. I happen to be a professor who studies writing and stories, but even as a professional student of words and letters, I am just beginning to learn about how to use language to express the Divine.

The story of what to call a Christian, a follower of Jesus, has evolved over time. For the first five centuries of Christianity, followers of Jesus called themselves *People of the Way* as they sought to enact the teachings of Jesus. The phrase *People of the Way* speaks deeply to me because it describes those who seek to engage in meaningful action. Bishop Michael Curry has offered "The Way of Love" as a rich but simple way for describing a Christian life. (See page 6.) What language for religious practice and spirit speaks to you and to your loved ones? As you use *Seasons of Wonder,* you and your loved ones will have many opportunities to talk together about finding language to describe the divine presence.

Toward the end of her life, Dr. Maya Angelou gave an interview in which she said:

> God loves me. It still humbles me that this force that made leaves and fleas and stars and rivers—and you—loves me. Me, Maya Angelou. It's amazing. I can do anything—and do it well! Any good thing—I can do it. That's why I am who I am, because God loves me, and I'm amazed at it and grateful for it.

Dr. Angelou's words ring true. As my years increase, my beliefs seem to be deepening. But also as my years increase, the absolutes and rules that make up the ecosystem of my beliefs seem to be waning. Talk about a surprise! As time goes on, my amazement and gratitude for God's love grows: for the people, the creatures, the land, the Earth, the stars that blanket us from above whether it's day or night. I lean on three essential teachings: Jesus asks that we love one another as "I have loved you." Jesus asks that we wash one another's feet. And Jesus asks that we share bread and wine together. Together, we can respond to those three wise and simple requests—to share, to serve, and to love—as we reflect on stories of the past, dwell in moments of the present, and care for creation together as the seasons ahead unfold.

A WORD ABOUT LITURGY

In May of 2007, I had been facilitating a study abroad trip in southern Africa with thirty undergraduate students and two faculty colleagues. I was thirtysomething, tired of leading, ready for respite, and dusty from walking the dirt roads of Gaborone, Botswana, when we arrived for Mass that Sunday morning. The Anglican Cathedral of the Holy Cross is a contemporary sanctuary near the central business district of Gaborone, and on that May morning, many from our group were attending the service. Though we were on the other side of the world from our home in America, the service, which alternated between Setswana and English, proceeded exactly the same as it did back home in Nashville. The order of service was common, the readings from scripture were the same all around the world, and following Holy Communion, we were sent out with the same fortifying words: "Send us now into the world in peace, and grant us strength and courage to love and serve you with gladness and singleness of heart."

I have been refreshed, restored, and fortified by liturgy in similar ways throughout my life. There are many liturgical churches in the Christian tradition: Catholic, Episcopalian, Anglican, Lutheran, Disciples of Christ, American Baptist, United Methodist, United Church of Christ, to name but a few. I have spent my entire life as a devoted member of a liturgical church. Over many years kneeling, listening, learning, leading, I have come to believe that faith is not only something we feel; faith is something we *do*. Faith is *work*, and in this sense, faith is like love or hope. We don't *feel* it so much as we *show up for* it and *do* it. And liturgy is part of the faithful work of the people.

The word *liturgy* derives from the Greek word *leitourgia*, which means "work for the people." Many are stunned to learn that *leitourgia* comes from *litus ergos* or "public service." I wrote this book because I believe that when we conceive of liturgy as public service—as work for the people—new possibilities, understandings, relationships, and practices emerge. Liturgy enables a small gathering or a larger community to craft praise, prayer, remembrance, and communion together. In those times when you cannot summon the words or when your voice shakes, the liturgy is there. Perhaps most important, liturgy reminds us that we can be collaborators with the Creator.

In my life, the cadence and rhythm of *The Book of Common Prayer* forms worship, and without a doubt, it is the most important work of literature on my bookshelf. I have a copy in my bedroom, a copy on my desk at home, and a copy on my office desk. Without *The Book of Common Prayer*, I am convinced I would not have become an English professor. *The Book of Common Prayer* is the link between my chosen profession and the wonderings about my calling. It's the language of my heart, my faith. I reach for it when I cannot summon the words. Samuel Johnson told James Boswell that he knew of "no good prayers but those in the Book of Common Prayer." Centuries later, American writer Elizabeth Gilbert wrote, "There's no trouble in this world so serious that it can't be cured with a hot bath, a glass of whiskey, and *The Book of Common Prayer*."

In 1549, Thomas Cranmer, the archbishop of Canterbury, compiled and composed *The Book of Common Prayer*, the first corpus of worship in the English language. James Wood, a staff writer for *The New Yorker*, tells us that Cranmer "wanted a prayer book in English, one that could be understood by ordinary people, even those who could not read." Cranmer borrowed from *The Sarum Missal*, a handbook for monks written in Latin, as well as Byzantine rites and liturgies from the Reformed church in Cologne.[3] And, as Wood reminds us, Cranmer "wrote dozens of new prayers and collects, in a language at once grand and simple, heightened and practical, archaic and timeless."

Engraved on my own heart are lines like this one from the liturgy before Holy Eucharist found in the 1979 *Book of Common Prayer*: "At your command all things came to be: the vast expanse of interstellar space, galaxies, suns, the planets in their courses, and this fragile Earth, our island home." I've said those words thousands of times, and the repetition makes me feel the fragility of *our island home* deep in my bones. My passion for creation stems from thinking of our Earth as a fragile island. And these lines from the burial service cast grief as a praise song: "All we go down to the dust; yet even at the grave we make our song: Alleluia, alleluia, alleluia." It's hard to express how much these very words have shaped my own theology and way of being in the world; thanks to the burial liturgy, I truly cannot pass by a cemetery or see a gravestone without thinking about making an Alleluia.

Liturgy, which is the work of the people, can root and form us. Furthermore, liturgy frees and liberates our imaginations. In this book, readers will be introduced to or reminded of the liturgical seasons and invited to orient time around liturgies. The circle of the liturgical year transforms our days into sacred time.

DISCOVER: STAYING GROUNDED THROUGH CYCLES OF YEARS AND DAYS[4]

The Revised Common Lectionary is a three-year cycle of readings that follow the life of Jesus. Year One focuses on stories about Jesus' life and teachings from the Gospel of Matthew, Year Two focuses on the Gospel of Mark, and Year Three focuses on the Gospel of Luke. Stories about Jesus' life and teachings from the Gospel of John are intertwined throughout the three-year cycle.

The circle of the church year begins on the first Sunday of Advent and ends on the Saturday preceding the first Sunday of Advent. Christmas is a fixed date (December 25). Easter is a moveable feast that occurs the first Sunday after the full moon that falls on or after March 21, the spring equinox. The date of Easter determines both the beginning of Lent (Ash Wednesday) and the date of Pentecost (the fiftieth day of Eastertide). The seasons of the church year are Advent, Christmas, Epiphany, Lent, Easter, Pentecost, and "the green season" or Ordinary Time. The calendar of the church year can be found on pages 15–33 of *The Book of Common Prayer;* additional feast days and holy days can be found on pages 880–85 of *The Book of Common Prayer.*

Many years ago, my boys and their little friends at church memorized "The Liturgical Colors Song" by Holly Tosco:

Purple and green, red and white,
Special colors of the year.
Purple and green, red and white
Remind us of the Light.

Green is for growing time
Purple in preparation.
Red is for Pentecost
White is in Celebration.

Purple is the color for preparation—the seasons of Advent and Lent in which we prepare for Christ's birth and resurrection. The fancy gold-and-white chasubles and vestments are worn to celebrate Easter, All Saints' Day, Christmas. And bright red comes out for Pentecost, recalling flames and the fiery energy of the Holy Spirit. By far, the color green is worn and displayed most often, for green symbolizes "the green season," the growing season of Ordinary Time. Ordinary Time is a time for the Earth to grow but also offers opportunities for *us* to learn, change, take root, and flourish.

The Book of Common Prayer provides liturgies for each day, beginning with Morning Prayer through Compline. The order of daily liturgies is: Morning Prayer, Noonday Prayer, Evening Prayer, Compline.

Advent

Advent, a time of preparation, takes its name from a Latin word for "coming." Advent begins the fourth Sunday before Christmas and concludes the day before Christmas.

Christmas

Christmas lasts twelve days, from Christmas Day until January 5, which is the day before Epiphany. The season of Christmas includes Christmas Day, as well as the Feast of the Holy Name of Jesus (January 1).

Epiphany

Epiphany (January 6) is a season to celebrate the manifestations of Christ to the people on Earth: his birth, the visits of the Magi, Jesus' baptism, and the Wedding at Cana.[1] February 2 is Candlemas or the Presentation of Jesus in the temple.

Lent

Lent takes its name from an Old English word meaning "spring" and is the season of penitence and fasting in preparation for the Paschal feast or Easter. Lent is forty days from Ash Wednesday through Holy Saturday, omitting Sundays. The final three days of Lent are the Triduum: Maundy Thursday, Good Friday, and Holy Saturday.

Easter

Easter takes its name from the Anglo-Saxon spring goddess Eostre and is the annual feast celebrating the resurrection. The Great Vigil of Easter begins at sunset on Holy Saturday. Easter Day is the first Sunday after the full moon that falls on or after March 21, the spring equinox. Ascension Day is celebrated on the Thursday that occurs forty days after Easter Sunday.

Pentecost

Pentecost occurs fifty days after Easter and celebrates the Holy Spirit. Trinity Sunday is the Sunday following Pentecost.

Ordinary Time

The "green season" or Ordinary Time indicates those parts of the liturgical year that are not in Advent, Christmas, Epiphany, Lent, Easter, or Pentecost. Ordinary Time is called the "green season" because it's a time for growth and for living out the callings of the Christian faith by focusing on Jesus' life and teachings and discovering how we encounter, embrace, and embody the Holy Spirit and the Way of Love in our lives today. August 6 is the feast of Transfiguration. November 1 is All Saints' Day. Christ the King Sunday, the Sunday before the first Sunday of Advent, marks the last Sunday of the church year. Ordinary Time is between Pentecost and the first Sunday of Advent.

Honoring Mary

We especially honor Mary, the mother of Jesus, on the Annunciation of Mary (March 25) and the Visitation of Mary (May 31).

A HYMN TO WONDER

I was born in the American South in 1975, and I didn't even know of a woman who was a priest or a minister until I was in my mid-teens. To this day in 2022, I still have relatives who would let a woman teach a Sunday school class full of girls but don't believe a woman is fit to teach teenage boys in Sunday school, much less preach about the good news, stand behind an altar, or dare to write a book like this one. My mother sometimes quips that the only women who were allowed behind the altar in her day were the women who were pushing a vacuum cleaner. She jokes, but I can hear pain in her voice.

Though she did find her way behind the altar as a lay minister, that's not how I picture my mom at her most wondrous: Instead, I think of how she can be walking along a path at breakneck speed, and, out of the corner of her eye, she will spy one four-leaf clover among a massive cluster of the common clover that has only three leaves. She'll stop, bend down, gently pry the four-leaf clover out of the earth, and keep on moving, as if nothing particularly unusual or astonishing has just happened. Over the years, she has amassed hundreds—if not thousands—of four-leaf clovers and preserved them between two pieces of clear tape or carefully pressed them between the pages of a book. In a world that hasn't always welcomed her gifts, she has taught me not only to be on the hunt for such astonishments but to *expect* to be awed by that which appears ordinary. Time and time again, she has shown me sacred wonders that others might simply pass right on by.

Likewise, I've collected quotations, voices from many different times, places, cultures, and traditions. As a member of Generation X and a child of the 1980s, I can't help but see myself as a maker of mixtapes. In my younger days, I would spend hours writing letters to my nearest and dearest friends . . . and I'd really sweeten the effort by folding those handwritten letters around mixtapes I'd labored over for hours. Just as I once worked hard to assemble the mixtapes I'd spend hours making, decorating, and wrapping up to mail off to my kindred spirits or give to my secret crushes, I've worked hard behind the scenes to hunt for, select, and orchestrate the placement of the diverse voices you'll find throughout this book.

But I'm also a professor of English, so I have tried very hard not to rip quotations out of their contexts or mischaracterize them for my own use. Like my mom will gently pick those four-leaf clovers out of the earth, I have attempted to gently pry quotations out of their original sources so that *they* can stand before you in their glory and distinctiveness for a few moments in time.

Above all, I have tried to assemble a chorus of voices from many different times, places, and traditions that come together in this book to sing a hymn to wonder. And as your days, months, and years increase, I hope you and the people you love will add your own voices to that hymn.

JANUARY

TRANSCEND DUALITIES

There are more things in heaven and Earth, Horatio, than are dreamt of in your philosophy.
—WILLIAM SHAKESPEARE, *Hamlet*, act 1, scene 5

Welcome to January! January is named for Janus, a Roman god known for having two faces. One of Janus's faces peered backward to the past, and the other looked forward to the future. Sculptures of Janus were often attached to gates, and like Janus, we are perched at the end of one year and at the beginning of another. What better time than now to think through some of the deep ideas and beliefs many of us hold? For this month, consider what it might mean to *transcend dualities*. That's a very fancy phrase, so let's simplify.

Right/wrong. Mind/body. Me/you. Male/female. Heads/tails. Tradition/ change. Visible/invisible. These are just a few common examples of dualistic thinking, and many of us find ourselves deeply rooted in such *either/or* thinking. Some Christians even define themselves by asking dualistic questions like: What do you believe? What don't you believe? Who is in our club? Who is out? What if, instead of centering Christianity around checklists of beliefs, we centered Christianity around the practice and ritual of gathering and celebrating together in hope, respect, and friendship?

Dualistic thinking burdens the imagination. Minds and systems constructed around dualistic thinking have prompted many to separate, fight, and be defensive instead of embracing the mystery, the wonder, and even the wildness that characterized Jesus' life and teachings.

For example, ponder the parables Jesus used in his teachings; just when you think you might understand one, you realize you actually have no idea what the lesson is supposed to be and you find yourself back inside the mystery. Or, imagine Mary Magdalene's eyes wide with wonder when she realized the stone at his tomb had been rolled away. And how wild it was when Jesus spit in the dirt and knelt down to make mud to rub in the eyes of that blind man he healed!

Leave *good/bad, right/wrong,* and *us/them* behind for the time being, and give your imagination permission to exist and to wander. Jesus taught mercy, grace, reconciliation, forgiveness, healing, hope, and love, and these radical ideas surmounted dualities like a January snowstorm overcomes the landscape.

- ✦ What if we embarked on this new year with a resolution *not to settle for easy answers?*
- ✦ What if we consider that being faithful is more about *what we do* than what we believe?
- ✦ What if we set aside those false choices that dualistic thinking forces us to make?
- ✦ What if a period of confusion can lead to a state of illumination?

January Creation Care Challenge: Enjoy your leftovers! All the time, energy, and resources it took to plant, grow, harvest, transport, purchase, and prepare the food is wasted when we don't reuse. We all have leftovers after the holiday season, so get in the habit of eating leftovers regularly this month. You don't necessarily have to rely on a recipe. Use your imagination, and challenge yourself to transform your leftovers into casseroles, salads, stir-fry, sandwiches, or soups.

GATHER & RESOLVE

We cannot love God unless we love each other, and to love we must know each other.

—DOROTHY DAY

A New Year's Resolution: Welcome to this new year. Each family member gathered in this space is beloved by God. What if, at this special time each and every week this year, you resolved to look in the eyes of these people you hold dearest in this life and remind them of their belovedness? By spending this short amount of time together every week this year, you are transforming an ordinary meeting into a sacred gathering. You are blessing and consecrating one another by dwelling in God's presence. Isn't that a resolution worth keeping?

Resolve to gather weekly in the ardent hope that, by gathering, we will learn day by day to love each other more and more. Where shall we gather? At what time? What shall we wear? I recommend keeping everything as casual, fun, and simple as possible. Maybe someone will bring a snack, and maybe someone will light a candle. Think together about how and when your gatherings will occur. But most important, think together about the atmosphere you'd like to create during your gatherings of loved ones. One of my mentors says that when she gathers people together, she works hard to create environments where trust exists. Why? Because where there is trust, *risk* occurs. And when we feel free to take a risk, we are more likely to speak the wild truths that live deep in our hearts. May this weekly gathering become an ecosystem where you and your families can be real, can be vulnerable, and can dwell in the presence of God's liberating love.

WONDER: What is something that makes you beautifully unique at the table? After you speak about yourself, go around again, and point out something about each other person at the table that you find uniquely beautiful. Listen, and let this discussion inspire you to proclaim something new you'd like to try to learn, do, or express as this year begins.

TRY: Use paper and markers to write a blessing that can begin each of your weekly gatherings this year. Find a way for everyone to contribute, and display your finished blessing nearby so you can say it together at the beginning of each weekly gathering. If you'd like an example, the template below might help:

We are gathered together at this table to_____.
We thank you for_____.
We praise you for_____.
We look to you for_____.
With joy and hope, we look forward to_____.

DISCOVER: THE WAY OF LOVE

The Most Reverend Michael Curry, presiding bishop of the Episcopal Church, reminds us that in the first century, those who were followers of Jesus of Nazareth were not called "Christians." They were called "followers of the Way." Bishop Curry invites us all to nurture families and communities devoted to the liberating, life-giving love of Jesus by following these practices, or the Way of Love:

TURN: Pause, listen, and choose to follow Jesus

LEARN: Reflect on Scripture, especially Jesus' life and teachings

PRAY: Dwell intentionally with God each day

WORSHIP: Gather in community weekly to thank, praise, and draw near to God

BLESS: Share faith and unselfishly give and serve

GO: Cross boundaries, listen deeply, and live like Jesus

REST: Receive the gift of God's grace, peace, and restoration

You can find a wealth of resources on the Way of Love at episcopal church.org.

The Way of Love is an aspirational invitation. How might you and those you love respond?

DISCOVER: EPIPHANY

The Magi were overwhelmed with wonder and joy when they found baby Jesus after following a star. The Christian calendar commemorates their visit on January 6 with the Feast of Epiphany. Traditionally, Christmas decorations are left up until the Eve of Epiphany (or Twelfth Night).

Celebrate Epiphany together by chalking your door, building a fire, and hosting a Twelfth Night party. Chalk the door above the main entrance to your home on Epiphany with a blessing and as a way to commemorate the hospitality Mary and Joseph showed to the three kings. Use chalk to write, for example, the pattern "20+C+M+B+23." The first and last numbers stand for the year (i.e., 2023), the crosses stand for Jesus, and the letters stand for the Latin blessing *Christus Mansionem Benedicat* (May Christ bless this home), as well as Caspar, Melchior, and Balthazar—the names of the Magi. Learn about the Magi's gifts of gold, frankincense, and myrrh. Gold, of course, was a gift for a king. Frankincense is derived from the Boswellia tree and promotes a feeling of relaxation and well-being. Traditionally used in prayer and meditation, frankincense has strong healing and cleansing properties; see page 33 to learn how to make candles infused with frankincense. My friend Jen makes a soothing body butter using frankincense because it is known to calm inflamed skin, as well as alleviate feelings of grief, lonelinesss, and anxiety. Myrrh is a resin extracted from thorny Commiphora trees, and was and is extremely valuable. Myrrh was an oil used for purification rituals and to anoint bodies, including Jesus', at burial.

As you gather together, light candles and say the Epiphany prayers found in *The Book of Common Prayer* or the Revised Common Lectionary. Have everyone make their own crown! Light candles or light incense, and have each person wonder aloud what it feels like for a king to come to the world in the form of a baby. Finally, bring the Christmas season to a close by banging on drums or playing any instruments you have while singing a loud and boisterous version of "We Three Kings."

You can also mark Epiphany with your loved ones by watching or reading the story of *Amahl and the Night Visitors* by Gian Carlo Menotti. In the story, a poor boy and his mother host the three kings who are on their way to Bethlehem to see the newborn baby Jesus.

DISCOVER: CARNIVAL SEASON

Celebrated in many cultures around the world, Carnival begins when Epiphany closes on January 6 (sometimes called Kings' Day) and continues until midnight on Mardi Gras (or Fat Tuesday or Shrove Tuesday). Carnival is a time for parades, parties, masks, and general revelry. Traditionally, Carnival is a season to consume all the animal products, butter, and sweets in the home so they won't be wasted when the Lenten season of fasting and sacrifice begins. King Cakes are a special Carnival tradition that originated in France and made their way to New Orleans in the mid-nineteenth century (see page 10 for recipe).

At midnight on Mardi Gras, Carnival comes to an abrupt close as Ash Wednesday marks the first day of Lent. In New Orleans, firefighters and police officers sweep Bourbon Street at midnight on Mardi Gras, and the party comes to an end because the solemn season of Lent has begun.

MAKE: A KING CAKE

A King Cake is an audaciously rich and vibrant cake made of a brioche dough and topped with icing decorated with purple, green, and gold sugars. King Cakes can be served on January 6 (Kings' Day) through Mardi Gras (Shrove Tuesday). To add to the wildness of the King Cake, a plastic baby symbolizing baby Jesus is tucked in the cake before it's served. In France the youngest person at the gathering determines who gets which slice of cake, and then whoever gets the baby Jesus wears a crown and gets to be "king" and boss everyone around for the rest of the day. At some gatherings, whoever gets the baby buys the next King Cake or hosts the next party. In Mexico whoever gets the baby Jesus has to buy everyone tamales at Candlemas!

KING CAKE[1]

SERVES 10 TO 12.

INGREDIENTS

For the cake

> 1 cup lukewarm milk, about 110°F
> 3 tablespoons sugar
> 2 tablespoons dry yeast
> 3¾ cups all-purpose flour
> 1 cup melted unsalted butter
> 5 large egg yolks, beaten
> 1 teaspoon vanilla extract
> 1 teaspoon freshly grated lemon zest
> 1 tablespoon ground cinnamon
> Freshly grated nutmeg

For the icing

2 cups confectioners' sugar

¼ cup condensed milk

1 teaspoon freshly squeezed lemon juice

Purple, green, and gold decorative sugars

1 plastic baby to hide in the cake after baking. You can find these in the baby shower aisle at party stores.

DIRECTIONS

Make the cake: Pour the warm milk into a large bowl. Whisk in the sugar, yeast, and a heaping tablespoon of flour. Mix until both the sugar and the yeast have dissolved, bubbles develop on the surface of the milk, and the mixture begins to foam. Then whisk in the butter, egg yolks, vanilla, and lemon zest. Add the remaining flour, the cinnamon, and the nutmeg. Fold the dry ingredients into the wet ingredients with a large rubber spatula. After the dough comes together, pulling away from the sides of the bowl, shape it into a large ball.

Knead the dough on a floured surface until it is smooth and elastic, about 15 minutes. Then put the dough back into the bowl and cover with plastic wrap. Set the bowl aside in a draft-free area to let it rise until the dough has doubled in volume (about 90 minutes).

Preheat the oven to 375°F. Once the dough has risen, punch it down and divide it into three equal pieces. Roll each piece of dough between your palms into a long strip, making three ropes of equal length. Braid the three ropes around one another. Then form the braided loaf into a circle, pinching the ends together to seal. Gently lay the braided dough on a nonstick cookie sheet. Let it rise until it doubles in size, about 30 minutes. Once it has doubled in size, place the cookie sheet in the oven. Bake until the braid is golden brown, about 30 minutes. Remove the cake from the oven. Carefully transfer the cake to a wire rack and allow to cool for 30 minutes.

Make the icing: While the cake is cooling, whisk together the confectioners' sugar, condensed milk, and lemon juice in a bowl until the icing is smooth and easy to spread. If the icing is too thick, add a bit more condensed milk. If it's too thin, add a little more confectioners' sugar. Once the cake has cooled, spread the icing over the top of the cake and sprinkle with purple, green, and gold decorative sugars while the icing is still wet. Tuck the plastic baby into the underside of the cake and, using a spatula, slide the cake onto a platter. *Laissez les bons temps rouler!*

STARGAZE

If the stars should appear one night in a thousand years, how would men believe and adore; and preserve for many generations the remembrance of the city of God which had been shown! But every night come out these envoys of beauty, and light the universe with their admonishing smile.

—RALPH WALDO EMERSON

We just celebrated Epiphany on January 6, and this week marks an opportunity to consider the wondrous stars that shine above. As you gaze toward the heavens with your loved ones, imagine the Magi, who followed a star to find the holy family. Planet Earth has been around for about 4.5 billion years, and the galaxies are filled with brilliant, shimmering stars. Sometimes it looks as if the stars have been thrown across the night sky by some ancient gardener scattering luminous seeds. Planting our feet on the ground and gazing up at the sky helps us put ourselves, our prayers, and our stories in perspective! We exist in a moment that's microscopic when you consider the massive expanse of space and time.

WONDER: Stars surround us, whether we see them or not. We often think of the stars "coming out" at night, but they are there all the time. Just knowing that the stars and their light blaze above while the sun shines during the day gives me a jolt of awe. In his resplendent poem

"The Peace of Wild Things," Wendell Berry refers to "the day-blind stars waiting with their light." How might recognizing the steadfast presence of starlight help us resist dualistic, on/off, either/or types of thinking?

TRY: Wayfinding is the art and science of determining your place in the cosmos and navigating where you want to go, and you can learn more about wayfinding by watching the wonderful film *Moana*. After you watch the film, bundle up and stand outside under the winter starlight with the people you love. There's nothing quite so wonderful in the world! If you can, try to find a place where there's not much light pollution and give your eyes about twenty minutes to adjust to the dark. Stand together silently and gaze up at the starry heavens. What do you see? Can you spot the Pleiades? Orion? What does stargazing stir up inside of you? If you are in an urban environment with a lot of light pollution, you can visit a planetarium, or try to find a rooftop with dark sky overhead, or even just focus on the moon or more visible planets like Venus or Saturn. Apps like SkySafari or Star Walk will help you locate and identify the stars shining above you.

MAKE: A CONSTELLATION LAMP[2]

Celebrate Epiphany by making a constellation lamp. This is a great way to end a day after tidying up after Christmas, especially when kids are still out of school. If you don't have a lamp around your house that you can use, a thrift shop is a great place to find an inexpensive option for this project.

EQUIPMENT

Blue and black acrylic paint
Paintbrush
Painter's tape
Lampshade (with a plastic barrier inside so paint doesn't bleed through)
Lamp that works with the lampshade
Printed constellation map
Needles (3 or 4 of varying widths)
Silver or white embroidery thread

DIRECTIONS

Paint your lampshade using blue and black paint. As you paint, try to make it look multidimensional like the night sky. Be patient . . . the lampshade absolutely must dry completely before you do the next step.

In the meantime, print out a map of the constellations. Use scissors to cut the map into several pieces, and, once the paint has dried, use painter's tape to fasten the map around the circumference of your painted lampshade.

Notice how some of the stars on the map are bigger (closer) and some are smaller (farther away). Use your needles of varying widths to poke holes right through the lampshade where the stars are located on the map. Vary the size of the holes by using needles of different widths so you can tell the different magnitudes of the stars. You don't have to punch a hole for every single star, but do make sure you have several constellations. Carefully remove the map.

Thread your smallest needle, using three strands of silver or white embroidery thread. Tie a knot in the end, and stitch through the holes you punched that comprise several of your constellations. Choose some of your favorite constellations to connect through your stitches, or choose some of the most recognizable constellations, like the Big Dipper or Orion, the Hunter. Leave lots of stars and constellations unconnected and unstitched. Find a spot in your bedroom for the lamp. Secure the lampshade on your lamp, turn on your lamp, and turn out the lights to see how the constellation lamp lights up the walls of your bedroom.

The constellations you punched and stitched into your lamp are the same stars the Magi gazed up at as they sought out the baby Jesus.

WRESTLE

Do I contradict myself?
Very well then I contradict myself,
(I am large, I contain multitudes.)
            —WALT WHITMAN, "Song of Myself"

D oes this week's theme, the word *wrestle,* surprise you? Maybe the
    word conjures up a vision of brothers and sisters rolling around on
the floor together, half fighting and half laughing. Or maybe you think
of a story from Genesis in which Jacob wrestles with God and receives
a blessing when morning comes after a long night of struggle. To wonder is also a kind of wrestling, and it is good when loved ones resolve
that it's healthy to wrestle together. We all wrestle with doubts, questions, and complex feelings that we have within us. We all wrestle with
unbelief and unknowing, especially when the world seems unkind or
unfair and especially when people or creatures or the land is disre-
garded or unloved.

Rachel Held Evans eloquently wrote about her own spiritual journey, often wrestling openly and publicly with herself and others by
asking wise and genuine questions about the systems and structures of
faith. Held Evans wisely pointed out that a God who asks us to "love
with all our hearts, minds, bodies, and souls does not suddenly de-
mand we suspend the use of those faculties the moment they challenge
long-held beliefs or power structures."[3] She left her family and this
world entirely too soon, and though I did not know her, I felt con-

nected to her because we were raised about twenty miles away from each other in similar conservative towns in East Tennessee. Tragically, she died at a Nashville hospital less than a mile from the home where I live now. For many years, I have assigned her books in my classes, followed her lively interactions on Twitter, and I always felt a sense of kinship with her. She showed many, many people how to be honest and candid about our doubts, questions, and unbelief. I personally struggle with the loss of her honest presence in this world, and we are all left with the legacy of her writing, which models *wrestling* so wisely and so well.

As we gather together this week, let us resolve that this home and this table will always be a place where we can dwell in unknowing and wrestle honestly, candidly, and openly with our faith as Rachel Held Evans did. Consider how two truths can be held at the same time. I can simultaneously feel the truths of grief and joy: I feel sorrow at the passing of time or the tragic loss of a life like Rachel Held Evans's. I can simultaneously feel a sense of joy as a new year begins or as I pick up one of her beautiful, wholehearted books. It may seem like grief and joy should wrestle each other, but maybe instead they fuse—existing at the same time, in the same consciousness.

WONDER: One by one, follow in Rachel Held Evans's example and say one thing that you are struggling to understand, one ideal you are grappling with, or one thing you wish you could believe. Is your "one thing" connected to dualistic, either/or thinking? Dwelling in unknowing can feel scary, so listen respectfully and honor what each person is wrestling with today.

TRY: Take a five-minute break for a scavenger hunt around your home, and find one object that embodies the hard question or problem you just told your family about. If you have little ones, you might tell them to go to their room and find one thing that makes them feel happy and sad at the same time. A family album or scrapbook can be a source of wrestling since it can conjure up feelings of loss and joy from one page to the next. If you're doing this with your friends, give them free rein to open and search through your kitchen cupboard, bookshelves, or family room. Return to the gathering place to show your example to the others. End your weekly gathering by reciting this prayer together, or write your own family prayer about the importance of wrestling together with hard things:

May this family forever be a safe harbor where we can bring our anger, our hard questions, our doubts, our contradictions, and our silences. May this family forever be a sanctuary where we know that faith and doubts are not opposites. May this family be made up of loving critical thinkers who embrace the shades of gray when it might be easier to just see things in black and white. May we wrestle openly together with all the respect and kindness we can muster. Sometimes the path is hard and rocky, so help our family, O Divine Spirit, to walk in the Way of Love as honestly and openly as we can.

Conclude with these words from the Tao Te Ching:

Tonight we reflect on paradox:
Water wears away rock
Spirit overcomes force
The weak will undo the mighty.
May we learn to see things backwards, inside out, and upside down.

SET THE TABLE

> Jesus never asked anyone to form a church, ordain priests, develop elaborate rituals and institutional cultures, and splinter into denominations. His two great requests were that we "love one another as I have loved you" and that we share bread and wine together as an open channel of that interabiding love.
>
> —Cynthia Bourgeault, *The Wisdom Jesus*

Jesus asks us to *love* and to *share*. These two verbs sum up his teachings. So literally and symbolically, tables are beautiful places to do both of those things. Tables are where we all bring our yearnings. We come to the table craving delicious food to fill up our hungry bellies. We come to the table eager to connect with the people we love most. Sometimes we come to the table joyful, and sometimes we come to the table when we feel sad or broken. At the table, most families do their best to put down their devices, look one another in the eye, practice their golden manners, share inside jokes and laughs, and talk about what happened during the day. When it comes to transcending dualistic thinking, the table may be the most meaningful piece of furniture in a home because it's the place where we come together with common longings and shared rituals.

WONDER: Imagine a perfectly bare table with no one yet gathered. How can you prepare the table so that it can be a place of deep love, blessing, sharing, and listening? What might you need to make the table feel welcoming to people who don't look or believe like you? Ask any children at the gathering to describe their perfect table. What shape might the table be? How might it look and feel? ·

TRY: Sit together and listen to the song "Crowded Table" by The Highwomen. The song is built around the majestic image of a table where everyone comes back together when the day is done, everyone has a seat, and everyone belongs. After the song ends, go around the table and talk a little bit about a "crowded table" you'd like to join. Who would be there with you? Is there anyone you *wouldn't* want to be there, and why? Can you think of anyone who might feel unwelcome or uncomfortable at your table? What would be on the table? What food would be served? What might be some topics of conversation at your ideal crowded table?

FEBRUARY

DISCOVER CONTEMPLATION

I have abandoned all particular forms of devotion, all prayer techniques. My only prayer practice is attention. I carry on a habitual, silent, and secret conversation with God that fills me with overwhelming joy.

—Brother Lawrence, *The Practice of the Presence of God*

February arrives amid wintertime for those of us in the northern hemisphere. If we cast our eyes ahead, we can catch a glimpse of the vernal equinox—the hopeful beginning of springtime that will soon come. During this shortest month of the year, brave hellebores, commonly known as Lenten roses because they bloom during the season of Lent, peep out from the cold earth and herald the wonder of a new season.

February received its name from the Latin *februum*, from which our word "fever" derived, so it's not surprising to learn that February got its name from ancient Roman rituals held near the middle of the month to promote purification, healing, and fertility. In fact, many scholars suspect the Church replaced Lupercalia, a particularly bawdy and violent pagan fertility festival that occurred in the middle of February, with St. Valentine's Day, a day to commemorate an early martyr who has become associated with romantic love. These days, when we enter stores this month, we find aisles full of chocolates and valentines to purchase for sweethearts and classmates—temptations that are clearly tied to romance and fertility but seem completely disconnected from anything resembling *purification and healing!*

On the Christian calendar, Epiphany offers us three Sundays of light and joy, a broad boundary of time before we enter into the thoughtful, sober season of Lent. Ash Wednesday and the beginning of Lent almost always fall during February, so this month often marks the beginning of the Lenten season, a time set aside for reflection, purification, and fasting. Every once in a while, Ash Wednesday comes at the very beginning of March. Since Lent often begins in or near February, this month is an ideal time to explore and encounter the role that attention and contemplation can play in our lives.

Contemplation is a deep way to pay attention—to be open to this very moment. Contemplation is dwelling with what *is,* instead of recalling what *was* or imagining what *will be.* When I pay attention in this way, I almost find that I am praying without ceasing. Contemplation offers me permission to stop analyzing, to stop trying to understand, to stop critiquing myself and others and *just rest*—just dwell in awareness of the moment. There are so many ways to encounter contemplation, and the Lenten season offers us the perfect opportunity to try out some contemplative methods with our family or families of choice. Along with prayer and meditation, contemplative activities can include reading (specifically, a practice called *lectio divina*), dancing, drumming, chanting, singing, looking, breathing, walking, housecleaning, gardening, or even petting a beloved furry friend.

A story to ponder as you encounter contemplation this month: When Jesus was about twelve years old, he was lost for three days in Jerusalem. When his parents finally found him, he was praying in the temple. I don't think I really grasped the "lost for three days" detail of the story until I became a mother—and then it rocked me to my core. Once, on a bright winter morning when my son Henry was three, I lost him in a crowded playground for a mere five minutes, and I don't think I breathed even once; tears sprang to my eyes as I screamed his name, so full of breathless panic I thought I would come right out of my skin. To search for a lost child over the course of three days must have been absolutely terrifying for Mary and Joseph. And yet, when they found him, perhaps they felt a teeny bit of pride in him for seeking out the quiet within the city and dwelling in the quiet within himself. He would do it again at different times in his life, going into the wilderness for stillness, prayer, and contemplation.

And Jesus encouraged others to be more contemplative. Consider his visit to the home of sisters Mary and Martha. While Martha busied herself with all the various tasks that need to be performed while a visitor is in the house, her sister Mary simply sat at Jesus' feet, dwelling in the present and listening to what he was saying. When Martha complained to Jesus that her sister wasn't helping out, Jesus told Martha that there was need of only one thing and that by dwelling in the present, Mary had chosen "the better part," something that would not be taken from her. Now, when I start to meditate or dwell in awareness of the present, I sometimes begin my need for contemplation by imagining the very human Christ who also sought out silence and rest. I try to recall his words to Martha about how being still and aware was "the better part." I seek to rest in Christ, as opposed to forming words or thoughts or concerns about outcomes. I silence myself, and find a place just to *be*. Sometimes I light a candle and focus on the flame or breathe in my favorite lavender or bergamot oils. Or, I ask one of my boys to tap our singing bowl with the wooden mallet, letting that unmistakable lingering ring call us into a time of awareness.

For two decades, I have taught many different versions of a class for undergraduates on ways of knowing; the fancy word for this topic is *epistemology*. The main question of a course like this is "How do we know what we know?" Well, we *know* through our firsthand experiences and the experiences our parents and even grandparents have passed down to us. We *know* through the wonders of language, through the intricacies of cognition, through deep wells of emotion, and through the stories, culture, and traditions we inherit. And on a basic level, we *know* through our senses, often relying heavily on that knowledge we make sense of through sight. But we also can *know* through stillness and contemplation, especially when we teach ourselves how to have a reservoir of inner calm within ourselves. We can always visit this place of stillness, this awareness of the Holy Spirit moving in and through us. We can always *know* by using our breath to rest in Christ's presence. And as long as breath moves through us, that will not be taken away.

In *Open Mind, Open Heart,* Thomas Keating explains that "contemplative prayer is the world in which God can do anything. Our private, self-made worlds come to an end; a new world appears within and around us."

Explore and encounter the new worlds that can emerge through contemplative methods such as:

 ◆ Centering Prayer
 ◆ walking meditation
 ◆ *lectio divina* (see page 53)
 ◆ dancing, chanting, breathing, laundering, looking, and *un*knowing

One February tradition my family and I have created is watching the marvelous film *Chocolat* together. *Chocolat* shows how sweetness, light, and love can invade and penetrate the somber season of Lent.

February Creation Care Challenge: At work, school, or even just walking down the sidewalk, keep your eye out for trash. Pick up a piece of trash and contemplate its origins as you place it in the garbage can. Bonus points if no one sees you do it!

BREATHE

We rarely think of the air we breathe. Yet it is in us and around us all the time. In similar fashion, the presence of God penetrates us, is always around us, is always embracing us.
—THOMAS KEATING, *Open Mind, Open Heart*

Many years ago, my heart would start racing unexpectedly. Tests revealed that it was a nonthreatening fluke in my body's electrical system, but my heart's sudden unpredictability made me terribly anxious. My wise doctors taught me how to use my breath to slow my heart rate and calm my nervous system. Around the same time, friends introduced me to the practice of Centering Prayer (see page 54), which is a way of praying in silence and using your breath to welcome the presence of the Divine. When we inevitably become distracted during the silence, we can use our breath to return, to rest, to surrender to the divine presence of Christ, that presence that is always longing for intimacy with us. The experiences of learning how my breath could calm my emotions, slow my racing heart, *and* bring me into a deeper relationship with the divine Holy Spirit truly changed my life. Breathing is gospel; breathwork is good news.

WONDER: In the second of the two accounts of creation found in Genesis, the Creator formed man "out of the dust of the ground" and then "breathed into his nostrils the breath of life," setting in motion the drama of the human story. In John's account of Jesus' life after the resurrection, Jesus breathed on his disciples and said, "Receive the holy spirit" (John 20:21–22). What do you and your loved ones make of these two stories about breathing? Our breath is a friend and partner we can call upon to "receive the holy spirit" for all of our days. The force of life that is breath should be honored and revered. In the past few years, I have made a startling realization about my own breathing habits: I often inadvertently *hold* my breath, especially while I'm in deep concentration at work, feeling anxious, or responding to emails! To address this problem, I've started using an app on my smartwatch that reminds me to take breathwork breaks, and these little pauses feel like I'm cleansing my spirit from within. Have you ever noticed that you hold your breath? Do you ever use your breath to soothe your emotions, quiet your thoughts, and center your spirit?

TRY: Like many religious traditions, Christianity has incorporated incense into prayer rituals for millennia. This week, connect to our olfactory past by lighting some frankincense incense at the table. For more than five thousand years, frankincense has been used by Greeks, Romans, Egyptians, and Israelites for purification, healing, and relaxation. If you don't have or cannot find frankincense, any incense or even a favorite candle will do. Notice the air as it enters your nostrils, and experiment together with a few cycles of 4-7-8 breathing. Breathe in for a count of four, hold the air for a count of seven, and breathe out for a count of eight. Imagine that you are not just doing the breathing; you are also *being breathed.* Isn't it a wonder to imagine the Divine embracing, nourishing, and loving you through this fragrant air you breathe?

DISCOVER: FEBRUARY 2, CANDLEMAS

My mission is to keep the light in your eyes ablaze.
—ALANIS MORISSETTE, "Ablaze"

February 2 is about halfway between the winter solstice and the spring equinox. On the Christian calendar, this date is forty days after Christmas Day and marks the feast day commemorating the infant Jesus' presentation in the temple in Jerusalem, as well as Mary's own rite of purification following childbirth. Both rituals were in accordance with the laws of the time. Mary and Joseph traveled with their baby to Jerusalem and gave a humble offering of two turtledoves, and when they were in the temple, they encountered Simeon, a man who had claimed he would not die until he had seen the Christ. Simeon cradled Mary's infant in his arms and said the words we now know as the *Nunc Dimittis* or the Song of Simeon:

Lord, you now have set your servant free
to go in peace as you have promised;
For these eyes of mine have seen the Savior,
whom you have prepared for all the world to see:
A Light to enlighten the nations,
and the glory of your people Israel.

This song is often sung at evening vespers (prayers), and since Candlemas is a day to bless the candles in your home, you can mark the day with a simple ritual around the table in your pajamas. Make candles together if you'd like, using the guide on page 33. Light all the candles you can find in your home, and say a small prayer of thanksgiving for the wax, the bees, the soy plants, the wicks, and, most of all, the light. While you watch your home candles burn, listen to two complementary songs about children and light:

First, listen to a traditional choral arrangement of the *Nunc Dimittis*.
Second, listen to Alanis Morissette's song "Ablaze" and watch the ac-
companying video together.

As you experience these two very different songs, consider how
Mary might have felt as that elderly stranger Simeon held her tiny baby
and said that he could now die in peace because he looked into baby
Jesus' eyes and saw "a light to enlighten the nations." Contemplate together what it means to keep one another's eyes ablaze. What is one
thing you can do tomorrow to enlighten and uplift others?

End vespers by saying the short service for Compline, which can be
found in *The Book of Common Prayer*. Carefully extinguish your candles, and consider them blessed and ready for the year to come. [Read
more about Compline on page 196.]

MAKE: SIMPLE SCENTED CANDLES
FOR CANDLEMAS

Make these at least a day before Candlemas!

EQUIPMENT

Saucepan

Cooking thermometer

1 pound soy wax flakes

Large Pyrex measuring cup or other heat-resistant cup
    to pour from

Potholder

8-ounce canning jars

Candlewicks

Glue

Small wooden kebab skewers or pencils to hold the wick in
    place when you pour the wax

Essential oils of your choice

Scissors

DIRECTIONS

Put water in a saucepan and heat the water to 180°F, using the thermometer. Put the soy wax in the large Pyrex measuring cup and place the measuring cup inside the saucepan to make a double boiler setup. Using the thermometer again, melt the wax to 180°F. Then remove the measuring cup from the heat with a potholder and allow the melted soy wax to cool to 100°F.

While the wax is cooling, place a wick inside each of the canning jars. You can use little dabs of glue to secure the wicks to the bottoms of the jars. Wrap the tops of the wicks around the kebab sticks to secure them in place. Rest your wick-wrapped kebab sticks on top of the prepared jars.

Add essential oils to the cooled wax. Honor the magi and their gifts to the baby Jesus by making frankincense candles. Use 15 drops of frankincense, 10 drops of lavender, and 7 drops of chamomile. Or, a combination of balsam fir (10 drops), eucalyptus (5 drops), and lavender (3 drops) is especially lovely this time of year!

Carefully pour your scented wax into the prepared jars. Allow to sit for 24 hours. Trim the wicks to about ¼ inch.

EMBARK ON A PILGRIMAGE

Restore us to our truer, wilder stories, O God.
In this wilderness, may our hearts be shed
Of the insulating layers of daily routines, of
The duties and comforts that distract and lull us,
Of the numbing surplus of our possessions.
—Douglas Kaine McKelvey, "A Liturgy for
Those Who Sleep in Tents"

Jesus was a pilgrim throughout his life. We know that he traveled to Jerusalem at the age of twelve on pilgrimage with his parents and family friends. Later, his ministry was composed of long walks during which he observed, befriended, listened, taught, and preached. Have you wondered about the wild places he must have camped or slept in? Have you imagined how the soles of his sandals must have gotten worn down and how the blisters on his feet must have hurt? I've wondered what he carried in his bag and where he washed and dried his clothes. And, on the many miles he walked, as he looked up at the sky and felt the breeze on his skin, did he often sense he was in the midst of what the ancient Celts would call a "thin space"?

Thin spaces are those places where heaven feels oh so very close to Earth. Picture a dark room with a door cracked open to another room, and in that other room, there is light: That threshold space between the dark room and the lit room is thin space; it's the place where you feel the in-between, a world elsewhere. In a thin space, you might throw

off your sandals, like Moses on the mountaintop, because you immediately sense you're standing on holy ground. I've felt thin spaces in
dramatic landscapes like the Cape of Good Hope in South Africa or in
Manhattan at the Cathedral of St. John the Divine, but the thinnest
space I ever encountered was under the blinding bright lights of the
delivery rooms where my boys were born; it was like a portal to another world, and I often return to that portal in my heart and in my
dreams. It strikes me that I remember the thinness of these places because they were all *edges:* The Cape of Good Hope is a cliff of rocks,
edged among sky, earth, and sea. Like walking across the threshold of
many massive urban worship spaces, entering the Cathedral of St.
John the Divine is passing from the edge of the boisterous city into the
sanctuary's serenity. And those delivery rooms: What edges they are—
borderlands where it's not clear where mother's skin ends and baby's
begins—sites of emergence mapped by blood, tears, and the first drops
of foremilk.

Like wildflowers that spend February preparing to rise up from beneath the surface of the earth, the season of Lent can be a time of unseen fermentation and growth. During Lent, we may become more
mindful about patterns of our behavior. Many of us "give up" something like eating meat, or take on a simple new practice like saying a
nightly bedtime prayer. And more than any other season in the liturgical year, Lent invites us to embark on a pilgrimage. To make a pilgrimage is to set out, often on foot with a few humble belongings in a
backpack, for a place we have heard or known to be special. In a class
I teach on walking and writing, we view *Walking the Camino: Six Ways
to Santiago,* a documentary profiling pilgrims from around the world
who, for various reasons, have dropped out of their so-called regular
lives in the so-called real world. They've set off as pilgrims on ancient
paths through Spain for a mere five-hundred-mile walk on the Camino
de Santiago, or the Way of St. James, from the Pyrenees to Santiago de
Compostela. An older Canadian widower walks to mourn and honor
his wife; a Brazilian woman in her thirties has cut off her hair, sold her
possessions, and bought a one-way ticket to go on pilgrimage because

she feels her life has become stagnant and she needs to "create some motion." In search of a deeper, richer, more authentic connection with God, a young French mother pushes her three-year-old son in a stroller across the miles and miles of rough terrain. As we watch the documentary during the Lenten season together, my students and I talk about the usually foreign concept of pilgrimage and wonder together what it might be like to make a pilgrimage to a place we hope will be "thin."

Later during Holy Week, we wander a few blocks from campus together to a labyrinth, perhaps to be jolted out of our everyday existence and planted smack-dab beside the heart of God. Like Jesus of Nazareth likely did as he walked through the landscape of Palestine in the first century, pilgrims allow themselves to be astonished by the sunrise even though they really want to grimace at the pain of a blister. They're on the hunt for signs, symbols, and beacons along the path because they're not worrying about the tasks that tend to consume us in our regular lives. Whether we're going to a cathedral in the middle of New York City, the Holy Land, the Way of Saint James, or a labyrinth a few blocks away, the first step of a pilgrimage is taken in trust and wonder because we don't know how encountering the edges could forever change us.

WONDER: Together with your loved ones, make a list of places that are "thin." Where are some places you have been that have stirred your soul or shaken you up? For children in the group, name some places that feel otherworldly, unusual, or special. They need not be magnificent or grandiose.

TRY: Take a Lenten pilgrimage together. You can go to a place like a city park that is completely new to everyone, or you can explore a friend's backyard. You can go to a place that one person has found to be "thin." Keep it simple; take a water bottle, a map, and a snack. Look for signs and symbols along your way. When you arrive, kick off your shoes and spend some time in silence together. After you have had some time to be silent, compose a prayer together that makes use of these words: Earth, stumble, transformation, way, find. Perhaps the Lenten practice in your household this season can be to say your pilgrimage prayer together each night before bedtime.

MAKE: A HIKING STICK FOR YOUR HIKES AND PILGRIMAGES

Whenever we go on a family hike, the first thing our son Peter wants to do is get the perfect stick. Of course, you can just choose a stick off the forest floor, but it's fun and simple to make your own. Never, never cut a branch off a live tree! Cutting off a branch from a live tree inhibits the tree's growth, and who are we to do something like that?

Since saws and knives are involved, all children require adult supervision when making a hiking stick.[1]

EQUIPMENT

Small saw to trim the stick

Relatively straight branch, at least 2 inches thick and about 5 feet long

Sharp pocketknife

1-inch piece of ¾-inch-diameter copper water pipe

Epoxy glue

Hiking medallion, sandpaper, and polyurethane (all optional)

DIRECTIONS

1. With your small saw, cut the branch to a length about 8 inches taller than your elbow.
2. Take your time and be patient as you use the pocketknife to whittle the bark away from your stick. If there's an inner layer of bark, carve that away as well.
3. Whittle down the bottom end of your walking stick so the copper piping will slip onto it, and secure the copper pipe with epoxy. (This step is to protect the bottom end of your stick.)
4. If you'd like, personalize your hiking stick with a hiking medallion.
5. Optional: Use sandpaper to smooth out the surface even more. Let it dry indoors for a month or so, and apply a protective coat of polyurethane.

LAUNDER

Before enlightenment, chop wood, carry water.
After enlightenment, chop wood, carry water.
—ZEN PROVERB

There's an old saying that everyone wants a revolution, but no one wants to do the dishes. Or—if you're in my household—no one wants to do the laundry. But like the Zen proverb suggests, the chopping of the wood, the carrying of the water, and the laundering of the clothes will still be there after enlightenment arrives! The contemplative in me sees dirty clothes as an opportunity to notice how the day-to-day lives we lead show up in the laundry.

Is there any action more appropriate than laundering to embody the grittiness of the day-to-day lives we lead? Day after day, we launder clothes that have embraced the bodies we love most. I often reflect on how the sweaty, dirty clothes my family brings home hold little mysteries of what their lives away from me are like. Little clues emerge when I take my boys' things out of the dryer: wrappers from granola bars, little blue foam cylinders from Nerf gun wars I wasn't there to witness. Those chubby little hands cram the flotsam and jetsam of their lives into their pockets, and the laundry brings these little wonders back to me the way a tide washes pieces of sea glass to the shoreline. The task of laundering offers an opportunity to be fully present if we will only pause, consider, and allow it.

* * *

WONDER: Be mindful of the inevitable laundry that enters your life. How did you get the clothes you are wearing? Whose money purchased them? In what fields were the fibers grown? Where were the threads, fabrics, buttons, and zippers made? Imagine the factories where your clothes were assembled and sewn. If children are present, ask them about their clothing and if they know how to do laundry. (If not, this is a wonderful week to teach older children how to do laundry!) What do you do in these clothes that have touched the lives of so many people and places? Are your actions honoring all the hands that labored to produce these garments before they made their way to you?

TRY: Experiment with the contemplative method, *lectio divina* (see page 53), by closely reading Matthew 6:25–34, in which Jesus speaks on the mountain to his friends. He speaks of clothing, laundry, and worry. Zero in on a line or two. Perhaps you'll choose to focus on these magnificent lines: "Why do you worry about clothing? Consider the lilies of the field, how they grow; they neither toil nor spin, yet I tell you, even Solomon in all his glory was not clothed like one of these." How might *lectio divina* offer you and your loved ones a glimmer of insight about the relationship you have with your clothes?

MAKE: PANCAKES FOR SHROVE TUESDAY

On the liturgical calendar, the last day before Lent begins on Ash Wednesday is called Shrove Tuesday, Fat Tuesday, or Mardi Gras. Shrove Tuesday is a day to make merry, eat sweet and delicious foods, and burn the palms from the previous year's Palm Sunday service into ash. Tomorrow, Ash Wednesday, those ashes will be used to remind us that we are dust and to dust we shall return. But before we begin the penitential season of Lent, let's follow those who have come before us and make a delicious dinner of pancakes to use up the butter, eggs, and other rich foods in the pantry or refrigerator. It's also a night to wear beads, masks, or costumes. Like Easter Sunday, Shrove Tuesday is a moveable feast occurring forty-seven days before Easter. (See more on lunar cycles and why Easter falls when it does on page xxix.) Find out when Shrove Tuesday will occur this year, and mark your family calendar for a pancake supper!

SHROVE TUESDAY PANCAKES[2]

SERVES 4 TO 6

INGREDIENTS

2 large eggs

2 cups all-purpose flour

2 teaspoons baking powder

2½ tablespoons honey

1 teaspoon baking soda

1 teaspoon kosher salt

2¼ cups full-fat buttermilk

4 tablespoons melted unsalted butter, plus unmelted butter for serving

1 teaspoon vanilla extract

Nonstick cooking spray or vegetable oil

1 cup frozen or fresh blueberries (optional)

Maple syrup, for serving

DIRECTIONS

Preheat the oven to 200°F and get out an electric griddle or a large skillet. Beat the eggs using an electric mixer or by hand until frothy. Add the flour, baking powder, honey, baking soda, salt, buttermilk, butter, and vanilla. Stir with a wooden spoon just until the batter is smooth and no flour lumps remain. Make sure you don't overmix! Heat the electric griddle or skillet to medium-high heat and grease with cooking spray or the oil. It's ready when a little drop of water dances across the surface.

Ladle about ⅓ cup batter for each pancake, and put a few blueberries on top of each pancake if you wish. After 1 to 2 minutes, bubbles will form on top of the pancake, and when they do, flip the pancake and cook until it's golden brown (2 minutes or so). Transfer the pancake to an oven-safe plate or baking sheet and keep warm in the oven while cooking the remaining pancakes. Serve with butter and maple syrup.

Wear festive masks and beads, and decorate the table with green, purple, and gold! Feast on pancakes with your loved ones, and know that as you feast on your delicious pancakes, you're using all the rich foods in your fridge (butter, buttermilk, and eggs) and are now ready for your Lenten fast.

DISCOVER: ASH WEDNESDAY/LENT

. . . you shall be called the repairer of the breach,
the restorer of streets to live in.
> —ISAIAH 58:12

Remember that you are dust and to dust you shall return.

Ash Wednesday marks the first day of the Lenten season. This solemn day immediately follows the sweet extravagance of Shrove Tuesday. The Lenten season is the forty days—minus Sundays, Maundy Thursday, Good Friday, and Holy Saturday—before Easter Sunday. And forty days holds importance because it's said to be the length of days Jesus spent in the wilderness fasting and praying before beginning his ministry. When you think of "forty days," think "a long time." Forty days is also said to be the length of the flood and the time the prophets Moses and Elijah spent fasting and praying in the wilderness.

Many of us immediately associate Lent with giving something up—often meat or chocolate or wine—but I wonder if Lent could be better imagined as a time of *letting go:* Letting go of the armor we wear to protect ourselves from being vulnerable. Letting go of our worry that if we do, or do not do, something we somehow lose our belovedness. We are beloved in the eyes of God and those who love us most no matter what.

A SIMPLE HOME LITURGY FOR ASH WEDNESDAY

Make ashes: If you have palms from last year's Palm Sunday, burn them into ash on Shrove Tuesday. If not, simply take a little ash from a firepit or candlewick, or simply go outside and get a little dirt. Add a few drops of olive oil and mix it up in a little dish.

Read Isaiah 58:1–12 aloud together at the table: Isaiah's ideas for what a fast means are extraordinary: Shout! Don't hold back! Share your bread with those who are hungry. Bring the homeless into your house. Let the oppressed go free. *Then* your light shall break forth like the dawn. *Then* your healing shall spring up.

After reading and thinking about Isaiah together, take some time to contemplate in silence. What feels hard? Think ahead to Easter morning: How might you feel renewed like that watered garden Isaiah imagines? What might you let go? Make a note for yourself and seal it. Put it in a bowl or basket on the table; open it up and reread it on Easter morning.

Conclude by marking each other's foreheads with a cross made of the ashes: One by one, use the ashes to make a cross on each and every forehead at the table as you say these poignant words: "Remember that you are dust and to dust you shall return."

UNSEE

A twenty-two-year-old girl was dazzled by the world's
brightness and kept her eyes shut for two weeks. When at the
end of that time she opened her eyes again, she did not
recognize any objects, but, the more she now directed her gaze
upon everything about her, the more it could be seen how an
expression of gratification and astonishment overspread her
features; she repeatedly exclaimed: "Oh God! How beautiful!"
—Annie Dillard, *Pilgrim at Tinker Creek*

In the lines above, Annie Dillard recalls reading a book about blind
men and women of all ages who were operated on to become newly
sighted, and these stories illuminate a very mystical form of knowing.
Dillard tells us that when she saw for the first time, the young woman
was so stunned by the brightness of creation that she literally had to
unsee. Her sudden new way of knowing through sight was all too
much, so she had to shut it right down and cover her eyes.

But the newly sighted girl tried again, and after some time, she re-
opened her eyes. Becoming newly sighted enabled her to be agog by
what she was seeing. This story makes me wonder what it would be
like to become unburdened by all my previous definitions for things,
for all my prior associations to vanish, for the weight of old meaning to
vaporize. What newness might emerge?

Oh, to be dazzled by light, to be astonished by color and beauty, to
know what it's like to see for the first time! What would it mean to walk

around seeing this world raw? How might I behave? What choices would I make differently, unseeing all that has become cooked in my mind and seeing it anew, just like she did—flabbergasted by the magnitude of colors, the lights, and the awe-filled beauty? Could I find the perfect words to tell about it? Or, like her, would I just fall back on, "Oh God! How beautiful!" (After all, maybe "Oh God! How beautiful!" *are* just the perfect words.)

Over the years, I've read and heard a lot of tales—both fictional and true—about people who blow up their lives. Maybe they blow up their lives by asking for a divorce and breaking up a family. Or maybe they blow up their lives by quitting a job. Or by moving to a new city or even escaping to the end of the earth. And after they've blown up their life, sometimes it seems that the main thing these humans wanted wasn't so much to be husbandless or wifeless or childless or jobless or uprooted; they really just wanted to unsee, unhear, and unknow for a while. Maybe they needed and wanted time and space and permission for contemplation . . . or even just a Sabbath! Maybe many of us need standing appointments with ourselves to stare out in silence at a broad expanse of earth, to feel the cold wind on our cheeks, and to be aware of our presence in the midst of something wondrous, wild, mystical, and intuitive. Perhaps what many of us need and want is time to *unsee* and *undo* so that, refreshed and unburdened, we can see and do again.

WONDER: Consider what it means to unsee, to unhear, to unlearn, to unknow, and to undo. To make this more real for children (or those blessed with a childlike willingness to play), have everyone close their eyes and plug their ears for what will feel like quite a long time—at least seven minutes if possible. When your experiment concludes, ask each other: When you close your ears, is it easier to listen? When you close your eyes, can you see better? What do the answers around the table reveal?

*   *   *

TRY: Eat a meal entirely in silence with your loved ones at the table. It's useful if one person silently brings the food to the table and puts it in front of everyone else before sitting down. Another person can be in charge of clearing the table in silence. Notice how things taste. Notice how you can hear and feel the crunch of your lettuce, how the tastes and essences of the foods are moving on your tongue and through your mouth. No need to verbalize, no need to make sense of anything that's happening. Just let it be awkward. If you need to exchange a smile or a smirk to acknowledge the strangeness of eating in total silence, so be it. Keep going. When you're finished, you can talk a bit together about what this different way of experiencing both eating and gathering was like and how this meal differed from a typical meal shared with others.

MAKE: TWO SIMPLE SOUP RECIPES FOR LENT: EFFORTLESS CARROT SOUP & SISSY'S POTATO SOUP WITH EARLY SPRING HERBS

Lent is the perfect season for simple soups, and these two recipes can easily be made for dinner—even by older kids.

EFFORTLESS CARROT SOUP

I made up this ridiculously simple recipe one spring Saturday when I had accidentally bought extra bags of baby carrots!

SERVES 4

INGREDIENTS

  2 bags of baby carrots or 2 pounds regular carrots
  Olive oil
  Sea salt
  1 yellow or white onion, chopped
  2 to 3 tablespoons fresh thyme leaves
  3 cups broth or water
  2 to 3 tablespoons freshly squeezed lemon juice
  3 tablespoons unsalted butter
  Freshly ground black pepper, if desired

DIRECTIONS

Preheat the oven to 400°F and line a rimmed baking sheet with parchment paper to make cleanup easy. Put the baby carrots on the prepared baking sheet and toss with 1 tablespoon olive oil and a little salt. Even the carrots out in a single layer and roast for about 30 minutes. When you can smoosh them in half or pierce them easily with a fork, you know they're ready.

In a large pot, heat 1 tablespoon olive oil over medium heat and cook the onions for about 5 minutes, until they are translucent. Stir in the thyme and cook until fragrant, about 1 minute. Add the broth or water to the pot, making sure to stir the onions so they don't stick. Add the roasted carrots to the pot and bring the soup to a boil. Reduce the heat to medium-low. Let simmer for 15 minutes or so.

Turn off the heat. Use an immersion blender to blend the soup until it's smooth. If you don't have an immersion blender, simply mash the cooked carrots in the pot. Add the lemon juice and butter. Taste and check your seasonings. Add black pepper, if desired. Blend again and serve! This is a perfect soup to have with bread and a green salad.

SISSY'S POTATO SOUP WITH EARLY SPRING HERBS

My sister Kelly's simple soup of potatoes, onions, and herbs makes an ideal Lenten meal, using up what's left of the winter pantry while taking advantage of the first signs of spring.

SERVES 4

INGREDIENTS

1 pound potatoes
1 small yellow or white onion
2 tablespoons unsalted butter
½ cup chopped herbs (such as parsley, chervil, chives, carrot greens, or
    a mixture)
Salt and freshly ground black pepper
3 cups chicken or vegetable broth

DIRECTIONS

Peel and dice the potatoes and onion. Add the potato peels and onion skin to your kitchen compost bin if you have one.

Melt the butter in a soup pot over medium heat until foaming lightly. Add the potatoes, onions, and ¼ cup of the herbs. Toss in the butter to coat, then season with salt and pepper. Reduce the heat to low, cover, and cook for 6 to 8 minutes, until the potatoes are tender, stirring a few times to prevent sticking.

Warm the broth in the microwave or on the stovetop. Add the broth to the vegetables and simmer over low heat, covered, for another 6 to 8 minutes.

Transfer the soup to the bowl of a blender or food processor and purée until smooth. Add more salt and pepper to taste. Serve topped with the remaining ¼ cup of chopped herbs, divided among four bowls.

DISCOVER: *LECTIO DIVINA*

Let us ruminate, and, as it were, chew the cud, that we may have
the sweet juice, spiritual effect, marrow, honey, kernel, taste,
comfort and consolation.

—THOMAS CRANMER, advice on how to read scripture, 1547

Read those lines from Thomas Cranmer aloud slowly so that you can
really get a feel for the meaning of *lectio divina* (or "divine reading"), an
ancient practice of contemplation that uses reading to be open to the
divine presence of Christ. Chewing on the cud, sucking out the marrow, savoring the sweet honey, getting down to the kernel . . . in a world
filled with bright screens, continual information, and never-ending
analysis, this extraordinary description of reading as an overture to
your unfolding relationship with God seems radically refreshing.

Lectio divina is not a method of exegesis in which you read a text
and attempt to solve what it means. It is not Bible study or literary in-
terpretation. Instead, it's an ancient method of reading that liberates
the reader to slow down, meditate, and contemplate how the divine
presence is unfolding through the words, right here and right now.
Lectio divina is probably like nothing you ever learned in school, and I
like to imagine it as a mash-up of "reading" and "wonder."

Lectio divina is so liberating because when you contemplate this
way with your loved ones, you are not trying to persuade anyone of
anything. No one need comment on what anyone else has said. You're
not trying to win an argument or come up with the best idea. Furthermore, no one even needs to share their thoughts out loud.

This contemplative method has four steps:

Lectio/Read: Choose a small passage from scripture, poetry, prayer,
song—anything that you or your loved ones feel called to—and
read it slowly several times.

Meditatio/Meditate: Be still. Close your eyes and ponder the words in silent meditation. Listen for the Spirit to illumine their meaning.

Oratio/Pray: Use words to form a prayer. Your prayer can be a silent conversation between you and what you understand to be God, or you can choose to say the words out loud so that others may hear.

Contemplatio/Contemplate: Return to silence, and breathe deeply in communion with the Spirit. You may choose a word from the original passage to return to if your mind wanders.

DISCOVER: CENTERING PRAYER

You cannot attain pure prayer while entangled in material things and agitated by constant cares. For prayer means the shedding of thoughts.

—Evagrius Ponticus, *The Praktikos*

How do you define prayer? Prayer is not simply using language to talk to God. Sixteenth-century mystic St. John of the Cross said that the first language of God is in fact *silence.* And Centering Prayer is simply an invitation to *let go.* Some other ways to describe Centering Prayer include: Lay aside your thoughts. Consent to the presence of the Divine. Nurture an intention within yourself to be present with the Holy Spirit.

Centering Prayer upends my preconceived notions about what prayer is because it's not about forming words but rather it's about letting words go. This practice takes me away from what has happened in the past and frees me from anticipating what may happen in the future. Centering Prayer is simply about sitting in silence, gently returning again and again to a sacred word, and dwelling in God's presence.

When we sit in Centering Prayer, we sit in silence, often alone but perhaps in a small circle with others. Begin your Centering Prayer practice by choosing a word or short phrase that is sacred to you, like

Jesus, Mary, Be still, love, peace, grace, or *mercy.* My sacred word is *loving-kindness.* Gordon Peerman writes that "your word is a symbol of your intention to rest your awareness on the stream of consciousness itself rather than on the objects or thoughts floating down the stream." Whenever you become aware of a thought, memory, image, or distraction, you simply bring your sacred word to mind. Centering Prayer is often described as *consent,* as being open to God. You use your sacred word like an anchor that returns you to that intention.

The directions for "doing" Centering Prayer are simple:

1. Find a place to sit comfortably so you'll be alert but relaxed.
2. Set a timer for twenty minutes. I use Insight Timer, an app on my phone.
3. Close your eyes and rest in the silence.
4. Open your heart to an awareness of the divine presence.
5. Whenever you find your thoughts wandering—and please kindly accept without judging yourself that you will—return to your sacred word.
6. At the end of the twenty minutes, you might stretch a bit, or reflect on the day's psalm (which you can easily find using an app like The Daily Office), or say a short prayer of thanksgiving before you go on with your day.

In *Open Mind, Open Heart,* Father Thomas Keating wrote that Centering Prayer is "designed to withdraw our attention from the ordinary flow of thoughts. We tend to identify ourselves with that flow. But there is a deeper part of ourselves . . . the inner stream of consciousness which is our participation in God's being." Centering Prayer helps me identify that deeper well within myself. So much "prayer" is characterized by talk, words, and conversation. But Centering Prayer is *communion.*

MARCH

EMBRACE MYSTERY

Blessed be you, universal matter, unmeasurable time, boundless
ether, triple abyss of stars and atoms and generations: you who
by overflowing and dissolving our narrow standards of
measurement reveal to us the dimensions of God.

—Pierre Teilhard de Chardin, *Hymn of the Universe*

In the words above, Pierre Teilhard de Chardin praises the mysteries of the cosmos as one would say the opening words of the Mass: "Blessed be . . ." As both a paleontologist and a priest, he knew exactly what he was doing. March is a tremendous month to say "blessed be." It's a season to invoke the holy, to welcome the divine, and to encounter the mysterious. March brings wind, rain, bright green shoots of grasses emerging from the earth, brave little wildflowers, bright yellow daffodils, muddy shoes.

March gets its name from Mars, the god of war. Long, long ago in ancient Roman times, March (then called "Martius") was the first month of the year, the time for armies to march again after a break during winter. March is also the season of Lent, which calls us to ponder, to prepare, and to transform. For their wedding date, my parents chose March 21, the first day of spring or the vernal equinox, and I've always thought it was a perfect date to take a naïve but courageous vow to love and cherish, to consent to play the leading roles in a story that will unfold in ways you cannot fathom.

Church has kindled my interior life and my own sense of wonder, marvel, and joy. Since I was a very little child, church has been a place where I have been invited to dwell in unknowing. I grew up around priests and Sunday school teachers who told me it was okay to have doubts, and I was encouraged to live with rather than quickly solve the big questions I had about God. I fell in love with the mesmerizing language of *The Book of Common Prayer* when I was very young, and I asked to be confirmed when I was nine years old because I wanted to kneel at the altar with the adults and taste the bread and wine. Back in those days, children were not allowed to share in the bread and wine, and I remember craving to understand what those mysterious substances would feel like on my tongue. Since those days, many churches have made the marvelously inclusive decision to allow children who aren't yet confirmed or at the so-called age of reason to fully participate in the Holy Eucharist, so they aren't longing to taste the bread and wine like I did for so many years.

For the most part, my Episcopal upbringing was a little love affair in which I encountered a vision of church as a place where anyone who walked in the door was welcome—and, in general, welcome to bring their baggage. Church was probably the most intellectually liberating place in my life, a place to bring all of myself, all of my doubts, and all of my questions. Learning about ritual, liturgy, and history alongside the sacred stories about Jesus' teachings and love made me hungry to say yes to more: Saying yes to helping the priest prepare the bread and wine before the Eucharist when I was ten. Saying yes to more scholarship about the authors of the Pentateuch when I was in college. Saying yes as a young professor to studying the early Christian theological speculations about materiality that led to the concept of the trinity. Saying yes as a single woman in her twenties to running the Episcopal summer camp of Tennessee and welcoming young people (along with their hiking shoes, art supplies, guitars, doubts, fears, love, and questions) to a glorious mountaintop setting every summer. Saying yes in my thirties and forties to leading contemplative retreats on hiking and wildflowers, to serving on boards, to leading stewardship campaigns, to writing new liturgies, and to creating art for the altar. Christianity has earned a rather poor reputation over the years, but for me and for some of my family and friends, church has been a place to cuss and to laugh, to dance and to cry, to investigate, explore, and take risks.

But not everyone has a happy love story with church, and that is precisely because church is not always a place that allows people to dwell in mystery and foment a connection with the Eternal. I long for religious experiences that nurture the capacity for wonder in my children, my students, and my adult self. I long to say yes to the Eternal, to dive into the mysteries headlong and just *dwell* with them for a season. I don't want my children or my students or myself to fear *unknowing*, for *unknowing* is a seedbed of dirt where new growth can emerge like bloodroot braving the cold earth of March.

As we enter the month of March, consider what it could mean to encourage and nurture an ecosystem of unknowing for the people you lead and the people you love. Consider what it means to stretch out your arms and embrace mystery. Shouldn't our faith communities be places where mystery and unknown are welcome? Where we offer trust, hospitality, and welcome to the very real questions our beloveds bravely bring to us?

I believe church should be a sanctuary for embracing mystery, welcoming questions, and basking in that other seedbed—the seedbed of silence. For some, church always has been this sort of sanctuary, but for many, mystery, questions, and silence are the unlikeliest things encountered in institutionalized religion. Many, many people have been hurt by a church that is too certain, a church that has robbed them of their capacity to *wonder*. What's more, the scourges of authoritarianism, homophobia, colonialism, racism, and misogyny have battered and violated so many people and thus formed traumatic experiences of *church*. And who can blame them for leaving, for who wouldn't want to leave a "church" that is so certain that *certain people* should be excluded, "fixed," or shamed?

For those who have needed to leave harmful church institutions, the tables in our homes or the tiny gardens in our backyards can be safe, nurturing sanctuaries where we can embrace mystery. In January, we contemplated the magic that emerges when we dissolve dualities. In February, we encountered contemplation as a way to dwell in the present, to be radically open to what *is* instead of what *was* or what *will be*. And so in March, we exercise those muscles we developed in January and February to embrace mysteries and let go of certainties. To embrace mystery means to get comfortable with that which is unknowable, inexpressible, contradictory, and boundless. To embrace mystery is to reach out our arms toward endlessness, toward spaciousness, toward multiplicities, toward faith itself. At once humbling and liberating, *embracing mystery* means we can be faithful and doubtful at the same time; we don't have to don the arrogant armor of certainty to be faithful creatures. We cannot presume to know the mystery of God.

I have spent my entire life in school as a student and a professor, and I can think of no greater barrier to learning than certainty. The brightest, most interesting students are not on the quest to be certain; they are curious, open, full of wonder, and known for their humility—not for their certainty. Even the hardest of rocks allow the cool mountain streams to smooth their surfaces. Perhaps certainty is the opposite of wonder: I've noticed that when I feel absolutely certain about something, I literally have no room for wonder; I have squeezed out all that I couldn't name, weigh, measure, define, or quantify and put it out of my sight so that there's nothing left but my precious, unbending, obstinate, absolute certainty.

As we walk through the weeks of March together, let's welcome the God that Pierre Teilhard de Chardin invokes in the lines that open this chapter: God is revealed not through the absolutes and the measurements but through the immeasurables, in the mysteries and marvels that we can see all around us if we will only risk opening our eyes, our hearts, and our minds.

As we embrace mystery during the month of March, ponder how:

- ✦ The Holy Spirit often speaks to us in the language of poetry, not prose. We don't have to understand everything.
- ✦ Institutions can discourage or encourage us to dwell in mystery.
- ✦ Wondering about something you don't understand can get you out of your head and closer to experiencing the Divine through your breath, through your existence, and through the flora and fauna with whom we share this world.

*   *   *

March Creation Care Challenge: Watch creation come alive by start-
ing a little garden with your loved ones. *Vegetable Gardening Wisdom*
is a colorful, family-friendly guide written by brilliant master gardener
(and my sister!) Kelly Smith Trimble. You can easily grow herbs or
veggies in little pots if you don't have space outdoors. My young boys
are in charge of growing veggies, flowers, and herbs in our Aerogar-
den, a hydroponic system that sits on the kitchen countertop year-
round.

DISCOVER: PALM SUNDAY
AND HOLY WEEK

Depending on the year, Palm Sunday and Holy Week may happen in March or April. Many think of Christmas as the primary Christian observance, but Holy Week is the most important week in the church year, and it commences on the evening of Palm Sunday, forty days after Lent begins. As we will discover in Week 47 later in the year, Christmas became popularized in part by the efforts of Francis of Assisi in the thirteenth century. Francis secured permission from the pope in the thirteenth century to re-create the nativity of Jesus of Nazareth because he wanted to inspire and kindle a sense of wonder about Jesus' birth. Many years later, in the nineteenth century, Charles Dickens's instant bestseller, *A Christmas Carol,* helped solidify the practice of families being together for the Christmas holiday. But prior to that, Holy Week was a far more important observance in the Christian tradition. As worship resources provided by the Church of England explain, the Christian participates in the sequence of Holy Week and "shares in Christ's own journey, from the triumphal entry into Jerusalem on Palm Sunday to the empty tomb on Easter morning." All of the fundamental themes of Christianity—incarnation, suffering, death, resurrection, glorification—can be pondered, re-created, discussed, and even felt as Christians observe Holy Week and Easter.[1]

PALM SUNDAY

Holy Week begins with Palm Sunday. We process together and wave palms to commemorate Jesus' triumphant arrival in Jerusalem. Consider purchasing palm fronds that are sustainably sourced or simply using leafy branches from your native surroundings. It's traditional to sing, act, or read the Passion narrative on Palm Sunday.

MAUNDY THURSDAY

We remember the Eucharist at the Last Supper. Maundy derives from *mandatatum,* signaling the "mandate" or new commandment Jesus gave us to serve and love one another by washing each other's feet. See page 107 for more on foot washing. At the conclusion of the service, the altar is stripped bare. Church bells are silenced and the organ does not play until Easter morning.

GOOD FRIDAY AND STATIONS OF THE CROSS

We enter the church in silence and remember the details leading up to Jesus' crucifixion on Golgotha. In many traditions, we observe the Stations of the Cross, a devotional exercise, by walking, meditating, remembering, and praying about the Passion of Christ in a church or other setting such as a park, a cemetery, a hospital, or a school. The Stations of the Cross illustrate fourteen images depicting the movements from Jesus' condemnation up until he is placed in the tomb. Walking the fourteen stations of the cross take us through the worst—the capture, the condemnation, the anguish, the murder. There is no "fifteenth" station of the cross, but followers of The Way know that Easter morning is coming, so there is hope in moving through those stations of the cross. Instigate a community art project depicting the stations of the cross. Even if you don't have an installation of the Stations of the Cross accessible to you, you can really get creative and walk the stations of the cross as a group in a natural setting like a park or on a hiking path on Good Friday. Do so by designating someone to print out fourteen images or artwork that your group can stop and ponder in collective silence along the path. The spiritual "Were You There When They Crucified My Lord?" is a deeply moving song to sing or listen to on this day.

EASTER VIGIL

After sunset on Holy Saturday, the vigil or watch begins. In some traditions, a Paschal fire or candle is lit to show light in the darkness as Jesus moves from death into life again, and this marks the first moments in which Easter is celebrated. Symbolically, the Paschal fire chases away darkness and brings the light of Christ into the world. You can easily begin a Paschal fire in a firepit, or light a candle in your own home. The Easter Vigil continues until sunrise on Easter morning.

Light a fire in the fireplace or firepit, or build a bonfire for the Easter Vigil. One of my favorite Holy Week traditions is to watch the Italian film *Il vangelo secondo Matteo* (The Gospel According to Matthew), directed by Pier Paolo Pasolini in 1964. Pasolini hired nonprofessional actors to make the film feel more realistic. He famously cast his own mother as the elderly mother of Jesus.

DISCOVER: THE LITTLE MYSTERIES
OF THE PARABLES

The seasons of Lent and springtime are an ideal time to encounter the little mysteries of the parables, the stories Jesus used when he was teaching. He often opened a lesson with similes like "The reign of God is like . . ." to try to communicate about the radical new world he wants to bring us.

Try contemplating one parable per week during March.

HUSH

Contemplate the parable of the sower and why Jesus wanted to tell stories in a new way (Matthew 13:1–14) (NIV).

> "Why do you speak to the people in parables?" He replied,
> "Because the knowledge of the secrets of the kingdom of heaven
> has been given to you, but not to them. Whoever has will be
> given more, and they will have an abundance. Whoever does
> not have, even what they have will be taken from them. This
> is why I speak to them in parables: Though seeing, they do
> not see; though hearing, they do not hear or understand."
> (Matthew 13:10–14)

POLLINATE

Contemplate the parable of the mustard seed and how little actions can be transformative (Matthew 13:31–32).

> He told them another parable: "The kingdom of heaven is like a
> mustard seed, which a man took and planted in his field.
> Though it is the smallest of all seeds, yet when it grows, it is the
> largest of garden plants and becomes a tree, so that the birds
> come and perch in its branches."

FEED

Contemplate the parable of the leaven, the marvelousness of bread, and the ways kitchens bring God's children together (Matthew 13:33–34).

> He told them still another parable: "The kingdom of heaven is like yeast that a woman took and mixed into about sixty pounds of flour until it worked all through the dough." (Matthew 13:33)

COMPOST

Contemplate how efforts to bring matter to the compost heap instead of the landfill resemble the parable of the lost sheep (Matthew 18:10–14).

> "If a man owns a hundred sheep, and one of them wanders away, will he not leave the ninety-nine on the hills and go to look for the one that wandered off? And if he finds it, truly I tell you, he is happier about that one sheep than about the ninety-nine that did not wander off." (Matthew 18:12–13)

HUSH

What has happened to our ability to dwell in unknowing, to live inside a question and coexist with the tensions of uncertainty? Where is our willingness to incubate pain and let it birth something new? What has happened to patient unfolding, to endurance? These things are what form the ground of waiting. And if you look carefully, you'll see that they're also the seedbed of creativity and growth—what allows us to do the daring and to break through to newness.

—SUE MONK KIDD, *When the Heart Waits: Spiritual Directions for Life's Sacred Questions*

"Catch a bubble!" Most teachers have a method for quieting their students, and I loved learning this delightful command from my children's kindergarten teachers: They can silence an entire procession of five-year-olds walking down the hallway by simply asking them to pretend to put a big bubble in their mouths. Lent is a season for all of us to "catch a bubble," to hush, to pause the endless chatter, and welcome some wide-open silences. It's okay not to talk, letting those awkward silences lengthen into spacious minutes when you can hear only the crickets. It's okay to have an unexpressed thought. It's okay not to engage with someone's opinion or idea. Let it be. Let language go and be on the alert for signs and symbols you might encounter on the Lenten path.

Use this season to get acquainted with your own secret well of silence, a source of strength, mercy, and wonder that lives deep within each of us and is right there waiting for us to draw from. I think of my own well as a vast, deep, sweet sea within. I can close my eyes and use my breath to tap into my secret sea like a sugar maker who knows just how and where to tap a maple tree for syrup. When we choose to calm the noise around us, hushing allows us to return to that well to draw strength again and again.

Poets can teach us how to hush and connect to our interior worlds, especially when they strategically employ blank space and line breaks. Such blankness on the page is often a gift to readers since it provides a pause, a wee moment of silence, access to an unwritten story unfolding in the margins. It's so important to become acquainted with the blank spaces, to tap into our secret seas so that we can become more attuned to the exterior marvels that await us: Marvels like bees that navigate by the position of the sun. Marvels like a ruby-throated hummingbird, which weighs less than a nickel and can migrate across the Gulf of Mexico. In a world filled with such wonders, being quiet from time to time and simply revering it all with a bit of humility seems an appropriate way to pay homage.

WONDER: Are there any people in your life who practice silence in a way that stirs you with awe? Who are they? Are they people who speak few words, or do they have some other qualities that encourage you to hush? Are there places in your life that encourage you to be quiet? Can you name rules, boundaries, or customs that encourage silence? Encourage little ones at the table to have a contest to see who can hold silence for the longest, or take them on a silent walk during the soft light of dusk to see if they can notice the rustling leaves or chirping whip-poor-will.

*   *   *

TRY: Master the art of hushing and practicing calm, and it will serve you well for a lifetime. Blow some bubbles with a bubble wand and a solution of dish soap and water. Play with the bubbles for a bit, and then ask everyone in your gathering to get quiet enough to hear the bubbles pop in the air. Sit together in silence for as long as you can. Try to get so still and quiet that you can hear your own heartbeat.

MAKE: A ROSARY OR CHAIN OF BEADS FOR PRAYER, MEDITATION, AND CONNECTION

When my babies were little, I had to carefully choose the necklaces I wore. As I held my sons in my arms, they would inevitably reach for any beads I wore around my neck, wrap their tiny fingers around them, and put them in their mouths. Human beings have been making—and playing with—beads for more than a hundred thousand years. Have you ever wondered why? Playing with beads calms us down and occupies our minds, and beads are portable, easily carried wherever we go. In fact, the English word *bead* derives from the Old English *bede*, which means "a prayer," and strands of them are used to keep track of prayer in Hinduism, Buddhism, Christianity, Islam, and Sikhism.

Perdita Finn and Clark Strand, who together wrote *The Way of the Rose: The Radical Path of the Divine Feminine Hidden in the Rosary,* as well as American writer Mary Gordon, have commented on the rosary's powerful feminine associations. All three have pointed out that beads are a way to connect through circles to the divine feminine, the goddess, the lady, the soil, the mother of Earth.

Lay out a rosary on a table, and if you stretch your imagination, you'll see that it makes the shape of the traditional symbol for woman. Perdita Finn would likely speculate when my babies were reaching for my beads, they were engaged in a primal mammalian activity since beads are like our mother's nipples, and babies instinctively reach out to them so that they can be fed and stay alive. Holding a rosary or prayer beads is like attaching to the mother—mother Mary, Mother Earth, mama—however you want to think of the feminine divine.

Using a chain of beads to help us repeat our prayers or mantras allows us to drift between wakefulness, imagination, and reverie. I have fallen asleep on more than one occasion with my rosary in my hand. A 2001 study even found that reciting the rosary and yoga mantras slowed respiration and improved heart rate variability, suggesting that using prayer beads might be viewed not only as a religious practice but as a practice to enhance overall well-being.[2]

SIMPLE INSTRUCTIONS FOR MAKING A ROSARY

59 beads (53 of one size and 6 of another size). Choose beads that will
   slide onto your silk cording.
1 Sharpie or pen
3 feet of silk cording
Clear nail polish or adhesive
A cross or special medal, like a Mary medal

Sort your beads into two piles. A total of 53 are your "Hail Mary" beads and the remaining 6 are your "Our Father" beads.

Using a Sharpie or pen, mark a dot at about 8 inches from each end of your cording. Make a knot at one of the dots.

1. String 10 Hail Mary beads to your first knot.
2. Make a knot at your tenth bead, allowing a bit of room for your beads to slide.
3. String 1 Our Father bead.
4. Tie another knot.
5. Repeat this process until you have five sets of 10 Hail Mary beads and 4 Our Father beads. *Do not add the fifth and sixth Our Father beads yet.*
6. Make a knot at the end. Tie your rosary into a circle, leaving a length of cording about 8 inches long.
7. Brush a little clear nail polish or adhesive to your big knot and allow it to dry for a few minutes.
8. Take your fifth Our Father bead and slide it on the longer piece of cording.
9. Tie a knot.
10. Slide your last 3 Hail Mary beads on the longer piece.
11. Tie a knot.
12. Slide your final Our Father bead on.
13. Tie a knot.
14. Slide on your cross or medal.
15. Tie a double knot to secure it, and again, add a little bit of clear nail polish or adhesive and allow it to dry.
16. Clip off your excess cording.

Ask a member of the clergy to offer a blessing, or offer blessings together for your rosary.

DISCOVER: HOW TO PRAY THE ROSARY

There are many versions of the rosary prayer. I've listed a few here, but I encourage you to find your own way of praying and honoring the life-giving spirit the rosary embodies.

This is a traditional method:

First, make the sign of the cross or kiss your medal or cross. As you hold each large bead, contemplate the five holy mysteries and pray the Our Father. As you hold each smaller bead, pray the Hail Mary. Make your way around the rosary. When you get back to the beginning, make the sign of the cross or kiss your medal, and end with any concluding prayers.

HAIL MARY

Hail Mary, full of grace, the Lord is with you.
Blessed are you among women, and blessed is the
Fruit of your womb, Jesus.

OUR FATHER

Our Father, who art in heaven,
hallowed be thy name;
thy kingdom come;
thy will be done;
on Earth as it is in heaven.
Give us this day our daily bread.
And forgive us our trespasses,
as we forgive those who trespass against us.
And lead us not into temptation;
but deliver us from evil.
For thine is the kingdom,
the power and the glory,
for ever and ever.
Amen.

THE MYSTERIES

One tradition is to contemplate the mysteries on each day indicated.

The Joyful Mysteries

(Monday and Thursday; and the Sundays from the first Sunday of Advent until Lent)

1. The Annunciation to Mary
2. The Visitation of Mary
3. The Birth of Jesus
4. The Presentation of Jesus in the Temple
5. The Finding of Jesus in the Temple

The Sorrowful Mysteries

(Tuesday and Friday; and the Sundays of Lent)

1. The Agony of Jesus in the Garden
2. The Scourging of Jesus at the Pillar
3. The Crowning of Jesus with Thorns
4. The Carrying of the Cross
5. The Crucifixion and Death of Jesus

Glorious Mysteries

(Wednesday and Saturday; and the Sundays from Easter until Advent)

1. The Resurrection of Jesus
2. The Ascension of Jesus
3. The Descent of the Holy Spirit upon the Apostles
4. The Assumption of Mary into Heaven
5. The Coronation of Mary Queen of Heaven and Earth

WEEK 10

POLLINATE

Each year sees the disappearance of thousands of plant and animal species which we will never know, which our children will never see, because they have been lost forever. The great majority become extinct for reasons related to human activity. Because of us, thousands of species will no longer give glory to God by their very existence, nor convey their message to us. We have no such right.

—POPE FRANCIS, *Laudato Si'*

Whether we are aware of it or not, an exquisite love story is happening around us on this Earth. We are fed because of animals and natural forces that move pollen from one place to another so that plants can reproduce, flourish, and thrive. Water and wind are forces of pollination. But so are our bees, hummingbirds, butterflies, bats, beetles, and moths, creatures that perform the often risky work of pollination that *moves new life forward.* The wondrous process of pollination nurtures humans, birds, flowers, trees, and livestock.

Contemplate an apple, something that could be in your kitchen or backpack right now: That apple is here and ready to feed you because a bee once visited the flower of an apple tree. And our planet's bees are in trouble; every year, billions of bees are lost to a complex combination of forces like parasites, poor nutrition, pesticides, and viruses. Bees' habitats are also disappearing, but we can productively work together to create and tend homes for them. For example, at the university where I work in midtown Nashville, our president emeritus often ends his workday by putting on long gloves, donning a mesh veil, and going up to the rooftop of one of our academic buildings where he tends hives of bees that will pollinate flowers as far as a mile away. There's no shortage of scriptural evidence imploring humans to tend to creation and cultivate life.

WONDER: How can we respond to losing vital members of creation? Can you think of some physical ways you and your loved ones might care for creation by encouraging pollination? Can you help children at the table cherish bees by helping them understand the different roles of the queen bee, the worker bees, and the drones? See page 79 for some simple guidelines on how to create a pollinator garden.

TRY: Gather around a screen, and behold the mystery of pollination by watching the documentary *Wings of Life*. The astonishing photography in this documentary allows you to look carefully at a process that very few humans have ever had a chance to ponder—the reciprocal love story between animals and plants. After you finish watching the film, compose a prayer of thanksgiving and protection for our bees and flowers with those in your gathering.

DISCOVER: PLANTING A POLLINATOR GARDEN

Plant a pollinator garden to attract bees and butterflies. Some quick research will tell you about pollinator plants that are native to your area. You can start from seeds or plants. They'll also love a water source like a birdbath. Some other simple guidelines:

- Leave the dandelions in your yard alone.
- Avoid weed killer and synthetic herbicides and pesticides. Apply organic ones only when bees aren't out.
- If possible, plant flowers in your front yard, your backyard, your balcony, your courtyard, a community garden, a schoolyard— wherever you have access to the outdoors.
- If you have a windowsill, you can plant a little herb garden the bees will love. Fill a plant box with potting soil and plant herbs like chives, marjoram, rosemary, lavender, mint, lemon balm, or thyme.

COME WITH BREAD

In my living I have hitched myself to this nourishment. I have devoured it, botched it, buttered it, forgotten to salt it, burned it, and relished it. I have tried to take, bless, and give. . . . All these years I have been working out my own ways to come with bread for others and for myself.

—Tallu Schuyler Quinn, *What We Wish Were True*

I lived very near a bread-baking company until it was torn down in the name of progress. When I'd drive by as the bread was baking, I swear I could feel tears of joy spring to my eyes as I smelled that unmistakable, exquisite aroma of bread baking. Bread is life-giving, and it comes to us through mysterious processes that are worth pondering. Have you ever considered the astonishing microorganisms that can be found all over creation and throughout our bodies? Generally unseen by the human eye, fungi form networks and relationships that make all life possible. I'm not an evolutionary biologist, but I'm curious about the endless connections and the life that thrives as a result of fungal activity, and fungi have always seemed mysterious and magical to me. In particular, I'm in awe of bread; for millennia, we humans have fed a type of fungi known as yeast so that we can then *feed ourselves* with bread.

There's nothing like being nourished with good, warm bread that has been baked from a starter and comes to you straight from the oven. I love the way yeast bubbles, and don't even get me started on that funky, sweet smell of bread as it rises and bakes . . . if I could smell it all day, I'd be a blissful person. I love to think about how bread is crafted right out of the elements in the air.

My friend Tallu was the best bread baker, and she would literally and figuratively show up with bread at all sorts of gatherings and in all sorts of ways. When she was twenty-nine, she started the Nashville Food Project, an organization devoted to feeding people literally and spiritually—to growing, cooking, and sharing delicious, nourishing food. Tallu's inspiring presence and joyful spirit made people want to be around her; there's a monthslong waiting list of people just hoping for the chance *to volunteer* in the Nashville Food Project's kitchens and gardens! Tallu knew that bread and the art of bread making nourish both the maker and the people who are fed. And she loved the fact that *bread* was baked into the etymology of the word *accompany* (*au con pain*). My heart broke when my beloved friend Tallu died of brain cancer at the age of forty-two. Always a remarkable organizer, she arranged for a freshly baked loaf of bread to be given to each person as they walked out of her funeral. Even after she crossed over into the next life, Tallu found a beautiful way to bless, feed, and accompany her community.

WONDER: Yeast is one of the most marvel-filled substances in the cosmos. It's on our hands, and it's in the air. From yeast, we make bread and wine; we are nourished by these microorganisms that are all around us yet invisible to our human eyes. Yeast breaks down sugars, and carbon dioxide gas is released through a process known as fermentation. You can quickly show this process to children at this week's gathering by combining a teaspoon of sugar, a packet of yeast, and ¼ cup of warm water in a clear bowl. Within ten minutes or less, the mixture will begin to bubble and foam, which means the microbes are producing carbon dioxide. Wonder together: How does yeast and the scientific process of fermentation teach us lessons about scarcity and abundance?

*   *   *

TRY: Bread is wondrous, and you'd be surprised at how easy, fast, fun, and satisfying it is to make a sourdough bread starter. All you need is flour, water, and a glass container, since a sourdough starter pulls natural yeasts out of the air as it forms! It's truly an amazing process that you can watch unfold over a week's time. Find a good online tutorial, like the one from King Arthur Baking, and experience the ordinary theology of bread making this week. Once you have a strong, well-fed starter, you can "come with bread" to all sorts of get-togethers. Bread will sustain you and those you love throughout your whole life.

PRAYER FOR MAKING AND OBSERVING SOURDOUGH STARTER EACH EVENING

God of the life that teems and bubbles all around us,
We thank you for life-giving bread.
We thank you for the farmers who plant, weed, and harvest.
We thank you for the miller who grinds the grain into flour.
We thank you for the workers who stock the flour on the shelves of
    the store.
We thank you for those who keep our water supply safe.
We thank you for the mystery of our hunger,
And for the bread that bubbles to life in this jar to feed it someday
    soon.
Nourish us with joy, humility, creativity, and patience
so that we may bring a posture of wonder
as we cherish and savor every crumb.

MAKE: COMMUNION BREAD

Invite a priest to your weekly gathering, where he or she can have a small Eucharistic feast for your loved ones. Let the priest know that you plan to make the communion bread in advance. This recipe has been adapted and shared with gratitude (and permission) from the Society of St. John the Evangelist.[3]

16 TO 24 MEDIUM (3-INCH-DIAMETER)

AND LARGE (6-INCH-DIAMETER) LOAVES,

DEPENDING ON SIZE

INGREDIENTS

    8 cups whole-wheat flour, plus more for kneading

    2 tablespoons plus 2 teaspoons baking powder

    4 teaspoons salt

    1 cup milk

    1 cup oil (vegetable, canola, or other light oil)

    1 cup water

    1⅓ cups honey (1 16-ounce jar)

DIRECTIONS

Preheat the oven to 400°F. Use oil or cooking spray to grease a heavy, light-colored cookie sheet.

In a large bowl, sift together the flour, baking powder, and salt. In a separate large bowl, mix together the milk, oil, water, and honey. Pour the liquid ingredients into the dry ingredients and mix until thoroughly blended; the dough should be stiff and moist but not sticky. Turn out onto a lightly floured board and knead briefly, using additional flour as necessary. For ease of handling, divide into two portions and work one at a time.

Roll out the dough on a lightly floured board to about ⅜ inch thick. Cut into rounds of appropriate size (no larger than a 6½-inch diameter). Stamp firmly with a floured mold or incise with a cross, using a sharp, thin knife dipped in cool water. Place on the prepared cookie sheet and bake for 12 to 14 minutes. Repeat with the remaining dough.

Cool the loaves on a wire rack and wrap well before refrigerating. They may be reheated in the microwave—ever so briefly to avoid drying—before use.

SOME ADVICE FOR BAKERS BEYOND THE MONASTERY

Practice! Don't expect your first batch to be ready for prime time. You, your oven, and your kitchen all bring something to the process, so sort that out before you forge ahead to make the loaves to be used on the altar for Easter morning when the Bishop is there and the sanctuary is full. Besides, the birds will find your "practice runs" to be a special treat!

Before rolling out the dough, divide it into four portions rather than just two. Your home kitchen is probably smaller than the monastery kitchens, and you may find it easier to work with less dough on your kitchen counter. Try to roll the dough as evenly as possible and try rolling to ¼ inch rather than ⅜ inch—experiment with different size rounds and depths, so that you can find the combination that works for you and your oven.

Don't incise the cross too deeply and don't drag the knife across the dough. Rather, lay it on top and lightly imprint the dough with the knife. Rather than greasing the cookie sheet, parchment paper works well and does save the effort of cleanup. The goal in baking is to get a lightly golden brown top, but not toasted. You should find that once the bread has cooled and you break it apart, it is moist and slightly sweet inside.

The loaves can be frozen in tightly sealed containers (such as Ziploc freezer bags) well in advance. Allow 24 hours for them to defrost so that they are room temperature at the time of the service.

Finally, remember that these aren't just any loaves, but rather they will be made sacred when they are consecrated at the Eucharist. As you go along, take the time to notice the smells, textures, and colors of the dough and loaves. The process of preparing them is both mundane and holy and it involves all your senses. It is a very special way of sharing in the liturgical and spiritual life of your community.

COMPOST

The garden is our oldest metaphor. In Genesis God creates the first *Adam* from the *Adamah,* and tells him to "till and keep" it, the fertile soil on which all life depends. Human from humus. That's our first etymological clue as to the inextricable bond we share with the soil. Our ecological problems are a result of having forgotten who we are—soil people, inspired by the breath of God. "Earth's hallowed mould," as Milton referred to Adam in *Paradise Lost.* Or in Saint Augustine's phrase, *terra animata*—animated Earth.

—FRED BAHNSON, *Soil and Sacrament: A Spiritual Memoir of Food and Faith*

As a child, I couldn't help but equate the word *Lent* with the fluffy blue-gray matter known as "lint," the fibers from towels and clothing that my mother made sure we collected from the dryer basket after each load of clothes was emptied. The remnants. The leftovers. The cast-offs. So I was surprised to learn years later in graduate school that the etymology of the word *Lent* actually comes from the Old English *lecten,* which means "spring season." Orthodox Christians describe Lent as an atmosphere of "bright sadness"—a poignant expression that helps me grasp how mourning can lead to intense joy. Only those cold, brown-gray branches of winter can bring us to those dazzling, bright green branches of spring.

The Lenten season begins with the liturgy of Ash Wednesday and, depending on one's tradition, concludes on Maundy Thursday or Holy Saturday, the day before Easter. Ashes for Ash Wednesday are made from the palms from the previous year's Palm Sunday service, signaling the intentionality of a ritual to remind us of renewal and reuse. At Ash Wednesday services, I walk up to the altar, brush the hair off my forehead, and make eye contact with the priest. She dips her thumb in the little container of ash and draws a cross on my forehead, saying these sobering words: *"Remember that you are dust and to dust you shall return."* I'll never forget meeting my husband downtown at the cathedral on a cold Ash Wednesday with our two-month-old baby Henry in my arms. I wept as the priest imposed the ashes on his tiny forehead. It's one thing to think of my forty-something-year-old-self returning to the earth; it's an entirely different feeling to have grown and birthed a baby and been told out loud to remember that he, too, is dust, and to dust he shall one day return.

Ash Wednesday, the ensuing Lenten seasons, and the Good Friday liturgies are times when we go down to the dead only to find rebirth and new life. During Lent a few years ago, Susan, our chapel's director of community life and education, began a composting initiative. This was one of the budget items I was proudest to rubber-stamp during my years as board chair. *Compost* comes from Old French and Latin and is related to *compose,* to putting something together. My sister, a master gardener, has inspired me to compost in our own yard, a daily practice that I hope teaches my boys lessons about renewal as it nurtures our small urban yard and pollinator garden with a rich offering of soil. Composting is transforming waste matter like banana peels, coffee grounds, lettuce heads, yard scraps, cardboard, and even that dryer lint from natural fibers into resources, a rich offering that makes the soil more fertile. Composting is an ordinary sacred act reminding *humans* that we can help out with the *humus!* Composting is evidence that creation is not merely a historical event but an unfolding process. We are here to care for the soil. And furthermore, we *are* the soil; we are dust and to dust we shall return. We are bonded to the soil through that first creation story where Adam is created out of the dirt. In *City of God,* Augustine even describes human beings as *terra animata,* animated Earth.

WONDER: During the season of springtime, the very Earth animates and transforms before our eyes. During the "bright sadness" of the Lenten season, humans transform. Consider your own relationship with Earth. If you have little ones at your gathering this week, go on a short worm hunt outside. Find some wet dirt, look under a stepping stone or in sidewalk cracks for a worm friend, pick up the worm gently, then let the worm go back into the dirt after a minute or so. Look at the dirt on your hands and talk about how you respond to it. After you wash your hands well, consider together: Do you feel connected to the soil? How? Or why not? Have you heard about the hygiene hypothesis, which suggests that many homes and other indoor environments are *too* clean and that a little dirt actually stimulates a healthy immune system to develop? How might "this fragile Earth, our island home"[4] embody hope, health, and resurrection during these two overlapping seasons of springtime and Lent?

TRY: There's no doubt that food waste contributes to greenhouse gas emissions. Start a composting initiative at your school, workplace, or church. Join a compost collective in your town or start composting at your home.

A PRAYER FOR THE COMPOST BIN

Creator, Redeemer, Sustainer:
Here we sit on the ground in another springtime,
Here we anoint our palms with a little bit of dirt,
And feel more and more like your children.
As we return vegetables and fruits back to the soil,
as we partner with this fragile Earth to compose new humus,

may the bright sadness of Lent remind us

that we are bonded to you through this dust and this dirt,

that we are part of creation as it unfolds.

Bless us as we begin to know compost,

As we offer what we have to you,

And to this magnificent Earth that animates all.

DISCOVER: MARCH 25,
ANNUNCIATION OF MARY

The Feast of the Annunciation of Mary is celebrated exactly nine months to the day before Christmas. To annunciate is to announce, and typically, this day is regarded as the day the angel Gabriel "announced" to Mary, a young virgin engaged to Joseph, that she would be bringing forth new life, specifically the son of God! Quite understandably, she looked at the angel and said, "How can this be?"

In her poem "Annunciation," Denise Levertov makes an astounding point that the Spirit did not enter Mary without obtaining her consent. Because she was human, Mary had a choice and could have refused. *There was a moment when she could have refused!* The Spirit waited for Mary to say yes, and Levertov goes on in her poem to say of Mary, "Bravest of all humans, / consent illumined her." And so, Mary's yes was an annunciation, too. By saying yes to something when she really didn't know what it would entail, Mary embraced and consented to a mystery she had no way of understanding.

And it illumined her.

Mark this day by listening to Patty Griffin's song "Mary" and reading Denise Levertov's "Annunciation." Then, think deeply about Mary's voice by reading the *Magnificat* below responsively by half-verse; change readers when you come to the asterisks. The *Magnificat* is Mary's song of praise and justice. Does reading it aloud in the context of Levertov's poem and Patty Griffin's song cause you to resonate with Mary? Can you think of other songs, poems, paintings, or icons that help you connect more deeply with Mary and her story?

My soul proclaims the greatness of the Lord,

*my spirit rejoices in God my Savior; ***

for he has looked with favor on his lowly servant.

*From this day all generations will call me blessed: ***

the Almighty has done great things for me, and holy is his Name.

*He has mercy on those who fear him ***

in every generation.

*He has shown the strength of his arm, ***

he has scattered the proud in their conceit.

*He has cast down the mighty from their thrones, ***

and has lifted up the lowly.

*He has filled the hungry with good things, ***

and the rich he has sent away empty.

*He has come to the help of his servant Israel, ***

for he has remembered his promise of mercy,

*The promise he made to our fathers, ***

to Abraham and his children forever.

Luke 1:46–55

APRIL

WELCOME INCARNATION

Look at the animals roaming the forest: God's spirit dwells within them. Look at the birds flying across the sky: God's spirit dwells within them. Look at the tiny insects crawling in the grass: God's spirit dwells within them. . . . Look too at the great trees of the forest; look at the wild flowers and the grass in the fields; look even at your crops. God's spirit is present within all plants as well. The presence of God's spirit in all living things is what makes them beautiful; and if we look with God's eyes, nothing on the Earth is ugly.

—PELAGIUS, *The Letters of Pelagius: Celtic Soul Friend*[1]

The name for April comes from the Latin word *aperio*, which means "to open, to spread out, to uncover, to reveal, to lay bare." The language lover in me revels in this etymology, for it's hard to imagine a better way to describe the month of April. *Aperio* is a wise, poetic word that deepens our understanding with the month in which flora begin to bud out and a spirit of renewal takes over through the seasons of spring and Eastertide. April bestows the gifts of pink buds, rivulets of rain falling from branches, violets, clover, and evening walks when it's no problem at all if we forget our jackets.

Flowering the cross (see the illustration on page 105) is a tradition that dates back to the sixth century, and this evocative ritual can easily be adapted into your own observance of Eastertide. April is the flowering cross of my childhood Easter mornings. On our way to church services, we children would go outside in our Easter morning finery to gather stems of daffodils, azaleas, tulips, forsythias, or whatever was blooming in our yards. In the front yard of the church that formed me, a waist-high barren wooden cross was displayed near the street, and before walking into the nave for Easter services, the children would process in a line to place our bouquets in the little holes that had been drilled in the cross. Flowering the cross vividly transforms an instrument of torture and death into radiance and life.

Another way to think about uncovering, revealing, and opening is kenosis, which is God's way of outpouring and diffusing Love in the world. Richard Rohr and Cynthia Bourgeault have been great teachers for me on this topic. Cynthia Bourgeault uses the metaphor of a water-wheel to help us visualize the incarnation. Think of how on a water-wheel, water from one bucket flows into another bucket and then that water flows into another bucket . . . and so, the wheel turns. This keno-sis or "emptying" creates the energy; the energy of incarnation is Love itself. Or, imagine a garden metaphor like pruning: Plants such as rosemary, lavender, and sage need to be pruned in early springtime to encourage new growth; the pruning creates new energy. Rohr explains that the first incarnation occurred when God emptied into the uni-verse 13.8 billion years ago when the big bang happened. The spirit of God was infused through the flora and fauna, in the way Pelagius de-scribes at the opening of this chapter. So often, we skip over those 13.8 billion years and fast-forward ahead to the second incarnation, but doing so ignores God's presence poured into all of creation, through all the flora and the fauna and the cosmos.

The second incarnation is when God, who is Love, empties into the Son, who is Jesus. Jesus empties into the Spirit, and the Spirit empties into God: This is the "divine dance" of trinity that is inherent to God's nature. Rohr writes that Christianity is about the daring, audacious idea that God's presence was poured into creation and into one human being through incarnation: "When I know that the world around me is both the hiding place and the revelation of God, I can no longer make a significant distinction between the natural and the supernatural, be-tween the holy and the profane."[2] This is what it means to be trans-formed by an incarnational worldview.

I was born in East Tennessee smack-dab in the middle of April, and the story my parents always tell is that they mailed off their taxes on the way to the hospital. And on the way home from the hospital, they drove my newborn baby self through the dogwood trails that Knox-ville is famous for. How I wish I could eavesdrop on that car ride and see myself as my parents watched over me and looked up at the pink and white blooms opening up, as they transitioned as early twenty-somethings into their new lives as my mom and dad, as I got my first hazy glimpses of creation revealing itself to me through the enchanting dogwood trees that are so sacred to me now. During April, signs of life abound. That new baby under the April dogwoods that was me is in fact all of us, greeting the renewal, revival, and resurrection that abounds.

Like wind moving through those dogwoods that bloom in April, the breath of God *whoosh*es into all creation. Pause a moment to re-read Pelagius's bold declaration that opens this chapter: His urgent request that we *look* helps us begin to grasp the mystery and the wonder of incarnation. Over and over, God is merging with the visible, physical world. This world is sacred, and there are so many nonhuman neighbors to love: the oceans, the stars, the forsythias, the craggy mountains, the smooth limestone, the squirrels, the octopuses, the violets, the dragonflies, the sweet peas, the moths, the composts, and the clovers. God is not up in the sky or out there. God is here; act accordingly with compassion.

April is here. This month, we can welcome incarnation by:

+ Imagining how tending to one another is tending to the body of Christ.
+ Writing a collect that illustrates love for our nonhuman neighbors.
+ Pondering what it means to embody—not simply attend or belong to—something called "church."

April Creation Care Challenge: Celebrate Earth Day on April 22 by planting a bare-root tree (or plant any sort of flora if a bare-root tree is not possible for your living situation). If you can't plant the tree within a day or so of its arrival, put wet newspaper around the roots. If you can, place it in a bucket of water for 12 to 24 hours. Dig a hole at least one and a half to two times as wide as the tree's root ball, but just one time as deep so you don't bury the trunk and crown of roots. Place the tree in the hole, backfill the hole, and then stake the tree. Add mulch and water well as the tree gets established.

DISCOVER: EASTERTIDE/EASTER SUNDAY

Practice resurrection.

—WENDELL BERRY, "Manifesto: The Mad Farmer Liberation Front"[3]

The holiest day of the Christian year is known as Pascha in Aramaic, Zatik in Armenian, Pâques in French, IPaskia in Xhosa, and Easter in English. The English word *Easter* derives from the Anglo-Saxon spring goddess Eostre. On Easter Sunday, we celebrate Jesus' resurrection. For Christians, this is the most light-filled, joyful day of the year. This is the third day after Jesus' execution and death, the morning Mary Magdalene and other women took spices to the tomb to anoint his body and found that the large stone at the entrance had been rolled away. In John's gospel, Jesus meets Mary Magdalene, who recognizes him as her *rabboni,* which means "my teacher." Jesus tells her not to hold on to him but to go tell the others the news.

Easter celebrations are colorful, festive, and triumphant—a time to don finery, flower the cross (see page 105), and say *alleluia* repeatedly during the liturgy (after abstaining from saying *alleluia* during Lent). In many traditions and cultures, Easter Day is a day for egg hunts and feasts and, sometimes, sunrise services. When I was very young, our family friends Gayle and Danny would host a sunrise service at their farm on Easter morning. My sister and I were coaxed out of bed in what felt like the middle of the night and allowed to take our Easter baskets with us on the short ride up to the house situated on a picturesque ridge. Adults and children of all ages gathered on the lawn in the dark, and we watched the sun come up together on the holiest of mornings. After trading some Easter candy with the kids, we'd go back home and *then* get ready for Easter services at church.

In one of my favorite poems, "Manifesto: The Mad Farmer Liberation Front," Wendell Berry concludes with two words: *Practice resurrection.* These two words are at the heart of the Easter story. Easter teaches us to practice resurrection as a defiant discipline in a world that sometimes feels hopeless, scary, and full of death. Standing with our loved ones before the rising sun on a spring Easter morning grafts upon us the story Mary Magdalene was instructed by her teacher to tell: We must practice resurrection as a defiant, revolutionary discipline of hope because, even though death is certain, life finds a way. Alleluia!

In every Christian tradition, Easter Sunday is a moveable feast, which means that the date for Easter Sunday is not fixed. In the West, Easter can fall between March 22 and April 25. The spring equinox occurs on March 21; the Paschal Moon is the first full moon after that date. Easter Sunday is the Sunday that follows the Paschal Moon after the spring equinox. Eastern Orthodox traditions throughout the world—including Russia, Georgia, Greece, Serbia, Cyprus, and throughout the diaspora—calculate the date for Easter using the Julian calendar (as opposed to the Gregorian calendar), so Easter falls on a different date in those countries.

MAKE: HOT CROSS BUNS FOR GOOD FRIDAY

Queen Elizabeth I and her court apparently considered Hot Cross Buns too special to be eaten on just any day, so in 1592, she decreed that they could only be sold on Good Friday and Christmas Day.

YIELD: 1 DOZEN

INGREDIENTS

For the dough

   2 cups whole milk, plus extra for coating the buns
   ¾ cup sugar
   ½ cup vegetable oil
   1 package active dry yeast
   4½ cups all-purpose flour
   ½ teaspoon baking soda
   ½ teaspoon baking powder
   2 teaspoons salt
   1 teaspoon cinnamon
   ½ teaspoon nutmeg

½ teaspoon cardamom

½ cup dried cranberries

1 large egg white, for coating the buns

For the icing

2 tablespoons whole milk

½ teaspoon vanilla

½ cup confectioners' sugar

DIRECTIONS

Make the dough: Combine the milk, ½ cup sugar, and the oil in a medium saucepan and cook over medium heat. Stir until almost boiling, then turn off the heat. Allow to cool for 25 to 30 minutes. Sprinkle the yeast over the mixture, then add in 4 cups flour. Stir to combine, and don't worry if it seems sticky. Cover with a linen cloth and set aside for 1 hour. Then add the remaining ½ cup flour, the baking soda, baking powder, and salt. Stir until combined.

In a separate bowl, combine the remaining ¼ cup sugar, the cinnamon, nutmeg, and cardamom.

Lightly flour a work surface. Press the dough onto the surface and sprinkle with 2 to 3 tablespoons of the sugar-spice mixture. Sprinkle in about ¼ cup of the dried cranberries. Fold the dough onto itself and flatten. Repeat the sugar-spice–dried cranberry process on the blank dough and fold again. Repeat a third time. You should have some sugar-spice mixture left.

Flour your hands and pinch off a golf-ball-size piece of dough. Roll it quickly into a ball and place on a lightly greased cookie sheet. Repeat until you've rolled all of the dough into balls. Cover the cookie sheet with a linen towel and allow the buns to rise for about 1 hour until nearly doubled in size.

Preheat the oven to 400°F. Mix the egg white with a splash of milk and brush on top of each roll. Bake for about 20 minutes. The tops of your buns should be golden brown. Remove from the oven and allow the buns to cool on a cooling rack.

Make the icing: Combine the milk, vanilla, and confectioners' sugar and mix until smooth. Put the icing in a plastic bag and snip the corner. When the buns are cooled completely, make an icing cross on each roll.

MAKE: DEVILED EGGS

Eggs symbolize fertility and rebirth and are inextricably linked with Easter celebrations. In the Eastern Orthodox tradition, hard-boiled eggs are dyed red to symbolize Christ's blood. Icons and images of Mary Magdalene often depict her with a red egg in her hand because she is said to have used an egg to tell about Jesus' resurrection.

For many, cracking open an egg symbolizes cracking open Jesus' empty tomb. In some traditions, eggs were off-limits during Lent, thus making them a delicacy for Easter morning, and many dye hard-boiled eggs festive shades of red, green, blue, purple, pink, and yellow.

In our home, we take the hard-boiled eggs we have dyed and make deviled eggs for our Easter feast. A simple recipe follows.

YIELD: 2 DOZEN DEVILED EGGS

INGREDIENTS

    12 hard-boiled eggs
    ½ cup mayonnaise
    2 tablespoons yellow mustard
    Salt and freshly ground pepper to taste
    Paprika

DIRECTIONS

My mom's recipe for deviled eggs is as easy as it is legendary. Crack the eggshells and run the eggs under cool water, gently removing the shells. Rinse well. Cut each egg in half lengthwise. Remove the yolks and place them in a medium bowl. Use a fork to smash them into a fine crumbly texture. Gently mix in the mayonnaise, mustard, salt, and pepper. Scoop the yolk mixture into each open egg white hole. Sprinkle with paprika and, if possible, serve on a festive deviled egg platter.

MAKE: FLOWERING CROSS

[Illustration and brief directions for Flowering of the Cross]
Find or make a wooden cross 20 to 24 inches high, and secure it on a
stand. Drill (or have someone drill) holes of about ½ inch diameter all
over the cross. These holes will be the places where the flowers and
bouquets are placed. This method is the most sustainable, but you can
also get a moss-covered foam cross from a florist.

WASH FEET

Christ has no body now but yours. No hands, no feet on Earth but yours. Yours are the eyes through which he looks with compassion on this world. Yours are the feet with which he walks to do good. Yours are the hands through which he blesses all the world. Yours are the hands, yours are the feet, yours are the eyes, you are his body.

Christ has no body now on Earth but yours.

—ATTRIBUTED TO TERESA OF AVILA

All my life, even when I didn't know what to believe or what to do next, I have walked up to the altar at church with a hunger for Christ, an appetite for Love. I have stood or knelt to receive the bread and wine, the Eucharistic feast, and looked in the eyes of my priest as she cradles the bread in my hands and says, "The body of Christ." Receiving the Eucharist is a sacrament, a sacred act, in which we become the hands, feet, eyes, and body of Christ, of Love. Christ is literally embodied, physical, Earthy, sensual, sensory. Christ is where spirit, matter, and hunger come together in a mysterious but practical and loving feast.

But there is also a forgotten sacrament, and that is Jesus' new commandment to wash each other's feet. Like eating bread and sipping wine, washing feet is a practical act, a way to offer practical care and hospitality for one another. Jesus and his friends wore sandals, as would have been the custom, and as they walked the roads and traveled from place to place, their feet got dusty and dirty. I imagine feet so tough and gnarly from walking that even the blisters had blisters, and in my mind's eye, I can envision the "clean" skin that would have been revealed underneath the sandal straps. Everything else about the feet would have been covered with grunge and grime. So, when it's time to go inside a house for dinner or rest, the kind, loving, practical thing to do would be to offer a space for resting and cleansing the feet. In the context of Jesus' time, a servant would have been the person assigned the task of washing the feet of the guests. Transcending the old duality of servant-master, Jesus flips the script by washing his friends' feet himself.

If Christ is Love, then Love does the most practical, useful, kind thing by tenderly washing those achy, dirty feet that have finally come in from the road, hungry for friendship, food, laughter, and rest. I wonder how Christianity might evolve if followers of Jesus adopted *feet* as our symbol of sacrificial love, since *feet* recall Jesus' example and commandment to serve one another in a spirit of kindness, humility, practicality, and compassion.

WONDER: In her beloved poem "Wild Geese," Mary Oliver writes about the "soft animal" of our bodies. Read the short poem at the table and think about the material, physical, fleshy part of *you*. Can you think of a time another person has cared for the *you* that is your body? Who was it? What was going on in your life? How did it make you feel?

TRY: Foot washing services traditionally occur on Maundy Thursday (see Holy Week, page 64), but a foot washing can happen anytime and can be a beautiful way to embrace mystery and contemplation. If you feel squeamish about touching feet, reread the lines from St. Teresa above, reminding us that when we touch someone else's feet or let our own feet be touched, we are encountering "the feet with which [Christ] walks to do good." Yes, the "soft animal" of your body is *your* body, but it also takes on a mystical quality by becoming the feet of Christ on Earth. So when you tend to one another's feet, you tend to Christ, to Love, to all that is good and wondrous in the cosmos. Prepare your foot washing by gathering a washcloth for each person and a basin full of water. Leave shoes at the front door and sit in a circle. You might read John 13:1–18, the story of Jesus washing his disciples' feet and telling them that he is setting a new example for them. Take turns washing each other's feet, and as you wash another person's feet, offer a prayer in loving gratitude for the wonder of their existence. Conclude your foot washing by anointing each person's feet with your special oil. As noted on page xxi, I like to use fresh olive oil infused with a few drops of lavender essential oil, but any plant-based carrier oil you have on hand will do.

EMBODY

A funny thing happened on the way to the Kingdom. The
Church, the people of God, became the Church, the institution.
—Verna Dozier, *The Authority of the Laity*

Oh, how I love the bumper sticker that reads: GOD'S ORIGINAL PLAN
WAS TO HANG OUT IN A GARDEN WITH SOME NAKED VEGETARI-
ANS. As the story of Christianity has unfolded, we've built buildings,
written canons, sewn vestments, printed creeds, decided some songs
were "hymns," and made this thing called *church.* If you close your
eyes and imagine *church,* what appears in your mind's eye? Do you see
stained glass? Do you imagine pews and kneelers and altars and people at the front talking and singing? Or do you see something else?
What in the world is *church* anyway? If you want to get a sense of how
ancient and provocative this conversation is, take a class in church history!

Many of my favorite human beings on this Earth are members of
the clergy. In some ways, I long for the kind of life that is ordered
around the church and the sacraments; to this outsider, a clergy life
appears organized around and anchored by the most critical, most important moments of people's lives. I love the feel of the needlepoint
kneelers on my knees and the sight of stained glass coloring the hair
and faces of my fellow worshippers. But it seems to me that lay people
like me—people who are not ordained or otherwise employed by the

institutions we call "church"—too often defer to the clergy and the church buildings when it comes to doing and being *church*. At the risk of stating the obvious, neither you nor I requires a permission slip from the institutional church to connect with the Holy Spirit. I've made altars in delivery rooms where I silently pleaded for safety as our babies were being born. I constructed a pew all by myself on the sand at the edge of the Gulf of Mexico, sticking my toes in the surf and singing a litany of thanksgiving for creation. The starry night skies have been cathedrals under which I've prayed, *"O, God, be my light in this here darkness."*

Consider the example of the man we know as St. Francis: The excess and scandal of the church led Francis of Assisi to a different sort of relationship with God. Francis had renounced a comfortable life, cared for lepers, and never sought ordination.[4] In 1209 or 1210, he traveled to Rome to meet with Pope Innocent III, and a remarkable thing happened: The pope—the institution—gave Francis permission to found an order, to do something radical within the institution of the Church. Francis worked within the institution and with the authority structure to try to live a life in imitation of Jesus' teachings. We know Francis of the birdbaths, those statues often depicted outside with the animals. But he wasn't just a lover of nature; he was absolutely committed to embodying the teachings of Jesus and *doing something* about loving the world and loving his neighbor.

WONDER: Imagine you had no bills to pay or prior obligations to meet: If you could embody or take the shape of "church" in any way under the sun, what do you think you would do? Would you sing? Wash feet? Dance? Shout alleluia? Take a vow of silence? Feed hungry people? Go to prisons and simply listen to the stories of those behind bars? Where would you make your altars? For children who are part of this conversation, ponder this question, and then make a group collage portraying what "being and doing church" *could* look like.

*   *   *

TRY: Listen to "Life Is a Church," a beautiful song written by my friend Marcus Hummon. "Life Is a Church" describes altars and sacraments that can be found in our ordinary, everyday lives. Close by writing a prayer together—one that includes the answers that you gave to the question above about how you would audaciously embody church.

WALK BAREFOOT

Remove the sandals from your feet, for the place on which you
are standing is holy ground.

—Exodus 3:5

When I was a child, I was traveling with my family in New Mexico when I saw barefoot pilgrims traveling on foot to Chimayó, a small adobe church north of Santa Fe revered for its healing soil. It was Holy Week. Many of the pilgrims we saw used wheelchairs or crutches to make their way down the dusty roads. Some carried candles, rocks, or photographs of loved ones. Others bore large wooden crosses on their backs. I vividly remember seeing an old man crawling on his bare knees in the dirt. As I child, I remember being simultaneously fascinated and perplexed: What were they doing? Where were they going? And why? It felt like I was witnessing something from another world, another time.

In many traditions around the world, removing shoes is a sign of respect. A few centuries after Jesus' life, followers of The Way began making pilgrimages on foot to holy places like Jerusalem, Rome, Lourdes, Santiago, and Croagh Patrick. For many, Holy Week is a particularly important time to walk barefoot quietly in solidarity with Jesus, who himself walked to Golgotha, the hill outside Jerusalem where he was crucified. A similar kind of solidarity takes place during the Holy Week ritual of the Stations of the Cross, when we walk, pray, and meditate through the fourteen actions leading up to Jesus' death. You can walk the Stations of the Cross at a church in your town, or you can just download the stations on your smartphone and meditate the Stations of the Cross on a favorite walking path. Walking barefoot can remind us that we are rooted to this sacred Earth.

WONDER: Have you ever walked barefoot? Where did you go, and why were you without shoes? Think about all the places your bare feet might like to walk: on moss, on sand, on large rocks, in a stream, on a cool tile floor, or even down the long wooden aisle of a cathedral. How can a barefoot walk be an act of devotion? How does walking barefoot teach us about the divine merging with the physical?

TRY: Take out the map and find a place nearby to take a walk with your loved ones. You could walk to a shrine, a labyrinth, a church, or another sanctuary. You could even walk to a waterfall or an overlook, or along a lake path. When you arrive, consider taking off your shoes and walking barefoot together. In Germany and Austria, there are hundreds of barefoot parks where you can store your shoes and walk for miles with your soles on Earth! Consider how being barefoot, or what some call *Earthing,* connects us to the Earth and grounds us as pilgrims in a bodily way.

DANCE

I danced in the morning
When the world was begun,
And I danced in the moon
And the stars and the sun,
And I came down from heaven
And I danced on the earth,
At Bethlehem
I had my birth.

Dance, then, wherever you may be,
I am the Lord of the Dance, said he,
And I'll lead you all, wherever you may be,
And I'll lead you all in the Dance, said he.
        —SYDNEY CARTER, "Lord of the Dance"

Every Easter Sunday, my priest Becca Stevens dances down the aisle as we process out of the church. She stomps her bare feet with pure happiness; she dances with gusto, and she raises her hands to the sky. Becca pulls people out of the pews to dance, and she always finds the oldest, most dapper gentlemen at the crowded service to dance with her—and she gets them to dance funky. Her long white vestments cannot hide the fact that she's absolutely grooving. And, as we file out of the pews to dance down the aisle with our grinning, glowing, barefoot priest, it's clear why we should all be dancing. For we have gone down into the depths of Lent, and finally, Easter morning is upon us. The altar was stripped bare on Good Friday, but now spring flowers and festive banners explode with color and life. Finally, we get to say our *alleluias* again at the end of the sentences in the Eucharistic liturgy. The divine has burst through the rock in front of the tomb, and we should all be dancing for the world transformed.

Perhaps like you, I grew up singing Sydney Carter's "Lord of the Dance," which is to the tune of the old Shaker song "Simple Gifts." "Lord of the Dance" suggests that at both the first and second incarnations, there was dancing. Carter imagined a divine dancer who danced at the beginning of time, under the stars and the moon. The divine dancer danced all over creation with gusto and joy. And then, during the second incarnation, the divine dancer was born in Bethlehem as Jesus. Carter imagined Jesus dancing throughout his ministry and even after his death, and Carter once said in an interview about "Lord of the Dance" that Jesus is "the incarnation of the piper who is calling us. He dances that shape and pattern which is the heart of our reality."[5]

Dancing brings us in touch with our bodies, with beats and melodies, and with our intuition. Dancing can feel like freedom! Movement is a way of knowing that reminds us that our bodies are sacred, they have wisdom and knowledge, and they dance through a sacred cosmos. And dancing can inspire a cooperative spirit. Individually, we may hold separate sets of beliefs, but when we dance together, we are united in a common act that feels a lot like hope.

WONDER: Name some of the people in your life you'd consider dancers. What exactly makes someone a dancer after all? Do you sense that dance can be a way to merge your interior life and the divine? Have you ever witnessed one person get up and start dancing in such a way that inspires others to join in? Tell a story about your relationship with dancing. When? Where? With whom? If you feel compelled to get up on your feet and dance while you tell your stories about dancing, all the better!

TRY: Learn the Dubliners' version of Sydney Carter's "Lord of the Dance." Create a playlist of songs together, and have a dance party with your loved ones for ten minutes every night this week.

MAY

ADORE CREATION

Teach the children. We don't matter so much, but the children do. Show them daisies and the pale hepatica. Teach them the taste of sassafras and wintergreen. The lives of the blue sailors, mallow, sunbursts, the moccasin flowers. And the frisky ones—inkberry, lamb's quarters, blueberries. And the aromatic ones—rosemary, oregano. Give them peppermint to put in their pockets as they go to school. Give them the fields and the woods and the possibility of the world salvaged from the lords of profit. Stand them in the stream, head them upstream, rejoice as they learn to love this green space they live in, its sticks and leaves and then the silent, beautiful blossoms. Attention is the beginning of devotion.

—Mary Oliver, *Upstream*

I loved dreaming up names for my unborn children. When my husband, Ben, and I found out we were having our first baby, I went straightaway to the closest bookstore and purchased the *Oxford Dictionary of First Names,* since it was the book on the shelf that had the most pages (almost 500!), looked the most serious and scholarly, contained no pictures, had the smallest print, and dove deepest into the etymologies and histories of names. Ben and I took turns making marks next to names we loved, generating lists, and eventually even making a basketball-type tournament bracket for the names we had amassed—and then just going with our intuition when it finally came time to settle on names for our boys. The human impulse to name transcends space, time, and cultures, for names help us connect, bond, and fall in love. In the lines above, Mary Oliver begs us to teach the children the names of the flowers and berries so that they will then be motivated to adore and thus care for them; she wisely advises us to forge sensory connections between our children and the aromatic herbs so that they will *pay attention,* for attention is the seedbed for devotion.

If April is a time to acknowledge and welcome incarnation, May—as well as Easter, Pentecost, and springtime—can be seasons to *adore,* times to feel a sense of wonder for the Holy Spirit and for the aliveness of creation that surrounds us. May takes its name from Greek and

Roman goddesses of fertility, which is fitting, for we watch the Earth in all its lush fecundity during this emerald month.

In May, creation seems to want us to feel the wonder of being alive as much as possible. Purple finches wait at the feeders, and purple irises line the sidewalks. I'm old enough to remember a tradition for the first day of May that should be revived—leaving a May basket of flowers hanging on the doorknob of the home of someone you love. "May" is also a variant of the name Mary, and in many Christian traditions, this entire month is devoted to Mary, that divine mother. If you have a statue of Mary or another woman who embodies the feminine divine for you, May is a perfect time to encircle her with a little garden. May Day festivals around the world honor the return of warmth and outdoor gatherings. Maypoles and garlands of flowers pay homage to the divine feminine, and in May Crowning rituals like the one that takes place at my sons' school, children adorn Mary statues with a crown of flowers as they reflect on her story.

What does the idea of adoration conjure up in your mind? Adoration can manifest as deep love, affection, and gratitude. May is a perfect time to dwell on the idea of adoration, to motivate the ones you love to feel love and care, to get in touch with the deep part of yourself that cares, too. Within ourselves we contain multitudes of experiences and sensations. I am the child that I once was, the child my own parents got to name. That Bonnie-child is still in me, though I carry all the diplomas, passports, and licenses that squarely put her out of childhood. This second Bonnie-self has obligations, a career, deadlines, responsibilities. This second Bonnie-self—she shows up, and she gets things done. But there is also this third Bonnie-self, and I bet you have one, too: This is the part of ourselves who longs to simply adore and be adored, who hungers for something called eternity.

I have a part of myself who craves the eternal, who has been stirred up by the feel of the wind on her face or the lines of poetry she just read and called into something deeper. To awaken to this deep form of knowing is transformative. By greeting and getting to know that part of our self that hungers for depth, we can teach and model an important way of knowing for our children—and our third selves who have been hungering for eternity—that we are called into deep, joyful lives.

May we all experience Eastertide, Pentecost, May, and springtime as a wondrous season to rise in love. Adore creation this May by:

- Forsaking time for just a day by putting down your watch or phone.
- Learning the names for birds and plants you didn't know before.
- Pondering the idea that the Earth is God's body.

May Creation Care Challenge: Be mindful of the plastic you're using. If you're using plastic baggies for school lunches, switch to reusable silicone or beeswax-covered cloth. Trade out plastic shampoo bottles for shampoo bars. How might you make some shifts away from plastic?

DISCOVER: EASTERTIDE/ASCENSION
AND PENTECOST

The Feast of the Ascension is celebrated on a Thursday, forty days after Easter and ten days before Pentecost. Recalling that Christ fused with all creation, Ascension Day connects Jesus to the air and sky.

Pentecost is known as the birthday of the Church, the day the Holy Spirit inspires the disciples to share the story of Jesus, his life, and the revolutionary new world he dreams of for all of creation. Pentecost falls fifty days after Easter Sunday, and since Easter is a moveable feast, the date for Pentecost changes as well. Pentecost can fall as early as May 10 and as late as June 13. Pentecost is the day to recall and seize upon the energy of the Spirit moving and breathing in creation. Traditionally, Pentecost is a day for worshippers to wear red clothing and for clergy to don red vestments. Red banners adorn worship spaces, symbolizing the wind and fire and heat and vitality of the Spirit. But the Spirit is not merely historical or theoretical; it wasn't only present *then*—it's here *now*.

Fly a kite on Pentecost to experience what it feels like to be liberated by the wind for love, movement, and new possibility. Like the revolutionary new world Jesus imagines through his life and example, kites cannot take flight until they have been caught on the wind.

NAME

When Sugar Maple is an "it" we give ourselves permission to pick up the saw. "It" means it doesn't matter. But in Anishinaabe and many other indigenous languages, it's impossible to speak of Sugar Maple as "it." We use the same words to address all living beings as we do our family. Because they are our family. What would it feel like to be part of a family that includes birches and beavers and butterflies? We'd be less lonely. We'd feel like we belonged.

—ROBIN WALL KIMMERER, "Nature Needs a New Pronoun"

When Robin Wall Kimmerer entered school to become a botanist, she wanted to understand why asters and goldenrod looked so beautiful beside one another and why they were so often intermingled. She was told that if she wanted to study beauty she should go to art school, that science would not be teaching her about beauty. As time went on, she learned that there are important ecological reasons why asters and goldenrod grow next to each other; they have a mutually beneficial relationship in that their beauty and connection attract more pollinators.

Kimmerer, who now holds a PhD in botany, has said that when she studied botany in academic settings, plants were referred to as objects, described for their uses; when scientists refer to plants, they refer to them by "it," an object pronoun. But as a member of the Citizen Potawatomi Nation, Kimmerer understands indigenous ways of knowing, the kinds of knowing that focus on beholding, on storytelling, on listening, and on the inherent value of the plants that fill the Earth. To address environmental problems, we need both scientific and indigenous ways of knowing. Knowing with our intellect and with our sophisticated ways of seeing (i.e., knowing by looking through microscopes) are, of course, important, but there is also a cultural worldview that deeply values intuition and listening. In this way of knowing, other species are not just "it"—they are our teachers, our partners, and our living family.

Referring to a living being as "it" makes that being easier to dismiss or exploit. We really need a life-giving pronoun beyond him/her that acknowledges the being-ness of living things. In a beautiful essay from *Yes!* that can easily be found and read around the table, Kimmerer tells the story of how she has come to propose that ki/kin become our new pronouns for living beings. And like Kimmerer, Catholic priest Thomas Berry suggested transforming language by incorporating a life-giving pronoun. Berry wrote, "We can no longer hear the voice of the rivers, the mountains, or the sea. The trees and meadows are no longer intimate modes of spirit presence. The world about us has become an 'it' rather than a 'thou.'"[1]

Furthermore, Father Berry urged Christians to put their Bibles on their shelves for twenty years. Doing so, he dreamed, would shift the focus from individual salvation to caring for the Earth.

Language can transform the way we know and the way we act.

WONDER: Since he was old enough to walk, my son Peter has gathered rocks. His name, which derives from the Greek *petra,* actually means "rock," and of course when Ben and I chose his name, we had no idea that he would grow to become a lover of rocks, minerals, and gems. Sometimes he will spy a humble piece of gravel, crouch down to inspect it, and decide it's extraordinary and therefore worthy of inclusion in his growing "wock cowection" (rock collection). When Peter was eight, I took him on a special mother-son date to Cosmic Connections, a sprawling old house–turned–crystal store across the street from the university where I work. That day, Peter spent his allowance to buy an amethyst for my mother, his beloved grandmother; he chose amethyst because he knew it was her birthstone, and he is fascinated by the whole concept of a special gem being assigned to each person. I've asked him to tell me why he loves rocks—and how he thinks rocks love us in turn. He says he loves rocks because they make him want to know more about the story of the Earth, and that rocks and minerals *love us* by giving us something beautiful to stand on and, in the case of salt, something to add flavor.

If there are children present at your gathering, ask them to name the plants, animals, or other nonhuman beings they love—and then ask them to wonder aloud how those same beings they've named *love them* in turn. We have been so conditioned to think of plants and rocks as objects. We are accustomed to thinking what the land can do for us, not how it loves us. Yet, the mystery of the incarnation means that God is loving us through creation. Do you feel that the Earth *loves you as you love the Earth*?

TRY: With your loved ones, learn the names for ten plants that you didn't know before. The Seek app by iNaturalist is a great resource for identifying plants (and animals) and storing your finds. Choose one of them to study more deeply. Illustrate the plant. Learn the story behind your plant's name. If possible, visit a gardening center, seek out your plant, and feel your plant's texture. If possible, bring your plant home! List the ways your chosen plant loves us. Write a little prayer of thanksgiving for your particular plant. You might even choose to start keeping a nature journal to record your observations of the land and seasons.

BIRDWATCH

We are a species motivated by love. Our most powerful
work is done in the fervor of love; our most urgent effort is
born from the fear of losing what we love best. To save birds,
we need to make the whole human race fall in love with birds.
What if all the people with phones in their pockets could
suddenly hear beyond the sounds of their own machines?
What if we could all discover how surrounded we are by bright-
winged fairies and golden-voiced angels come down to live
among us?

—MARGARET RENKL, "This 'Shazam' for Birds
Could Help Save Them"

I want you to notice the birds that we share this world with. Sometimes simply noticing and being aware can help you fall more in love
with creation. In the piece noted above, Margaret Renkl laments the
staggering decline of bird populations due to human behavior. We
have lost nearly one-third of our bird populations in the past fifty
years. Renkl wisely speculates that if we could fall more in love with
birds by just listening to them and learning their names, we would be
more inclined to help save them.

Sales for birdseed, birdfeeders, and birding supplies like field guides
and binoculars soared during the COVID-19 pandemic. In the midst
of lockdowns, cancellations, and sickness, the sight of a bright red car-

dinal perched in the feeder at sunrise and the *cheer-cheer* sound of a singing robin offer a glimmer of hope.

Most every morning, I take my coffee out to our screened-in back porch and listen to the birds. One late spring morning, I was sitting out back with my coffee, feeling the wind on my face. I looked down at my phone when a text came through from my friend Jes. She texted a brief video of a hummingbird on a very small baby dogwood, accompanied by her words. "Mom's birthday is in ten days, and this little lady has been coming and perching on my sweet memorial dogwood that you all gave me all morning." Jes's mom had died earlier that year, and our small group of sister-friends had sent a little dogwood tree for her to plant. Sister Hummingbird was showing Jes the incarnate love of God with each and every flutter of her wings.

St. Francis referred to the moon as Brother, the birds as Sisters. The mystery of the incarnation is made real through our kinship with the natural world. Brother Moon lights up the path so we can refill the birdfeeders before bedtime. Sister Hummingbird helps remind us of our mother's love. Miracles happen everywhere, if only we take the time to look, to see, to study, to love, to listen, to *adore* . . . to use all of our faculties and senses to perceive the love that abounds.

WONDER: Consider the birds of the air with the people you love this week. After a lot of staring at branches and sky, and after a lot of quiet, come together for your weekly gathering and ask one another this generous question: "What did you hear? What did you see?"

TRY: Fall more in love with birds by getting to know them. Invest in a set of binoculars if you can, and keep them near a window with a bird-feeder nearby. See page 129 for directions on making a simple bird-feeder and birdhouse. Download an app—like iNaturalist from National Geographic or the Merlin app, developed by ornithologists at

Cornell—that will help you identify birds and their songs. Add David Allen Sibley's *What It's Like to Be a Bird* to your home library. And if you're keeping a nature journal, include the names of the birds you see, where and when you saw them, and your impressions of them. Try to describe the songs and sound they make.

MAKE: A SIMPLE BIRDFEEDER & BIRDHOUSE

EQUIPMENT

Peanut butter

Something cylindrical from the recycling bin (like a toilet paper roll)

Birdseed

Foil pan or dish to use as your work surface

Branch or dowel that's a bit longer than your cylinder

String

DIRECTIONS

Spread a thick layer of peanut butter all over the outside of your cylinder. Pour birdseed in your foil pan or whatever you're using for your work surface. Roll the peanut butter–covered exterior of your cylinder all through the birdseed. Put the branch or dowel through the cylinder's hole, and then attach string to the exterior end of your branch or dowel. Hang your birdfeeder in a tree at eye level from a window, if possible, so you can see the birds visit and enjoy your feeder.

If you're not a woodworker, the simplest way to get children involved in building a birdhouse is to purchase a prefabricated cedar kit. Let them decorate it and choose a place for their birdhouse, ideally within view of the house.

FISH

Fishing is merely an attempt to connect to something that you know is there but can't see—a perpetual series of occasions for hope.

—BRANDI CARLILE[2]

In Athens, the small East Tennessee town where I was raised, weekly Bible lessons were taught in our public elementary school by a kind-hearted woman named Miss Johnson. Every week, she was sent over to our school from the biggest, most powerful Baptist church in town, and she told us stories and lessons about Jesus, as well as carefully chosen characters from the Old Testament. We dutifully illustrated the stories and wrote sentences about their lessons in our little notebooks. Catholic and Jehovah's Witnesses kids would leave the classroom during Miss Johnson's Bible lesson to sit quietly in the library because their parents didn't want them to attend. Even then, it was audacious to have Bible classes taught in public school.

But my public school system also had something quite progressive for the 1980s—a spacious, beautiful camp situated on the edge of a scenic lake that they leased from the Tennessee Valley Authority for $1 per year. At the camp, kids in elementary school and middle school from all sorts of backgrounds learned how to build and cook on a campfire. They slept in cabins, hiked on trails, made crafts, and retold ghost stories and the "Jack tales" of Appalachian folklore. During those wonderful days at camp, I first learned how to fish. Fishing lessons were taught by Mr. Harrell, our PE teacher, who would start by having us go off into the woods to find the perfect fishing stick. Then, he would show us how to tie a hook and connect a weight and bobber to our lines. Finally, we would find our own spot to sit on the dock, pass around a plastic container of dirt filled with worms, and gingerly attach a squirming worm to the sharp barb on our hooks. I was ten at my first fishing lesson, and it didn't take long for me to feel the weight of a fish on my line, to learn the art of waiting a bit before pulling a small-mouth bass or black crappie right out of the lake.

So the public school in my conservative, Protestant community taught me both Bible stories and how to fish. In the New Testament, you'll find many stories about Jesus fishing and believing in things you can't see. In Luke's gospel, Peter has been fishing all night without success when Jesus tells him to move the boat out a little and put his nets down for just one more try. The nets come back up so heavy with fish that they break. And then in John's gospel, after the resurrection, Peter has once more been fishing through the night without any luck. Standing on the shore, the resurrected Jesus calls out to the disciples in the boat to cast their nets down again. When they do, another massive haul of fish comes in, and they immediately realize God's presence in Jesus. Joyful and giddy like a child, Peter pulls his clothes around him, jumps in the water, and runs to the shore to greet his beloved friend. The other disciples bring in the full net of fish. We are told that no one asks Jesus who he is; they just intuitively know that their friend is with them, and they share a breakfast of fish and bread by the fire Jesus has built—a beautiful outdoor occasion for hope, joy, abundance, communion, and connection.

WONDER: What if you decided that everything you connected to in the past twenty-four hours was an occasion for hope? What if all the people, places, and things you'd connected to in the past day are divine manifestations? If there are children at the gathering, let them wonder aloud about this before everyone else. Hearing children tell about their past day's connections can set the tone for an illuminating conversation among people of all ages.

TRY: Set aside an hour or so this week to go fishing with your loved ones. Put a line in a creek, lake, stream, ocean, or pond somewhere, and be still as you look out at the surface of the water. Can you connect with a fish? Ponder about all those before you who have fished, including Jesus and his friends. Or, if fishing is not possible for you at this time, ask each person at the gathering to use photography to *connect with something they know is there but cannot see.* At the gathering, go around the table and show your photographs. Explain what is there in your photograph that can't be seen with our eyes. Does this feel, as Brandi Carlile describes above, like an occasion for hope?

COMMUNE

Anyone who truly knows creatures may be excused from listening to sermons, for every creature is full of God, and is a book.

—ATTRIBUTED TO MEISTER ECKHART

These lines attributed to Meister Eckhart speak deeply to me—the idea that every creature is a book. And full of God! What glorious images to help us imagine how incarnation "works" in all creatures. All animals—not just the human animals—are infused with the divine. We are all full of pages waiting to be touched, read, understood. Even our language holds this secret, for the word *animal* derives from *anima,* the Latin word for soul!

Many years ago, when I was on safari in South Africa with my students, I saw a bird common to that region but utterly extraordinary to my North American eyes: a lilac-breasted roller. That bird was an audacious explosion of color perched all alone in some sparse branches we passed. That majestic, otherworldly creature had royal-blue tipped wings, a teal belly, and a pinkish-purple breast! Sometimes when I meditate, I envision the lilac-breasted roller and that moment of adoration and communion I feel certain we shared in our encounter. In my office, I even keep a copy of the photo I snapped, and from time to time, I look on it the way other people might gaze at an icon of a saint.

I want to know creatures, and I believe that, on some level, creatures want to know me. Just last night, I woke at three A.M., worried about an ill family member. My eleven-year-old miniature schnauzer Teddy immediately sensed that I was awake. Teddy got up and came over to nestle right next to me. I petted his furry body, and I tried to match my breathing with his until we both fell back to sleep.

WONDER: Consider the idea that whatever we are doing to the body of Earth and its creatures, we are doing to the body of God. Ask any children present at this gathering to put this idea in their own words. What can we learn out of the mouths of babes about the notion that all creatures—not just human animals—are part of God's incarnation? How do you and those you love respond to this ancient and faithful idea? Are there elements of your life that inhibit you from communing with nonhuman creatures? What are they?

TRY: Spend some time in the companionship of an animal this week— maybe a dog, a cat, a guinea pig, a hamster, a rabbit, a horse, or another nonhuman creature. There's a particular kind of energy, affection, ado- ration, and unconditional love we humans get when we commune with animals.

DISCOVER: MAY 31, VISITATION OF MARY

Your flesh rejoiced; like the blade of grass on which the dew has fall'n, viridity within it to infuse: so it was with you, O mother of all joy.

—HILDEGARD OF BINGEN, "Ave, Generosa"

After the annunciation, Mary went into the hill country to be with her cousin Elizabeth. Elizabeth was also pregnant, and when Elizabeth heard Mary greet her, Elizabeth reported that her own baby leapt for joy in her womb. The baby leaping in Elizabeth's womb, of course, would grow up to be John the Baptist.

Commemorate the Visitation of Mary by reading *Visitation*, an exquisite volume of poetry by Maggie Blake Bailey. Bailey's poetry explores the relationship between Mary and Elizabeth, examining themes of motherhood, family life, friendship, and the sacred feminine. Another way to commemorate this day is to plant red roses, rosemary, lavender, or daisies, flowers that often symbolize Mary.

MAKE: AN ICON OF MARY

The word *icon* comes from the Greek for "image," and icons are found throughout many religious traditions. Icons are images to focus on during contemplation or prayers. Icons can be images of Jesus, saints, angels, or other admired ones—and May is an ideal time to draw, paint, or collage an icon of Mary. Spend some time online looking at images of icons throughout different traditions, and then take your paints, crayons, pastels, or other art supplies and make an icon of Mary that speaks to you. Dive deeper into a family exploration of feminine manifestations of the divine by reading *Mother God*, the poignant, tender picture book written by Teresa Kim Pecinovsky and gorgeously illustrated by Khoa Le.

JUNE

COME ALIVE

Don't ask yourself what the world needs. Ask yourself what makes you come alive, and go do that, because what the world needs is people who have come alive.

—ATTRIBUTED TO HOWARD THURMAN

The light increases and crescendos in June, for this month holds the longest day of the year: the summer solstice of June 21. On the liturgical calendar, Ordinary Time begins after the Day of Pentecost and continues until Advent begins. Members of the clergy wear green vestments, and altars are adorned with green linens to remind us of the verdant life that waits for us beyond the walls of a church building. The long season of growing that is Ordinary Time invites us to learn from sacred (and not-so-sacred) texts and to reflect on the examples of saints (both saints that have been recognized and those not officially stamped as saintly). Ordinary Time is a season to become more rooted in our love for and connectedness to the greenness of creation. Hildegard of Bingen, a twelfth-century Benedictine abbess, mystic, healer, and composer, whispers an ancient secret across time and space: *The word manifests itself in every creature.* What if the wonder of this so-called ordinary season is to encounter the Holy Spirit—not only through liturgy, prayer, and contemplation—but through our own creatureliness?

According to legend, St. Francis was once walking in meditation in his garden, and he stopped at a bare almond tree. As he approached the almond tree, he asked the tree to tell him about God. Suddenly, the almond tree was covered in blossoms. To tell Francis about the nature of God, all the tree had to do was "come alive" in its inherent splendor.

While Francis's tree came alive by blossoming, many organisms come alive by glowing with light—a wondrous phenomenon known as bioluminescence. Jellyfish, gnats, shrimp, fungi, and beetles are but some of the organisms on this planet that produce their own radiant light. My parents live near the entrance to the Great Smoky Mountains National Park where, for two to three weeks a year peaking in early June, people from around the world make pilgrimages to witness a species of fireflies flash their light patterns synchronously. Through their elaborate, flickering mating ritual, the synchronous fireflies (*Photinus carolinus*) use astonishingly complex patterns to let their brothers and sisters know they have come alive for the season. Their twinkling little lights communicate that they are ready, waiting, willing, and able to bring about more generations of mysterious radiance in the darkness of the mountains.

Some days when I, like Hildegard and Francis, wonder about the nature of God, I close my eyes and imagine Love's breath filling up the valleys, spreading over the mountaintops, whipping across the surface of the sea, and inflating my own lungs. I imagine the animating breath that makes us all come to life. In *The Naked Now: Learning to See as the Mystics See,* Father Richard Rohr, a Franciscan, recalls the YHWH prayer a rabbi taught him many years ago: Jews traditionally do not speak God's name but breathe it with an open mouth and throat: Inhale—*Yah;* exhale—*weh.* And so, as we breathe, we are always speaking the name of God and participating in God's breath; it's how we enter this world and how we leave it. With each breath, we approach God through God's aliveness in the world.

Ordinary Time invites us to become more rooted, more alive, and more aware of Jesus' dynamic ministry, which culminates with his Sermon on the Mount, also known as the Beatitudes. In this intricate, radical, enrapturing sermon, Jesus boldly announces that the poor in spirit, those who are mourning, those who are meek, those who hunger and thirst for righteousness . . . these are the ones who are blessed! The peacemakers and the merciful and those who are insulted . . . these are the children of God! In the Beatitudes, the rebel Jesus turns the world upside down by flipping the script on who is "blessed." This unorthodox carpenter from Nazareth has come to catalyze a revolution, a movement of peace, transformation, and abundance, a movement based on love and justice. As I use my holy imagination to read these lines aloud to myself and conjure up that wondrous scene of him offering these upside-down tenets, I feel I am in the presence of a human being who has fully come alive.

Contemplate the idea that our families—or families of choice—are our Schools for Love. In our Schools for Love, we learn what makes us come alive, and we engage in practices that help us approach God's aliveness in the world. So, in your Schools for Love this month:

- Set your alarm clocks a little earlier than usual and wake up before the birds. Sit outside and start your day by "coming alive" when they start their morning songs, coos, warbles, and chirrups.
- Sing out loud from time to time.
- Spend some time with the Beatitudes.
- Take some time to contemplate, pray about, name, and share what makes you come alive.

June Creation Care Challenge: Caring for community can also be a way to care for creation. Invest in your community and reduce your carbon footprint by committing to buying local whenever possible, and eschew buying from nonlocal retailers when a local alternative is available. Furthermore, you may find that putting money back into the hands of local businesses brings you a sense of joy!

WAKE

The first chirps of the waking birds mark the "point vierge" of the dawn under a sky as yet without real light, a moment of awe and inexpressible innocence, when the Father in perfect silence opens their eyes. They begin to speak to Him, not with fluent song, but with an awakening question that is their dawn state, their state at the "point vierge." Their condition asks if it is time for them to "be." He answers "yes." Then, they one by one wake up, and become birds. They manifest themselves as birds, beginning to sing. Presently they will be fully themselves, and will even fly.

Meanwhile, the most wonderful moment of the day is that when creation in its innocence asks permission to "be" once again, as it did on the first morning that ever was.

—THOMAS MERTON, *Confessions of a Guilty Bystander*

Mornings are sacred to me. I often tell my husband, Ben, that the last thought I have before going to bed is how the sooner I go to sleep, the sooner I can wake up to the exquisitely hand-poured cup of coffee he brings me most every morning. My deep love of coffee—combined with birdsong, the changing light, Ben's steadfast gift of making it and bringing it to me—truly make mornings the loveliest part of my day.

And I'm not alone. Our son Peter often says, "The birds get up; I get up." At the age of seven, he once looked out a hotel room window and woke the whole family up so we could see "the rainbow sunrise" he was enjoying alone at daybreak. Our hotel room faced a nondescript line of strip malls on the city limits of Montgomery, Alabama, but all Peter could see was the beauty, and he couldn't wait to show it to us. I am a morning person, and it appears I'm raising at least one other morning person.

As I read Merton's words at the beginning of a sultry summer morning accompanied by coffee, candlelight, and quiet little clicks of my keyboard, I try to pry words out of the mud in my brain: Six in the morning is my favorite time to cobble together a praise song. I like the idea that each and every day, in my drowsiness, fresh from sleep, I can use mornings to form a hazy question for God. I'm not ready to be productive or tackle my to-do list, but I'm ready to *be*. The Creator gives me permission to "be" once again—to be fully myself in the newness of morning.

Each morning will provide me with wonder, if I let it. I have to watch myself—I have to be careful not to freak out if I come down to the kitchen for my coffee and find that the boys left their dishes in the sink. I have to will myself to walk right past any messes straight to the back porch where I can hear the birds manifest themselves as birds, as Merton says. I have to resist the urge to surrender my attention to a glowing screen. It takes a little work to wake this way.

WONDER: Turn to one another and ask: How do you feel when you wake? Is morning that most wonderful time of your day, or your least favorite part? Do your feet hit the ground running with courage and strength? Where is your attention in the morning? What does the best version of a morning look like to you?

TRY: Pick a day this week to wake up before the birds. Check the time for sunrise, and set your alarm for half an hour before, while darkness still covers the world. This might take some coaxing on behalf of some members of your family, but get the coffee ready the night before and know that it will be worth it. Find your perfect morning song, or make a morning playlist for yourself. "Morning Has Broken" by Cat Stevens, "O-o-h Child" by the Five Stairsteps, and "Dragons" by Drew Holcomb would be at the top of mine. Pray these words attributed to St. Patrick:

I arise each day
Through the strength of heaven:
Light of sun,
Radiance of moon,
Splendor of fire,
Speed of lightning,
Swiftness of wind,
Depth of sea,
Stability of Earth,
Firmness of rock.

SING

I will sing to the Lord as long as I live.
I will sing praise to my God while I have being.

—PSALM 104:33

I don't have a tattoo, but if I did, I think I might copy my friend Margie's. Her tattoo simply reads AND SANG. Margie inked these two words on her body as a reminder of the final two words of Mary Oliver's poem, "I Worried." The speaker of "I Worried" voices a litany of concerns: She wonders if the garden will keep growing and if the river will keep flowing. She worries that the Earth will stop turning, and she worries that her aging body will fail her. And she wonders if she should even dare to sing in a world where even the birds sound better than she does. The speaker of the poem concludes with the brilliant realization that worrying wasn't going to get her anywhere so she gave up worrying for good: She took her imperfect body out into the glory of the morning . . . "and sang."

And sang. It's shorthand for singing anyway. For singing in spite of. For letting the litany of worries go because there are songs to be sung, there are old bodies that need to go out into dawn and come alive alongside the finches, the robins, and the cardinals. Learning the story of Margie's tattoo marked a turning point for me. I sing in public now, without worrying if I am any good. I sing to my students at the beginning of class. I sing with the windows down in traffic and when I am cooking dinner and when I'm standing on a tarmac getting ready to board a plane.

We sing to praise, to mourn, to pass the time. We sing our stories, and we sing to tell our histories. We sing because we feel joy, and we sing to release tension. We sing because singing songs helps us memorize formulas, alphabets, the names of the states, the months of the year. We sing to soothe our babies, and we sing to reveal our love to other beings.

I live near the Ryman Auditorium, which was first built by a riverboat captain as a gathering place to glorify God and is now a legendary music venue. Stained glass windows and hard, wooden pews make the Ryman still feel like going to church, and there have been nights when I could get only one ticket for a show I wanted to see—so I've gone all by myself to hear the loudest of rock concerts, worshipped with electric guitars and ecstatic foot stomping so rhythmic I'd swear the building was vibrating. I love going to the Ryman-church to sing with strangers late into the night; it's not Compline, but as the liturgy says, leaving the Ryman late at night with my ears ringing and my throat sore from singing with strangers is "a perfect end." My theory is, music reveals a sustaining and life-giving part of me that I don't know well and want to know better.

WONDER: My colleague Andrea's mother had advanced dementia and was in a memory care unit. Every week, Andrea went to get her mother and took her to church, where her mother—who could not even recall her own name, the name of her children, where she was, or major details of her life—could sing every single word to every single hymn. Why do you think singing and songs are embedded so deeply in our beings? How does singing make you feel? Are there particular songs that are deeply part of who you are?

*   *   *

TRY: Explore the Revised Common Lectionary online and read this week's lessons. Then, imagine and decide on one, two, or three songs that connect to the readings. I'll freely admit my love of music is rather promiscuous and unrestrained, so when I do this, I find that I joyfully draw from a wide range of artists, styles, and genres that I happen to love with wild abandon. I certainly wouldn't stick to so-called sacred music. For example, if the Revised Common Lectionary called for the Old Testament reading of Isaiah's prophetic vision of beating swords into plowshares and spears into pruning hooks (Isaiah 2:1–5), I'd cue up Brandi Carlile's inherently political "Hold Out Your Hand," a song that has become an anthem for ending gun violence. Or if Psalm 31 was part of the appointed readings of the day, I would choose gospel artist CeCe Winans's rendition of "Goodness of God." Along with hearing "I love you"s from my beloved family, I think that listening to the glory that is CeCe Winans singing "Goodness of God" might be the last thing I'd want to hear before my body leaves this Earth.

Be sure to let the children at your gathering choose songs as well. Print off the lyrics if you need to. Read the lessons, and focus on singing together, thus making communal singing the focal point of this week's liturgy.

DISCOVER: EVENSONG

Now as we come to the setting of the sun, and our eyes behold
the vesper light, we sing thy praises. . . . Thou art worthy at all
times to be praised by happy voices, O Son of God, O Giver of
life, and to be glorified through all the worlds.

—"O GRACIOUS LIGHT," *Phos hilaron*, Evening Prayer, Rite II,
The Book of Common Prayer

The last two weeks have focused on coming alive through waking and
singing. It's a perfect time to discover the tradition of evensong, a gorgeous service of sung and chanted evening prayer that begins as the
sun is setting. Evensong originated in the candlelit cathedrals of England. A simple way to experience this entrancing service together is
to turn out the lights, light some candles, and watch Evensong on the
Washington National Cathedral's social media channels.

LAVISH

Wonder is the heaviest element on the periodic table. Even a tiny fleck of it stops time.

—DIANE ACKERMAN, *The Rarest of the Rare*

One of the wildest, most sensual stories in scripture is the account of the woman with the alabaster jar, a story that appears in Matthew, Mark, Luke, and John. Here is the scene: It's the week of Jesus' execution, and he is in Bethany at the home of Simon the Leper. Jesus is relaxing at the table, and an unknown woman, described as a so-called sinner, arrives uninvited with an alabaster jar—a white stone container—filled with nard, which would have been the finest perfume available to her. Surely, this jar of nard is the most expensive thing she owns. As she enters, time seems to stop. She interrupts dinner and goes straight to Jesus. She weeps. As her tears fall on his feet, she wipes his feet with her hair, and she cracks open her alabaster jar and pours the expensive perfume all over his feet. Shards of alabaster are all about. An exquisite fragrance fills the room as she lavishes and anoints Jesus with an amalgam of her tears and the costliest thing she owns. The absolute best of her material and embodied possessions have been shattered and poured out, flowing on Jesus' body. She's radically, extravagantly, and lovingly anointing a king and preparing him for his death.

This story of the woman who weeps, who anoints, who breaks the most expensive thing she owns and perfumes the whole room has always amazed me on multiple levels. It's earthy, shocking, sensory, unrestrained, dramatic, cinematic. It's the story of a woman who seems to have come alive in the presence of Love and could not care less what the others think. By all accounts, the disciples are annoyed with her because the perfume represents a year's wages, but Jesus defends her offering and welcomes her disruption. He tells the disciples not to bother her, that what she has done is a great offering.

"Do you see this woman?" Jesus asks. "I entered your house; you gave me no water for my feet, but she has wet my feet with her tears and wiped them with her hair." Jesus says she has loved much. She has offered her skin, her hair, her body, her perfume, even the shattered pieces of alabaster on the floor—all of this sensual, extravagant, ephemeral lavish offering has met with his total approval. For this woman, Love is not just a feeling. Love is a practice, something she does with her body. Love is not a state of being; Love is something she offers by pouring out the best that she has, and Jesus fully endorses her lush offering.

WONDER: Have you ever witnessed anyone "come alive" and make a lavish offering like the woman with the alabaster jar? Can you think of any offerings that are made with the best parts of someone's self? Have you ever made an offering that came from the best of what you had? Consider ways you experience abundance in your own life, and take this opportunity to wonder about a future offering you might make. Perhaps there is an offering your group can make to the wider world or someone you know who could use a lavishing surprise. Especially if children are present, bring out the art supplies and create a drawing, painting, or sculpture that represents what you consider the finest possession or quality you have to offer.

*   *   *

TRY: Make an offering that embodies Love. Maybe it's a letter to the group. Maybe it's a cherished possession like a special rock or a family recipe. Maybe it's something only you can imagine. Gather an offering from each member of the circle, and share it at the table or put it on the family altar (see page 152).

MAKE: A FAMILY ALTAR CLOTH

The bright summer day my husband and I got engaged, we drove over to see Becca, our priest. We couldn't wait to tell her our happy news. She didn't have any champagne, so she poured us beer in fancy glasses, and we sat gleefully on her back porch and talked about marriage. One of the pieces of advice she gave that I've never forgotten is how important it was to begin to create our own family rituals. She mentioned making a special altar cloth that we could use for our wedding, for baptisms, for confirmations, and even for burials. Inspired by Becca's advice, I went to the nicest fabric store in town and bought some beautiful embroidered white linen. I hemmed the edges, ironed it carefully, and brought it to the church the day we were married so I could place it on the altar. As the years have gone by, we've used our handmade altar cloth not only for our wedding but for both the boys' baptisms.

When the COVID-19 pandemic began to spread across the world and it was clear we would not be going to church in person for a while, I took a console table out from behind a sofa and cleared off the books, magazines, and bric-a-brac. I got out the lemon Pledge, got down on my knees, and dusted every surface and crevice. Since we'd be having "home church" indefinitely, I decided to put this nondescript table into service as our home altar. With help from Ben and the boys, we moved our altar in front of the fireplace, right under the television where we'd be participating in church via YouTube for the time being. We covered it with our family altar cloth, a candle, and flowers from the yard. In our church community, we started sharing photos of home altars on Instagram as a way to feel more connected to each other during an isolating time.

Make a family altar cloth. Begin by brainstorming with your loved ones about what sort of altar cloth you'd like to make together. You can get much fancier than I did. Consider color and texture. Choose fabrics that epitomize your unique story. You might even choose to incorporate appliqués or stencils. You might include a piece of a baby blanket or a hand-me-down tablecloth. Or you might embroider or appliqué flora, fauna, elements, or special words or symbols that are important to your family.

BLESS

When I understand Jesus' words in Aramaic, I translate like this:
Get up, go ahead, do something, move, you who are hungry and
thirsty for justice, for you shall be satisfied. Get up, go ahead, do
something, move, you peacemakers, for you shall be called
children of God. To me this reflects Jesus' words and teachings
much more accurately. I can hear him saying: "Get your hands
dirty to build a human society for human beings; otherwise,
others will torture and murder the poor, the voiceless, and the
powerless." Christianity is not passive but active, energetic, alive,
going beyond despair. . . . "Get up, go ahead, do something,
move," Jesus said to his disciples.

—ELIAS CHACOUR, *We Belong to the Land*

A s I've tried to learn more about the Beatitudes, Jesus' Sermon on
the Mount, I have learned that in Jesus' language of Aramaic, the
word *blessed* that he used repeatedly was *ashray*. To our ears, *blessed*
can sound passive, but *ashray* was really active; it means "to turn yourself around, to repent." If you read the *Blessed*s of the Beatitudes, Jesus'
sermon becomes a reflection on how to turn our own personal suffering outward—a "how to" manual serving others in love and peace.

Early one June morning in the midst of the uprisings for racial justice following George Floyd's horrific murder by a police officer, I
placed the biggest BLACK LIVES MATTER sign I could find in my front
yard in urban Nashville. My doing so was a ridiculously small gesture

in the greater context of more traumatic injustice and a long overdue reckoning with our nation's heartbreaking history of violence, white supremacy, and rampant racism. But I wanted a literal sign to express my solidarity, a poster board proclamation to say what I wanted to scream. A white woman, a literal neighbor of mine, walked by as I was pushing the sign holder in the dirt. She stopped and asked me what "woke" meant. "Woke" had rapidly entered the lexicon as a way to describe people who are learning to see the injustices all around the world, but by her abrupt question, I sensed that she was troubled by the idea of being "woke" and maybe she was troubled by my sign.

Wakening to our histories and wakening to our present realities are ways of coming alive. In later conversations on the sidewalk, I tried to tell my neighbor that when I was displaying my sign, I was thinking about all the Black geniuses who never got to thrive and come alive in their own brilliance. I was thinking of all the Black parents who had to teach their children how to interact with the police and others in a world under the relentless threat of racism. I was thinking about those Black mamas and daddies who didn't have time and space to nurture their own sense of wonder because they were too worried about their children's safety.

Maybe like you, I am thirsty for justice. Maybe like you, I'm not afraid of getting my hands dirty. But here I stand—a white woman of privilege who has experienced so many benefits and advantages that I'm walking around in a cloud more than half the time. I'm trying to learn how to be a justice-seeker, how to be energetic and not fall into despair; I'm trying to read, study, and listen. I'm trying to figure out how my life can mean something, how my life can offer a scrap of a blessing to someone else. I'm clumsy, I'm awkward, I'm inadequate, and I'm extremely imperfect, but just for today, I promise to get up. I vow to keep on walking, to pray with my legs.

WONDER: Do you have a deep yearning to do something that blesses other people? What is it? Some people might say that this deep yearning you feel is actually God yearning for connection with *you*. Ask any children present to tell a story about a time they blessed someone.

TRY: Listen together to Simon and Garfunkel's 1967 song "Blessed," which riffs on the Beatitudes. What does the last line, "I have tended my own garden much too long," mean to you? If you're feeling inspired, compose your own riff on the Beatitudes, like Simon and Garfunkel did.

THE BEATITUDES: MATTHEW 5:1–12 NRSV

When Jesus saw the crowds, he went up the mountain; and after he sat down, his disciples came to him. Then he began to speak, and taught them, saying: Blessed are the poor in spirit, for theirs is the kingdom of heaven. Blessed are those who mourn, for they will be comforted. Blessed are the meek, for they will inherit the earth. Blessed are those who hunger and thirst for righteousness, for they will be filled. Blessed are the merciful, for they will receive mercy. Blessed are the pure in heart, for they will see God. Blessed are the peacemakers, for they will be called children of God. Blessed are those who are persecuted for righteousness' sake, for theirs is the kingdom of heaven. Blessed are you when people revile you and persecute you and utter all kinds of evil against you falsely on my account. Rejoice and be glad, for your reward is great in heaven, for in the same way they persecuted the prophets who were before you.

DISCOVER: THE SACRAMENTS OF BAPTISM
AND THE EUCHARIST[1]

In the Anglican/Episcopal tradition, the sacraments are often explained as outward, visible signs of God's grace. Baptism and the Eucharist are sometimes described as the chief sacraments because they were given by Jesus to humanity. (As shared on page 106 of week 13, washing feet was also a sacrament given by Jesus to humanity; that humble, useful act of service and devotion is sometimes called "Jesus' forgotten sacrament.")

Eucharist derives from the Greek word *eucharistein,* which means "give thanks." At the Eucharist, which is also called Mass, Holy Communion, or the Lord's Supper, bread is broken and wine is shared. The Eucharist is a response to Jesus' words: "Do this in remembrance of me," which he spoke at the final meal he shared with his friends before his crucifixion and resurrection. The Eucharist is considered a foretaste of the love and nourishment God promises to all. At the conclusion of the Eucharistic feast, we are sent out in peace to love and to serve.

The outward and visible sign of Holy Baptism is water, and the inward spiritual grace is this: Through baptism, we are born into the family of the people of God (also known as "the church") and given new life through the Holy Spirit. Infants are baptized because they are members of God's church, and promises are made for infants by parents and godparents.

To be baptized is to join the people of God. Often, babies or children are baptized with godparents at their side, and the godparents speak for the babies and little ones who cannot yet speak. The sacrament of baptism begins with a prayer of thanksgiving for the gift of water because in water, the Spirit has lived and moved since the beginning of creation. Baptism often involves sacred water from a special font inside a church, but baptism can also take place outside in a beautiful moving river, under the sky and clouds as John the Baptist baptized Jesus in the Jordan River.

When we are baptized, we promise to break bread and share wine, to fellowship with one another, and to seek and serve Christ in all persons, loving our neighbors and ourselves. We promise to strive for justice and peace, respecting the dignity of every human being. We also assert, over and over again in the baptismal covenant, that we will need God's help; we promise to ask for it. In *A New Zealand Book of Common Prayer,* the baptism liturgy specifically calls for the celebrant to pray that the spirit of wonder will increase in the person being baptized.

Read the liturgies for baptism in *The Book of Common Prayer.* What do you wonder or wrestle about when it comes to the covenants and special prayers? My incredibly thoughtful father took the covenants of baptism very seriously, and he wasn't baptized until I was baptized as an infant. One of my favorite family photographs is of him at the age of twenty-six holding me, his baby girl, on the day we were both baptized. Does your family have any stories, special clothing, rituals, or photographs to share around the sacrament of baptism? What does baptism mean in your life?

JULY

CULTIVATE RESILIENCE

My religion is kindness.
   —His Holiness the Dalai Lama

In July, even the windows perspire in sweltering Tennessee. Though I love Mother Creation with all my heart, soul, and mind, I am not all that interested in being outside during these dog days of summertime unless I'm completely immersed in a cool body of water with a glass of homemade lemonade nearby. Likewise, I have mixed feelings about the fireworks that bring wide-eyed joy from my children (and especially from my pyrotechnics-loving husband); such dazzling displays bring loud booms that shock our neighbors who are veterans of combat and terrify our furry family members.

The name of this month comes from the Roman statesman Julius Caesar, whose tragic story was immortalized in Shakespeare's play, one of the works many of us read and enact in high school English and theater classes. Julius Caesar's friends are convinced that murdering him is in the best interest of Rome, that the common good is served by the horror of an assassination. The twisted argument Julius Caesar's countrymen make to rationalize "doing good" brings up a lot of complex emotions for me during the month of July. For in my homeland, the United States, this is the month that red, white, and blue flags start flying on porches, and if we are wise, we will thoughtfully consider our nation's complicated history alongside the meaning of liberation and independence.

I love and am deeply attached to this beautiful land. When I've been traveling out of the country, my heart swells with delight and relief when the customs officer stamps my document and says, "Welcome home." American democracy has so much to be proud of, but as a follower of Jesus and the Way of Love, I can't help but feel a bit squeamish about this month's displays of patriotism. Freedom, liberty, justice, and a devotion to the common good are absolutely worth celebrating, but we are all God's children, and I certainly don't believe some people are better than other people. Toni Morrison once said in an interview, "[I]f you can only be tall because someone else is on their knees, then you have a serious problem."[1] To me, Morrison's wise line sums up my mixed feelings about patriotic displays and expressions of national pride. I don't want anyone to be left out, mistreated, forgotten, or told they aren't as good as someone else. I tend to pray for inclusion and liberation, not reinforced power dynamics and oppression.

However, I do love the patriotism and unity of "Lift Every Voice," written in 1900 by James Weldon Johnson. Known as "the Black national anthem," "Lift Every Voice" tells a rich story of America:

God of our weary years, God of our silent tears,
Thou who hast brought us thus far on the way;
Thou who hast by the might led us into the light;
Keep us forever in the path we pray.

"Lift Every Voice" is about confronting the brutality of America's past and present, hoping through our weariness, and singing through despair to the "listening skies." It inspires desperately needed truth-telling about the past and a sense of hope and resolve about the years to come.

What does it mean to be part of a nation, to feel a sense of duty toward others, and to act on behalf of the common good? July is a good time to ask this question, perhaps while sitting near an air-conditioning vent. And I am vexed by the very question because Jesus' teachings point me not just to a love of those who live in proximity to me but toward a love of my neighbors near and far. The love of Christ extends toward all, not just some who happen to be born in a particular country. Becoming a mother in my mid-thirties deepened this yearning in me because I found myself looking at others with a new kind of tenderness. Each person was not just an American or a Russian or a Canadian or a Ukrainian but a *child*. Someone's child. Someone's baby ... *imago dei:* the image of God.

July is an opportune time to extend an understanding of our neighbors beyond national borders and also our neighbors from different faith traditions. Francis of Assisi provides us with a memorable example of interfaith dialogue. He went to Egypt on one of the Crusades and was horrified by the murderous actions of the "Christian" knights. Scandalously, he crossed enemy lines and sought out the sultan of Egypt in an effort to make peace. He found not a murderous enemy but a friendly sultan, thus showing him that goodness, mercy, and kindness were not unique attributes of Christians. And he found in this journey that Christians were not immune to hate, that some of his fellow Christians were actually murderous enemies.

Friendship, beauty, and strength arise from travel and interfaith experiences. My own path has taken me into spaces of learning from Buddhism. In college religion classes, I began learning about how Buddhist practices uniquely confront human suffering, and my curiosity for learning more has only grown in the past thirty years. Like Christianity, Buddhism teaches unconditional love, but Buddhism offers so many more "how-tos," methods, and concrete tools when it comes to real-life struggles with suffering and unconditional love. The practices Buddhism offers are serious but playful, too; smiling, laughter, humor, and joy are integral to Buddhist teachings. Buddhism proposes many specific methods for confronting the realities of the human condition and the nature of suffering. July is an opportunity to dive deeper into mystery by learning about Buddhist teachings of the Four Immeasurables, which are practices that cultivate resilience by showing specific ways to make room for other beings in our consciousnesses. The Four Immeasurables (*brahmavihārās*) are loving-kindness (*metta*), compassion (*karuna*), sympathetic joy (*mudita*), and equanimity (*upekkha*). There is literally "no measure" to the wonders of these ideas and how they invite us to see others inside of ourselves.

Given that Ordinary Time, the "green season" between Easter and Advent, is a season for growth and maturity, July is a good season to tap into the wondrous, immeasurable well that lives deep inside our beings, as well as to seek out ways to put ourselves in dialogue—and perhaps even find friendship—with those from different homelands and faith traditions. During July, ponder how three statements might live in harmony:

- I love and respect the land of my birth.
- I want my neighbors near and far to be free from suffering.
- I want to radiate compassion, connection, and joy.

July Creation Care Challenge: Animal agriculture places an immense burden on the environment. A plant-based diet is good for our health and for Earth's health, too. Find a local farmer's market or vegetable stand. How many plant-based meals from local farms can you eat during the bountiful month of July?

DISCOVER: ORDINARY TIME

Come, Thou Fount of every blessing,
Tune my heart to sing Thy grace;
Streams of mercy, never ceasing,
Call for songs of loudest praise.

Teach me some melodious sonnet,
Sung by flaming tongues above.
Praise the mount, I'm fixed upon it,
Mount of Thy redeeming love.
  —ROBERT ROBINSON, "Come Thou Fount of Every Blessing"

Also known as "the green season" or Sundays after Pentecost, Ordinary Time occurs between the Monday after Pentecost and the Saturday before the first Sunday of Advent. Green is the color of growth and life. And Ordinary Time is all about how *the church* can grow by living into the teachings of Jesus. I emphasize the words *the church* because *the church* is not merely a building or an organization or an institution: Rather, *the church* is the people of God. And *grow* doesn't mean to grow in number of people or in buildings—here, to *grow* is to mature, deepen, become more resilient and more alive. Ordinary Time offers us extraordinary space and time to contemplate Jesus' life, teachings, and encounters with people along the way.

RADIATE

The living Christ is the Christ of Love who is always
generating love, moment after moment. When the church
manifests understanding, tolerance, and loving-kindness, Jesus
is there. Christians have to help Jesus Christ be manifested by
their way of life, showing those around them that love,
understanding, and tolerance are possible. This will not be
accomplished just by books and sermons. It has to be realized
by the way we live.

—THICH NHAT HANH, *Living Buddha, Living Christ*

Imagine yourself sitting on the hub of a wheel where all the spokes
meet. There at the center, you're radiating beams of light in all directions. Keep this image of love in your mind during the week ahead.
Have you ever really let yourself wonder about inclusive, unconditional, multiplying loving-kindness? An openhearted, flabbergasting
type of kindness and love for yourself, for those you know, for those
you do not know now and will never know? Have you thought about
how love might not be portioned out like a dozen cupcakes but how
love bubbles and grows like a jar of bread starter?

Learning about the practice of *metta* or loving-kindness ironically
(but not accidentally) falls during the week of the Fourth of July, a day
set aside for celebrating the United States, a specific land and a specific
people. And so, we are offered this challenge to radiate loving-kindness
throughout the cosmos during a time of intense focus on what it means

to be part of a nation. *Metta* translates from Pali as "boundless friend-liness," "goodwill," and "loving-kindness."

So very much time and energy in my life have been expended toward doing *what I imagine* may please others. "What I imagine" is the key phrase there since, of course, I don't even know if all this energy spent trying to please others is in fact pleasing them. And furthermore, overtly or subconsciously trying to please others is not particularly kind to me. Loving-kindness meditation (or *metta*) helps us not please others but rather does something much healthier—it's a way of sending good thoughts, goodwill, and kindness toward others. In turn, exercising the muscle of loving-kindness may make us kinder to ourselves.

In one of the final songs he wrote before his death, John Prine imag-ined *boundless love* as something that's dumbfounding and confounding in the way that it surrounds us. I close my eyes and imagine myself in the center of a wheel, extending circles of love to others. To me, these words capture what it means to radiate loving-kindness to yourself and to others.

WONDER: In the United States, this week is often full of demonstra-tions of national pride and patriotism, and I worry about how national pride perpetuates dualistic thinking—*us* (Americans) and *them* (those who are not Americans). How can we balance national pride with a Christlike love for all? What does it mean to you to extend loving-kindness toward all beings? How might radiating loving-kindness cul-tivate Christlike love?

TRY: Exercise your muscle of loving-kindness meditation this week, perhaps while you're doing something mundane like waiting in line at the grocery store or in traffic.

First, radiate loving-kindness toward yourself: *May I be safe. May I be well. May I be happy. May I be peaceful and at ease.*

Then, bring to mind someone who cares for you: *May you be safe. May you be well. May you be happy. May you be peaceful and at ease.*

Next, radiate loving-kindness to someone with whom you have a hard relationship: *May you be safe. May you be well. May you be happy. May you be peaceful and at ease.*

Then, use your imagination to extend loving-kindness in more specific, boundless, inclusive ways, like this: *May those working in munitions facilities in the countries some call "enemy" be safe. May every sister and every brother in every nook and cranny of the world be well. May all children playing on the sidewalks in every country on Earth be happy. May all mothers and fathers, weary from worrying about their children, be peaceful and at ease.*

Ask any children at the gathering to go outside and use sidewalk chalk to make a community art project that radiates love toward passersby. Maybe the center of the art project is a heart radiating sparks of love, or maybe the center is the hub of that wheel you imagined. Consider making fresh lemonade (see page 169 for the recipe) to offer to anyone who happens to pass by. Finally, take a few moments to listen to John Prine's majestic song "Boundless Love" as you imagine yourself and the loved ones in your circle on the receiving end of someone else's loving-kindness meditation practice.

MAKE: HENRY & PETER'S FRESH LEMONADE

My sons love to make fresh lemonade, and they have been making it mostly on their own since they were nine and seven. I keep an eye on them while they're using the knives and the stove. If you start the first step when you wake up, the lemon peel can sit in the sugar for the morning hours and the lemonade will be ready to drink by early afternoon. This timeless recipe is easy for lemonade lovers of all ages.

YIELD: 8 SERVINGS

INGREDIENTS

6 to 8 lemons

1 to 1¼ cups sugar (depending on preference—I personally prefer more lemon and less sugar, but to the surprise of no one, the children like to err on the side of sweetness!)

6 to 8 cups water

DIRECTIONS

Wash the lemons well. Use a zester or vegetable peeler to remove the lemon peel.

Stir the lemon peel with the sugar, and let it sit for the morning. (You need to stir and agitate the peel a bit so the oils release into the sugar.)

Bring the water to a boil over high heat in a large pot. Make sure the children are supervised!

When the water comes to a boil, remove the pot from the heat and pour in the lemon-sugar mixture. Stir to combine and let sit for about 10 minutes, then pour the liquid through a strainer into a heat-resistant pitcher. Discard the lemon peel and let cool for 20 minutes.

Then cut the lemons in half and squeeze the lemon juice into the pitcher. Chill the lemonade and serve over ice for immediate refreshment!

RESONATE

> Travel is fatal to prejudice, bigotry and narrow-mindedness, and many of our people [Americans] need it sorely on these accounts. Broad, wholesome, charitable views of men and things can not be acquired by vegetating in one little corner of the earth all one's lifetime.
>
> —MARK TWAIN, *The Innocents Abroad*

More than 150 years ago, Mark Twain memorably argued that there's nothing quite like travel to teach us how to be aware of others and to appreciate the vastness of the world around us. By disorienting us, making us a bit uncomfortable, and showing us marvels we cannot even fathom, travel teaches us to resonate with unfamiliar ways of knowing, doing, and being.

I often tell students that the one thing I regret about my own undergraduate education is that I didn't study abroad, and I try to help as many students as I can to catch a case of wanderlust. I've worked hard to incorporate travel into the broader university curricula, as well as into individual students' lives. As an educator, I grow restless when I spend week after week in the confines of a physical classroom. I've taken my students on field trips to labyrinths, museums, state parks, and even to Robben Island, a political prison in Table Bay off the coast of Cape Town.

Travel has been transformative for my husband, and he often tells stories about the two years he lived in Japan as a young attorney in the

Navy JAG Corps. Ben learned so much experiencing Japanese culture, and baseball culture in particular offers a helpful study of Japanese values. In Japan, baseball fans are extremely passionate about their teams. Every bat is an opportunity for fans of the batter's team to cheer that player on with noisemakers and well-organized chants. Something remarkable happens each half inning. Once the last out of an inning is made, the home team's fans will raise one last cheer and then invariably sit down and rest their voices while the visiting team's fans take the opportunity to cheer on their team while batting. This is a courtesy that a visiting Boston Red Sox fan would never expect if watching a game at Yankee Stadium, or vice versa. Such a custom demonstrates the value of resonating with others through showing deep respect and consideration.

When travel isn't possible, we can be transported to other corners of Earth through our screens, an effort natural historian, writer, and documentarian Sir David Attenborough has been leading for eight decades. In 2020, then ninety-three-year-old Attenborough released *A Life on Our Planet,* a film he describes as his "witness statement" to the wonder of wildness. *A Life on Our Planet* is an urgent plea for compassionate actions on behalf of all species, and witnessing this film uniquely enables viewers to *resonate with*—to feel the vibrations of, to suffer with, to have compassion for—the vulnerable and stunning creatures, oceans, and human beings with whom we share Earth. To resonate with others is to feel their feelings, even when those feelings are frightening, distressing, or painful. And furthermore, you can resonate with yourself by having awareness of and compassion for your own suffering.

WONDER: Think back over the past week since you last gathered. Consider the Latin root *pati,* which means "to suffer" (as in a *patient* who is suffering), and *compassion,* which literally means "to suffer with." At what times during the week were you aware of others? At what times were you aware of others' suffering? Did loving-kindness meditation, radiating out love to others, have an impact on your week? Did it provide you with an opportunity to resonate compassionately (*karuna*) with other beings?

TRY: Experiment with compassion meditation and tonglen breathing. Similar to loving-kindness meditation, compassion meditation is radiating out wishes or prayers for freedom from suffering and extending those prayers to yourself, other humans, and even other species. Pema Chödrön describes tonglen breathing as visualizing "taking in the pain of others with every in-breath and sending out whatever will benefit them on the out-breath." So tonglen helps liberate us from selfishness and helps us feel love for ourselves and for others.[2] Watch Attenborough's *A Life on Our Planet* this week, and have a conversation with your beloved circle about the idea of resonating with other beings, the nature of thriving, and this wondrous world we share.

REVEL

A candle loses nothing by lighting another candle.
—FATHER JAMES KELLER

The writer and psychotherapist Amy Bloom wrote a short story slyly titled "Love Is Not a Pie." In Bloom's story, the narrator learns a powerful truth: There is not a finite amount of love we have to give or receive. Love is not divvied out like pieces of pie. I'd say a better image for love is a wellspring.

And Buddhism teaches the same is true for joy and happiness. Sympathetic joy is taking delight in the good things that happen to others, and when we sincerely feel joy on behalf of others (*mudita*), our own joy multiplies. We don't lose any joy or happiness when we rejoice when others rejoice. Just as resilience can be built from feeling compassion for another's suffering, feeling gladness when something good happens to someone else multiplies feelings of joy within ourselves.

I remember gazing in wonder the first time I saw a natural spring. Clear water flowed straight out of the earth, and it just kept coming and coming. I felt the same astonishment when I learned how sourdough bread starter was infinite; more and more bread could be baked, more and more mouths could be fed from the same bubbly concoction on the countertop. And laughter works the same way, as anyone who has ever seen a video of His Holiness the Dalai Lama giggling with Archbishop Desmond Tutu can attest.

Joy is limitless. The more we bury ourselves in false dichotomies like I/you or we/them, the harder it is to grasp this concept. If you are joyful, I can be joyful as well. If you have enough to eat, I, too, can eat. If you have great access to healthcare, so can I! My freedom and liberation are bound up in yours. When it comes to rejoicing with others, I hope I will learn to live with *mudita* rather than schadenfreude, with abundance rather than scarcity.

WONDER: Choose one person in your life who has had something good happen to them. Who are they? What's their story? Tell the gathering about them and how their joy brought you more joy. Then, work your sympathetic muscles a bit more by choosing a person who is difficult for you, a person whose success might stir up feelings of envy in you. Reflect upon how another person's success doesn't diminish your own.

TRY: In the documentary you watched last week, *A Life on the Planet*, David Attenborough makes an urgent plea for raising the standard of living around the world by improving access to excellent healthcare, allowing girls around the world to stay in school, and raising people out of impoverished situations. "A species can only thrive when everything around it thrives, too," he says. What words come to mind when you talk with your loved ones this week about how raising up others increases your own joy? Make a banner of words, phrases, or symbols that come to mind when you discuss sympathetic joy! Hang it in your gathering space like a flag.

MAKE: A COLLABORATIVE CENTERPIECE INSPIRED BY CREATION

Ordinary Time is the perfect season for creativity and improvisation, so include everyone in creating a centerpiece for the table. Make the table ready for your weekly gatherings by first covering it with a tablecloth. Have a large empty bowl in the center, and fill a vase or two with water. Begin each weekly gathering by asking everyone to present their centerpiece offering and place it in the middle of the table. A heart-shaped piece of limestone, a slick green magnolia leaf, a perfectly formed pinecone, a fistful of bright zinnias, a plump homegrown tomato, a blue jay's feather . . . there are so many ways to decorate with the flotsam and jetsam of creation. Challenge everyone not to spend any money on their contribution to the centerpiece.

RELEASE

There is a secret place. A radiant sanctuary. This magnificent refuge is inside you. Be brave and walk through the country of your own wild heart. Be gentle and know that you know nothing. Be still. Listen. Keep walking. No one else controls access to this perfect place. Give yourself your own unconditional permission to go there. Waste no time. Enter the center of your soul.
—MIRABAI STARR, Introduction to *The Interior Castle*
by St. Teresa of Avila

July has been a month to dig in to the Four Immeasurables—loving-kindness, compassion, sympathetic joy, and, finally, this week's immeasurable, *equanimity*. Imagine them as a wheel; the Four Immeasurables rely on each other to make the wheel turn. Each speaks of the boundlessness and freedom of love. Some ways to describe equanimity include: composure, balance, and the steady realization that everything changes. Equanimity is active peacemaking in ourselves and others. The more we practice meditation or Centering Prayer, the more we are prepared to respond with composure and equanimity when the unexpected inevitably comes our way. Equanimity releases us from holding on so tightly to our pride, jealousies, and desires.

I'll be the first to admit that finding and making peace can be extremely challenging; this has been particularly true for me during the COVID-19 pandemic as my husband and I—like many, many parents—have attempted to manage our careers from makeshift home offices while overseeing young children who are learning remotely. Canceled plans, constant anxiety, and uncertainties abound. But above all, I have struggled with one particular realization that has come during the pandemic: No matter how hard or how reasonably I try to make the case, I just cannot make people—even members of my own family—care about others. I cannot force other people to care for strangers. I cannot force other people to get vaccinated or show compassion for those who could be severely compromised by COVID-19. I cannot make others care for my friends and colleagues who are enduring chemotherapy, for my brother-in-law the lymphoma survivor, or even for my ninety-two-year-old grandmother. And this is absolutely maddening to me. Furthermore, I cannot force other people to want good things for strangers; I cannot force you to support a good education or access to excellent healthcare for people you do not know. I believe God dreams of a beloved community in which we care for and act on behalf of others, a world that we love without judgment.

But I cannot coerce others into equanimity. I can only go to the country of my own wild heart, the "magnificent refuge," St. Teresa describes in the words above from *The Interior Castle*. In Episcopal services, between the Liturgy of the Word and Holy Eucharist, there is a wondrous time set aside for active peacemaking, known as The Peace. The Peace is a few moments in time devoted to greeting one another in the name of Love. In my tradition, we mark the time of The Peace by exchanging kisses, by shaking hands, and by coming out of our pews and gathering merrily in the center of the aisle to greet one another. Newcomers might mistake The Peace for the conclusion of the service, but it's really the middle of things, the time of releasing and reconciling ourselves with others (and with our own selves), a time of preparing to go to the altar to receive bread and wine. The active peacemaking of The Peace harkens to the practice of equanimity. It's actively finding peace together in the exact moment in which we find ourselves, a glimmer of the "magnificent refuge" made public.

* * *

WONDER: Are there situations in your life that instantly make you feel defensive or off balance? How can you respond rather than react? What are some ways you can strive to cultivate peace or composure within yourself?

TRY: Practice releasing that which makes you unsteady and takes you farther from peace. Pick one, two, or even all three of these activities with your loved ones tonight:

- Physical activity like running around the house or punching the air
- Practice 4-7-8 breathing (breathe in for a count of four; hold it for a count of seven; breathe out for a count of eight)
- Light your candle, and meditate on Jesus' words of peace as a way to cultivate equanimity in yourself: *Peace I leave with you; my peace I give you. I do not give to you as the world gives. Do not let your hearts be troubled and do not be afraid.—John 14:27*

MAKE: TALLU'S COMFREY SALVE

Comfrey is the common name of a flowering plant in the borage family used for gardening and healing, especially bug and spider bites and minor itches, scrapes, aches, and pains. The Latin name for comfrey is *Symphytum*, which derives from the Greek *symphis*—growing bones together—combined with *phyton*—plant. (I imagine J. K. Rowling knew all about the etymology of comfrey since she created a character named Madam Pomfrey, a healer from the Harry Potter series who could repair broken bones in a flash.) Comfrey even heals the soil since its roots promote aeration and water absorption. Comfrey relieves pain because it contains an anti-inflammatory called allantoin, and I have made this simple comfrey salve for friends and relations who absolutely love it for minor muscle aches and discomforts. As you would with any herbal remedy, check first with your doctor, and use sparingly on the surface of your skin. **Never ever ingest comfrey.**

One July afternoon in her bright farmhouse kitchen while our four young children played together in the next room, my dear friend Tallu taught me how to make comfrey salve. You can harvest comfrey leaves or purchase dry leaves. Tallu suggested I go to a thrift store and purchase a crockpot that I designated solely for making salves, and I found one for about $4.

YIELD: ABOUT 8 OUNCES OF SALVE

EQUIPMENT AND INGREDIENTS

1½ cups comfrey leaves (or about 1 cup dried)

Thrift store crockpot—to be used only for salve making—or a double
boiler set up on the stove

About 8 ounces olive oil

Salve tins or 2-ounce mason jars

1 ounce beeswax pistils

Begin by making your infusion. Place the comfrey leaves in the crockpot. (You can substitute a double boiler setup if you don't have a crockpot.) If you harvest fresh comfrey leaves, tear them up. Cover the
comfrey leaves with about an inch of olive oil and "cook" on low for
about 3 hours. (If using a double boiler, put water in a heavy pot, and
bring the water to a low simmer. Place a heat safe bowl on top of the
simmering water so the water covers about two-thirds of the bowl.
Cover, and let the oil and comfrey mixture simmer for a couple of
hours.) Prepare for an unusual and exquisite smell to permeate your
home.

After your infusion is complete, strain the oil through a fine mesh
cheesecloth into a mason jar. You should have about 8 ounces of
comfrey-infused olive oil. Turn off the crockpot, and wipe it clean of
any remnants of comfrey leaves. Return the hot oil to the crockpot.
Turn the crockpot back on low. (If using a double boiler, turn off the
heat and remove the comfrey leaves from the oil with a fine mesh
strainer spoon. Return the hot oil to the double boiler and proceed
with the directions below.)

Using a ratio of 8 ounces of oil to 1 ounce of beeswax pistils, stir in
the beeswax and warm gently in the crockpot (or in the double boiler,
if you're using that method). The beeswax pistils will melt, and your
salve will be complete. Pour the salve in your small jars or tins, and
allow it to harden and cool. Small jars of comfrey salve make wonderful handmade gifts, and children can easily assist in this process.

DISCOVER: REFLECT ON THE DAY
BY PRAYING THE EXAMEN

Ignatius, the salty saint of the imagination, had a solution for
days when the day escaped you. He suggested a small examen, a
ten-minute reflection where you begin with connecting with the
source of all Goodness, and then tell yourself the story of your
day before noting the consolations and desolations, the uplifting
moments and the pitfalls of the day before then preparing for
the next day. Even the uncontained can be a container for the
rhythm of hope.

—Pádraig Ó Tuama, *Daily Prayer with the Corrymeela Community*

St. Ignatius of Loyola, the founder of the Jesuits, taught the Examina-
tion of Consciousness (or the Examen) as a way to connect with the
Divine, reflect on our day, and develop inner strength, purpose, and
resilience. There are five steps to praying the Examen, which is often
prayed at the conclusion of the day:

1. Ask God for light, insight, and a way of seeing your day through a
   sacred perspective.
2. Be grateful for the day you have just lived.
3. Review the day in your mind, asking for guidance from the Holy
   Spirit. Pay special attention to the moments of the day that
   brought joy, worry, or a sense of opportunity.
4. Focus on a particular part of the day and offer prayers of gratitude
   or adoration, prayers for intercession or help, or prayers for re-
   pentance or forgiveness.
5. Conclude the Examen by praying for tomorrow, for the day that is
   to come. What do you hope for?

In *New Directions for Holy Questions: Progressive Christian Theology
for Families,* Claire Brown and Anita Peebles wisely suggest that the

Examen can be easier to explain to children by having them picture a rosebush, which contains roses, thorns, and buds. Roses represent a joyful thing from the day; thorns represent a painful or challenging experience; buds represent an opportunity for growth. A child can pray the Examen by telling about the roses, thorns, and buds they encountered during the day.

AUGUST

CHERISH THE HOLY PAUSE

Recline with us today, Lord.
Show us how to relax our shoulders, breathe deep—
place a tender hand on our clenched jaws.
Help us to befriend our bodies today,
that we would hold space for every needing thing within us
and look on it with curiosity and kindness.
Grant us this salvation—this holy pause.

—COLE ARTHUR RILEY, Black Liturgies

August: a month to reflect, to stop, to pause. A time to embrace boredom, if ever there was one. A time to reflect on the nature of the attention economy, to realize that you and I are more than clicks, more than hashtags or likes, more than time spent online, more than the revenue we generate.

I can still feel my fingers run through the ridges in the wooden pews in the church I grew up in, St. Paul's in Athens, Tennessee. Sometimes I would sit during the sermon, tune out the priest, and run my fingers over the ridges in the oak pews. In my delightful boredom, I would take *The Book of Common Prayer* and start thumbing through it. All the prayer books at St. Paul's would open pretty easily to page 332, Rite I, the page in between The Word of God and The Holy Communion. The moment right after The Confession, right before The Peace. Right before the beginning of The Great Thanksgiving, the Eucharistic prayer. The liturgy is like a three-act play, and The Peace is like the glorious moment of intermission. But in Rite I, wedged between The Confession, when you unburden yourself, and The Peace, where you greet one another in anticipation for the celebration that is Holy Communion—wedged in between those two is something called "The Comfortable Words." Using those wooden pews, I can still feel the damask cushions on my bare knees, scraped from my summertime adventures. After we had confessed on our knees, the priest would say this: "Come unto me all ye that travail and are heavy laden, and I will refresh you."

Those words were a mouthful for the young me to get my head around, but when you hear them every week they become a part of you; they get written on your heart. Even more so when you sit that book in your lap and trace your fingers over them in boredom—glorious, generative boredom. "Come unto me" . . . "ye that travail" . . . "heavy laden" . . . "I will refresh you." As I reread those words and pray with my imagination and my memory, I find myself in a mystery; I'm seven years old, a relatively new reader, and I don't know what all the words mean. But I can see everyone in my community on their knees, and I can see their shoulders slacken, their necks relax. They are becoming unburdened, *together.* I'm learning in Sunday school that everyone in the Anglican tradition all around the world is hearing these same comfortable words, and we are all being invited to unburden ourselves and to rest, because the celebration—the communion—is coming next.

In his remarkable book *The Return of the Prodigal Son,* Henri Nouwen meditates on Rembrandt's painting of the parable of the prodigal son. Nouwen brilliantly uses his imagination to put himself in the place of the three main characters in the story—the younger son who is coming home after squandering his inheritance on pleasure and debauchery; the father, who welcomes that son back with open arms and a big party; and the elder son, who is jealous and frustrated by the whole situation because he has been working hard and "being good." In the section in which Nouwen uses his imagination to empathize with the father, he writes: "Here is the God I want to believe in: a Father who, from the beginning of creation, has stretched out his arms in merciful blessing, never forcing himself on anyone, but always waiting; never letting his arms drop down in despair, but always hoping that his children will return so that he can speak words of love to them and let his tired arms rest on their shoulders."

God knows we are tired. God knows we hunger for adventure and are jealous of those who get it. God knows we need unburdening, and so God offers it. It's up to us to fall into those arms, like the moment Rembrandt captures in his painting when the prodigal son collapses into his father's arms.

Songwriter John Hiatt once wrote the mystical line, "your love is my rest." I'm not entirely sure Hiatt was referring to God's love in that line, but for me, it sure does seem to sum up how the Holy Spirit can take the shape of rest. Love can feel like an unloosening, like an unburdened exhale—exactly like rest. This is the God I want to believe in. The God who, from the moment of creation onward, has been waiting with open arms to offer compassion, relief, and rest. This August, cherish the holy pause:

- Ponder the role of water in our lives, especially in terms of how water offers liberation and release.
- Use contemplative forms of reading when you need a break from thinking, analyzing, and solving.
- Close your days with the meaningful, dreamlike liturgy of Compline.

August Creation Care Challenge: Explore secondhand shops in your area for clothes, furniture, and books. Share back-to-school clothes with friends and neighbors. Instead of buying new and adding more and more of these items to the planet, find treasures you can reuse.

DISCOVER: AUGUST 6, TRANSFIGURATION

Suddenly they saw him the way he was, the way he really
was all the time, although they had never seen it before, the
glory which blinds the everyday eye and so becomes invisible.
This is how he was, radiant, brilliant, carrying joy like a
flaming sun in his hands. This is the way he was—is—from
the beginning, and we cannot bear it. So he manned himself,
came manifest to us; and there on the mountain they saw him,
really saw him, saw his light. . . . Then, perhaps, we will see
each other, too.

> —MADELEINE L'ENGLE, *The Irrational Season*

The Feast of Transfiguration invites us to entertain the radical idea that
God sees us the way that Aaron and the Israelites saw Moses when he
came down from Mount Sinai with the covenant: radiant, brilliant,
carrying joy in his hands and on his body like the sun. God sees us the
way Peter, John, and James saw Jesus when he was praying on the
mountaintop with them and his face changed; it shone like the sun,
and his clothing became dazzling white. This Feast helps us entertain
the fantastic notion that God sees the incarnate, mystical, wondrous
light glowing within you.

In 1958, Thomas Merton was walking down the street in Louisville,
Kentucky, running some errands for the monastery. At the corner of
Fourth and Walnut, Merton realized that when we stop and become
open to the holiness of everyday life, we can see the dazzling light in
our fellow pilgrims. If we truly believe that we are beloved by God and
if we truly believe that we are part of God's incarnation, then we are
becoming that light all the time.

When the world feels dim and heavy, it's sometimes hard to hear the
message that we are becoming God's light. It's sometimes hard to see it
inside yourself. I've stood at that exact corner of Fourth and Walnut.

I've gazed around that ordinary street corner in Louisville because I wanted to put myself in the steps of Merton and maybe feel a smidgen of what he felt. And it was surprisingly easy; all I had to do was stand still, breathe deeply, and notice light shining like the sun on the faces of those around me.

FLOAT

In the beginning when God created the heavens and the earth, the earth was a formless void and darkness covered the face of the deep, while a wind from God swept over the face of the waters.

—GENESIS 1:1–2

We humans are composed primarily of water, and so is Planet Earth, so memorably referred to in *The Book of Common Prayer* as "our island home." Water cleanses, heals, purifies, nourishes, sustains. And water calms.

There's an old adage for new parents that when your baby's fussy, you should put them in water, and that seems to work for me in my mid-forties as well. A few years ago, I started paying hard-earned money to float for an hour at a time in a sensory deprivation tank. Yes, that's what I said. "Float therapy" is what they call it, and for me, it works like a charm—and when I think back in time, it always has. The place where I pay for my float therapy has massive octopuses on the wallpaper, and before I go in to float, I stare at the octopuses for inspiration. After stripping down to nothing—naked as Adam and Eve—I step into a small tank filled with water that's my body temperature and one thousand pounds of Epsom salts. I put in earplugs, get in the tank, close the little door, rest my head on a doughnut-shaped float, and turn out the lights. Human-made starlight shines on the ceiling. I could listen to music or a guided meditation, but silence is really my favorite way to pass the hour. Actually, I do listen to something: I listen to the beating of my own heart, and I listen to my own breath. Floating on top of the water in total darkness like a baby in the womb, I fully and completely rest for sixty full minutes. There's nothing but me, lots and lots of salt, the water that matches the temperature of my body, and lovely faux starlight. I have had great talk therapy before, but float therapy really does it for me.

On sunny days when I'm fortunate enough to be on vacation with my family, I love to float on my back in the Gulf of Mexico and stare up at gray-blue clouds rimmed by sunlight. Alone with the elements and completely buoyant, I feel astonishingly less anxiety and stress—utterly relaxed on a cosmic molecular level. When I float, I pray, meditate, and stare at the clouds and the stars. Floating helps me get my head on straight.

Situated between Israel, the West Bank, and Jordan is the Dead Sea. Like my float therapy tank, the Dead Sea has an incredibly high salt content, and generations upon generations of people have gone there to be buoyant, to float, to find themselves suspended between heaven and earth. The Jordan River, which flows into the Dead Sea, is a great symbol for freedom. I can't help but feel connected to these old stories and traditions as I float, rest, and feel completely uninhibited by time, space, and convention.

WONDER: Water is a wondrous gift that's fundamental to the health of our bodies and our planet. Tragically, the Jordan River has become so polluted that, at times, pilgrims are discouraged from entering its waters. Contemplate the role water has played in your past. Do you like to float, swim, dive, or take long baths or showers? Ask any children at the gathering to say how they feel when they are immersed in a swimming pool, lake, ocean, river, or bathwater. What hopes do you have for water in generations to come?

*   *   *

TRY: Serve water from a pitcher this week, and pour it into your finest glasses, cups, or goblets. Turn together to the liturgy for Baptism in *The Book of Common Prayer*. Read aloud the "Thanksgiving over the Water." In part, the celebrant prays:

> We thank you, Almighty God, for the gift of water.
> Over it the Holy Spirit moved in the beginning of creation.
> Through it you led the children of Israel out of their bondage
> in Egypt into the land of promise. In it your Son Jesus
> received the baptism of John and was anointed by the Holy
> Spirit as the Messiah, the Christ, to lead us, through his death
> and resurrection, from the bondage of sin into everlasting life.

One by one, offer a toast to the gifts water has offered in your lives. From your list, compose your own group litany of thanksgiving for water.

MAKE: BATH SALTS FOR A
GOOD NIGHT'S REST

YIELD: 2 16-OUNCE JARS OF BATH SALTS. KEEP ONE, AND GIVE
THE SECOND TO SOMEONE IN NEED OF REST!

INGREDIENTS

4 cups Epsom salts

1 cup sea salt

⅓ cup baking soda

50 drops essential oil (chamomile, lavender, bergamot, or neroli—any
combination you like)

Handful of dried herbs (like chamomile or lavender), suggested but not
required

2 16-ounce mason jars with lids

DIRECTIONS

Combine the salts and baking soda in a large bowl. Stir in the essential
oils well, and then stir in a handful of dried herbs if you wish. Transfer
to each mason jar, and close the lid. These should keep indefinitely!
Add about ½ cup to your warm bath before bedtime to relax.

CHANT

Chanting is at the heart of all sacred traditions worldwide, and for very good reason: it is fundamentally a deep-immersion experience in the creative power of the universe itself. Because to make music, you must engage those three core elements out of which the earth was fashioned and through which all spiritual transformation happens.

—CYNTHIA BOURGEAULT, *The Wisdom Jesus*

*B*reath, *vibration*, *intentionality:* These are the three elements required to make the kind of music Bourgeault describes in her work on chanting as a wisdom practice. Chanting suspends time and space, carrying us into a holy pause. What comes to mind when you think of chanting? You can chant a psalm or a poem you love. You can chant the word *alleluia* or *ah-men*. You can chant alone, or you can chant in the company of others.

Thomas Cranmer wrote *The Book of Common Prayer* in the language of the realm, so that common folk could pray together. My friend Ellen says she secretly loves to drown out the sound of her own voice during common prayers and tells me that when she does so, the spiritual and physical elements of prayer come together for her in a meditative way. Ellen prays aloud, but she makes her voice very, very soft—so soft, in fact, that even she can't hear it. So soft that she knows she's making any noise at all only because she feels her own neck vibrating.

That way, worship transforms into a warm murmur of voices, all repeating the same ancient and lovely prayers for peace, for the Earth, and for one another by name. And so the genius of Cranmer's idea of common prayer becomes apparent and real in that it is still shared, still communal, and even still uniting.[1]

This idea takes my breath away. Ellen's description of drowning out her own voice so that she can literally resonate with others feels faithful, ancient, and mysterious. To silence yourself in a way that wholly delivers you into the common prayer feels generous and magnanimous, an almost noble form of surrender.

WONDER: Do you experience common prayer like Ellen does, or have you experienced it in a different way? What does it feel like to speak or sing in unison? Can you relate to the impulse to drown out the sound of your own voice? Have you ever chanted? How might chanting, praying together aloud, or singing communally be restorative and restful? For any children present at this week's gathering, connect the rhythm of chanting with other rhythmic activities like drumming or jumping rope.

TRY: Learn about Taizé, a French monastic community devoted to the ideals of kindness, reconciliation, and simplicity. Taizé services are known for beautiful repetitive chanting and simple candlelit services. Dedicated to dwelling in Christ's presence with others, the Taizé tradition is founded on service, singing, healing, and hospitality. Take a pilgrimage to attend a Taizé service in your area, or participate in prayers from Taizé at www.taize.fr/en.

DISCOVER: THE LITURGY OF COMPLINE

Guide us waking, O Lord, and guard us sleeping; that awake we
may watch with Christ, and asleep we may rest in peace.
                    —AN ORDER FOR COMPLINE

Night had fallen. The band was still playing loudly when I stepped
outside of the college party into the mist. Bells chimed, letting me
know it was ten o'clock, so I walked through the fog toward the massive wooden door of the small gothic chapel. In the silence, my ears
rang from the loud music at the party as I took my place in the pew
and knelt. It wasn't the first time I had ghosted a raucous party to attend Compline. Candles were the only light illuminating the stained
glass behind the altar. I breathed in the incense deeply. "The Lord Almighty grant us a peaceful night and a perfect end," the leader began,
and my mind switched into the cadence of the ancient words of the
Compline service I had been saying to mark the end of the day since I
was a little girl. "Keep watch, dear Lord, over those who work, or
watch, or weep this night. . . ."

Many religious traditions—including Judaism, Christianity, and
Islam—pray at dedicated times of the day. Discover the ancient, brief,
peaceful liturgy of Compline, the last prayer of the day. The word *Compline* derives from the Latin *completorium*, which means "prayers at
the close of day." Easily led by layfolk, the order for Compline can be
found in *The Book of Common Prayer*.

LAZE

Rest in your God-breathed worth. Stop holding your breath, hiding your gifts, ducking your head, dulling your roar, distracting your soul, stilling your hands, quieting your voice, and satiating your hunger with the lesser things of this world.
—SARAH BESSEY, *Jesus Feminist*

In 1935, British philosopher Bertrand Russell published an essay titled "In Praise of Idleness." I often wish I could put that on a T-shirt for my kids. And I'll admit it—for myself, too. It's okay to not be entertained; it's okay to not be rushing or learning or doing. Boredom, rest, idleness . . . these are some of the family values my heart wants to teach my children. And doing so feels countercultural because I was raised in a family and a culture that tends to praise hard work and rebuff any activity or state that suggests "laziness."

The neighborhood pool where we have taken the boys since they were babies has a delightful rule of life called "rest period." At fifty past the hour without fail, the lifeguard's whistle blows, signaling this glorious time, this rest period. Where else in this life are we mandated to stop, account for everyone, and rest? For ten minutes, we dry off and we stop. One August afternoon I witnessed a miracle during rest period: My two little boys grabbed their towels and a Ziploc bag of goldfish crackers and headed up to the grassy hill behind the pool, all the way to the fence line. They spread their towels out and lay on their bellies to have a conversation I could not hear. Eating goldfish together under the clouds, far away from me. Brothers at rest.

Rest and Sabbath are theological concepts that have interested me for years, since I learned a fascinating paradox early on in my academic career: The word *sabbatical* means Shabbas or "rest"—every seven years we are to rest, leave the land alone, and forgive all debts— yet to obtain a sabbatical you usually have to prove a program of work. You have to feed the machine to earn your rest. Rest, then, is never guaranteed in academic culture; it must be earned, and, let's be honest: A sabbatical is not really *rest,* but a time to execute a work plan to which a committee has given its stamp of approval. We are not programmed to rest in our culture at all, yet God's plan for us clearly includes rest.

What if reading scripture—being with a text or a story—could also be a form of rest, a relief from work? I like to think of reading as a way of resting with God, but that's not the way I was trained professionally. I was trained as an English professor to research etymology, to do deep work understanding purpose, audience, context, history, rhythm, pattern, rhyme. Reading is my work. I was even trained to look at the white space between the stanzas in a poem so that I could understand what was happening in the spaces between the printed words. The white space—now that's revolutionary. Those empty spaces often contain meaning. The empty space offers the hardworking reader an occasion to close her eyes, to luxuriate in the words that she has just read. A blank space to be lazy and take a rest.

And beholding something with my eyes can also be a form of rest. Whenever I'm in Chicago, I try to make a special pilgrimage to the Art Institute so I can simply behold an example of artistic creation that speaks deeply to me: Marc Chagall's *America Windows.* Chagall's installation of painted stained glass surprises me each and every time I stand before it. Installed in its own special room near a courtyard, Chagall's cobalt windows bathe me in a moody, mystical blue light as I stand and behold. His dreamscape honors the impulse to create music, painting, dance, theater, and literature, and furthermore, Chagall, who was a Russian Jew, made the windows to thank America for providing safe harbor for him during World War II. Something about resting in the presence of Chagall's exquisite *America Windows* mesmerizes me, allows me simply to be transfixed in space and time. I shut off all those hardworking critical faculties that live inside my brain. I don't try to appraise, judge, or compare his artwork to something else. I'm just standing before it, awed at its very existence and grateful that I can rest in its presence. Similarly, I can rest in the awareness of a watercolor painting Peter brought home from third grade. I can lazily behold a line in the Psalms. I can lose myself in the arc of creek water as it curls across an ancient rock.

WONDER: Of course, we don't have documentary footage of Jesus' life; we rely on human stories to help us understand. I like to imagine the gospels as portraits of Jesus' life that were painted by individual artists. Consider reading again: Have you been taught that reading scripture is an active process? Or have you ever read sacred texts in a quiet, restful way, somewhat lazily relying on your imagination instead of interpretive strategies?

TRY: Ignatian contemplation—a method encouraged by the Jesuits—is a way of praying with your imagination. Together with your group, choose a scene from the gospels and read in an active, sensory way. Spend some time in silence, daydreaming about the sights, sounds, and feelings of the scene. Put yourself in there, as if you're a character in a movie. Don't worry about being wrong or right, just place yourself in the story and imagine, remember, and wonder. Let your mind roam as if you're a little boy on a towel looking up at the clouds on a clear summer morning. Write a few words or draw a portrait of the scene, and go around the circle to share what you experienced.

CONJURE

In art we are once again able to do all the things we have forgotten; we are able to walk on water; we speak to the angels who call us; we move, unfettered, among the stars.
—MADELEINE L'ENGLE, *Walking on Water*

About ten years ago, my friend Paula was sitting beside me as I nursed my older son, Henry. We were sitting together in a shady spot outside on a late summer day. Paula's own son had just left for college, and as she watched me nurse Henry, she said that all these years later, she could still conjure up the memory of her own son nursing. Her body retained that memory, she told me, and thinking about nursing her son brought her a deep sense of peace that went all the way to the marrow. She said she hoped the same would be true for me. Now that my children are nine and eleven, I do find her words to be true. If I close my eyes and recollect the unique sensation of feeding them with my own body, I instantly feel a deep sense of peace. My body knows and remembers. The crook of my arm remembers what it felt like to nestle their heads, and my skin recalls their silky baby hair and velvety skin. The memory of their little bodies' heft embedded into mine. That flush and sensation of milk moving from my body into theirs: just like a little waterfall cascading down a mountainside into a stream.

I believe it is possible that when I conjure up the powerful memory of my babies' nursing, I am actually summoning my guardian angel.

Western culture is saturated with images of angels as blond girls in white dresses with wings, and these superficial images interfere with a deeper contemplation of angels, an idea that simply means "messenger of God." Angels are messengers between God, who is Love, and humans. Angels have also been known as servants, guides, protectors, and intermediaries. I have much to learn about angels, but I believe I am summoning my guardian angel when I think about nursing my boys because when I do so, I feel so close to God that it's almost as if a force field of love surrounds me.

WONDER: *Conjure* is an interesting word that emerges from the roots of the Latin words that mean "to swear or pledge together." To conjure is to bring something into existence. What memories bring you a deep sense of peace? Can you bring them into existence by telling your loved ones about them? What do you believe about guardian angels?

TRY: Making art tends to help us be playful, to come out of our egos and rest in our own playfulness for a time. Bring out your paints and give everyone a canvas. Conjure up a small painting of one of the memories you named that brings you a deep sense of peace. Place your painting near your bed, and let it be a reminder that you have an undeniable connection to Love.

MAKE: A PRAYER CARD FOR YOUR BAG, BACKPACK, OR BRIEFCASE

Shortly after the printing press was invented in the middle of the fifteenth century, prayer cards emerged as a way for people to carry around small prayers and images of saints. Usually, prayer cards are about the size of a playing card. On one side, there's a prayer, and on the other side there's an image—Mary, St. Christopher (the patron saint of travelers), a loved one, or another person who inspires you. Dive into the free resource *A Great Cloud of Witnesses* to learn about inspiring people who are commemorated throughout the entire year.[2]

All you really need is card stock, art supplies, and maybe some nice pens. Cut your card stock to about the size of a playing card (2½ x 3½ inches). Decorate one side with an image representing the person who inspires you. You could draw, use a photograph, or even make a collage. On the other side, write your own prayer. Or you could choose the Serenity Prayer, the Prayer of St. Francis, or some words from your chanting or Centering Prayer practices. If you're learning another language, you could include the prayer in that language as well.

Tuck your prayer card in your wallet or in your backpack, or use it as a bookmark. Prayer cards make for extremely personal, meaningful handmade gifts.

SEPTEMBER

GATHER COURAGE

Those who contemplate the beauty of the earth find reserves of strength that will endure as long as life lasts.
—Rachel Carson, *The Sense of Wonder*

Ah, September: It's time to prepare for winter, time to get ready for the weather to turn, because soon, all you'll want to do is stay inside by the fire in your jammies with a big pot of soup on the stove. "People Get Ready," written by Curtis Mayfield, is one of my favorite songs, a tune that absolutely embodies September in my mind. When I hear "People Get Ready," I feel like it's time to rise up and get my house in order. Released in 1965 in response to the assassination of President Kennedy and the bombing of the 16th Street Baptist Church in Birmingham, "People Get Ready" was the song Dr. Martin Luther King, Jr., called the unofficial anthem of the civil rights movement since it was often used "to get people marching or to calm and comfort them."[1] The iconic lyrics tell us we don't need to bring any of our belongings or our baggage; all we need to do is board the train. That's good news that someday, all the "stuff" won't matter, all the pain and sadness will end, and everyone will be welcome to board the train to the Promised Land. Songs like "People Get Ready" help us tap into our reservoirs and wells of strength and help us notice how God's love already and always permeates our lives.

Ordinary Time continues through September, a month that originally took its name as the "seventh" month back when the old Roman calendar was ten months. In September, we go back to school. Some of us do so literally; some of us watch the academic calendar resume from our nonacademic lives. Whether we resume teaching and learning formally or not, September is a season to continue to grow through Ordinary Time. As the temperatures begin to cool, I look forward to clearing out the summer yard and maybe discovering an errant tomato or pepper; I look forward to gathering the last bouquet of zinnias, to clearing out spaces to plant fall bulbs that we will have forgotten all about until they say "Here I am!" when they come to life aboveground months later. September is also a time to get rid of excess, to clean closets one by one. Always, always, I procrastinate cleaning out the closets, and it never takes as long as I think it will take, and it always feels better when I have finally done it. September is the ideal time to can tomatoes and green beans, to start putting up the harvest for the winter months.

This is a month to gather courage, too. Because I work with college students, my September calendar inevitably fills with appointments in which students come to my office to deliberate changing their majors or career paths. I have long wished that we wouldn't require such an audacious thing of eighteen- and nineteen-year-olds who have just left home for the first time, who are just figuring out how to manage their own laundry and social lives, who are just beginning to explore subjects they didn't even know existed. How can you know your major will be environmental studies when you've never had a chance to take a class in such a thing? Why would one write off theology or philosophy before ever having had the opportunity to study such spellbinding subjects? And so, I have appointment after appointment with young people who feel disappointed in themselves for changing a major, for not yet knowing (as they presume others know) their calling. I sign their forms. Over and over, I tell them that "undeclared" is the best major, especially for the short season of a semester. I encourage them to draw strength from the change to come and reassure them that altering a decision is not a letdown, a failure, or a catastrophe.

And then I tell them stories of my own ongoing sense of calling, that I'm not finished yet, either. To feel called is a process that goes on and on—a process that can shift as we evolve and change and grow like the seasons. American writer and theologian Frederick Buechner famously said that vocation is the sweet spot where our deep gladness overlaps with the world's deep hunger. And French Carmelite nun Therese of Liseux famously concluded that her vocation is Love!

Asking deep questions about our own gifts and callings requires courage. My friend Mary Claire introduced me to happenstance theory, which acknowledges that on our paths of discovering gifts and callings, the unexpected always happens, so we should be prepared. We cannot plan our entire lives, but we can cultivate certain traits in ourselves and those we love, especially these five: curiosity, persistence, flexibility, optimism, and risk-taking. When we cultivate these five traits and store them up like those summer tomatoes we've canned, they're at the ready when we encounter the inevitable happenstance. They've been stored up, they're at our fingertips, and they become instinctive. The more consciously I've stockpiled these five ingredients, the more ready I am to step forward, wholeheartedly and with courage.

Ponder:

 ♦ Are there special songs, words, or mantras that give you courage?
 ♦ Has changing your mind or encountering the unexpected revealed a new path for you? How might your story edify others?
 ♦ Consider postures, like kneeling or doing a sun salutation, that give you a lift of courage. Can you incorporate them into your ways of being?

September Creation Care Challenge: Identify something around the house that's broken, like an old picture frame that needs to be glued back together or a watch that's stopped ticking. Before you throw it away and buy another one, see if it can be fixed. Be of good courage! What's the worst that could happen if it's already broken? You'll find that YouTube is a great resource for repair tutorials.

DISCOVER: EXPLORING GIFTS AND CALLINGS

> Our baptismal vocation is to pay attention to how God is calling
> us as unique, unrepeatable individuals. We are saints here and
> now, practicing for our sainthood in heaven. Though we may be
> moving slowly and seem to make little progress, we are being
> transformed "from one degree of glory to another."
>
> —BR. KEITH NELSON, Society of St. John the Evangelist[2]

As part of my work as a professor, I lead the honors program, and so I work daily with extremely talented young adults who are also often quite driven. Many of them feel pressure (and honestly, many of their family members pressure them) to know exactly what they are to do with their lives at quite tender ages. I often wish these eighteen-year-olds felt freer to *explore* their gifts and callings and less pressure to *know* for certain their vocations. But I get it—the staggering expense of higher education combined with financial aid rules often don't allow for much experimentation or exploration.

In a passage about *vocare* or "calling" I alluded to earlier, theologian Frederick Buechner wrote, "The place God calls you to is the place where your deep gladness and the world's deep hunger meet." Often when I talk with college students about exploring their gifts and callings, I get very specific with Buechner's wise definition by showing them the UN Sustainable Development Goals (SDGs). The SDGs are the UN General Assembly's aspirational framework for 2030. Some of the seventeen goals include: eradicating poverty; improving health and well-being for all people on Earth; working for gender equality and high-quality education for all; addressing climate action and advocating for responsible production and consumption, and more. These goals represent the world's "deep hunger."

I give the college students a piece of paper with the goals and invite them to contemplate these hungers in silence for a while. Then, I ask them to set them aside, and after some more silence and prayer, try to name their *deep gladnesses,* to take all the time and paper they need to compose a list of the times, places, people, and activities that bring them a deep sense of peace and joy. What are you doing, for example, when you lose track of time? What are you doing when you feel most connected to Spirit?

Then compare your list of *deep gladnesses* with the vision for the *world's deep hunger* in the decade to come. Are there any places of obvious connection? If not, that's fine! But maybe you can use your imagination to find a meeting point or two. This exercise, which plays out over a couple of weeks, tends to bring about a good conversation about gifts and callings.

We are all works in progress, even in our forties, fifties, and sixties, so give yourself permission to watch your gifts and callings evolve just as your sense of faith and belief evolves over time. Longitudinal data from the U.S. Bureau of Labor Statistics data on baby boomers reveals that, on average, Americans have twelve different jobs in a lifetime.[3] Your deep gladnesses may shift when, like my friend Stacey, you discover birdwatching in your forties. Or when you begin to understand the grave injustice that not all girls around the world are allowed to go to school—*just because they are girls*—your anger might fuel the beginning of a young adult novel that you could write to educate others.

And furthermore, we are more than our gifts and callings, and the 2021 film *Encanto* is a poignant—and tear-jerking—reminder of this important truth. Watch *Encanto* together and reflect on the weight of expectations, self-worth, pressures we put on one another and ourselves, and what it means to explore, share, and celebrate our gifts within communities.

CLEAN YOUR CLOSET

Thank God for the things that I do not own.
—ATTRIBUTED TO ST. TERESA OF AVILA

How I have put off this day. I have imagined how it would end in my mind so many times: I've fantasized about the carefully dusted shelves, the neat stacks of colorful shirts, the labeled container meant only for winter socks, the dresses organized by length and hue, the woolen sweaters tidily placed in bags. But I have lingered and loitered in my imagination for far too long; it's well past time I stop fantasizing and procrastinating and actually do the work of cleaning out my closet.

When I really let myself wonder about it, it takes courage to examine my life in this way. I feel shame when I sit down on the floor in front of a messy closet and willingly confront all this matter that I have accumulated, to gaze upon all these things I own that seemed to make sense when I acquired them. That dress: Surely it would make me feel confident. That T-shirt: When I purchased it, I imagined that when I wore it I would make someone else smile, or it would immediately associate me with the right side, with the best team. So often, I purchase clothing because I think it will make me feel a certain way.

In the gospels of Matthew and Luke, Jesus says we shouldn't care so much about clothing; instead we should consider the lilies and how even Solomon in his glory was not as lovely as the beautiful flowers we see in the fields.[4] Why does it feel so good to get rid of things? Cleaning out the closet—finally—reminds me that I am free; I am so much more than this matter that surrounds me.

WONDER: Many of us devote so much time, energy, and resources to clothing. Once I dreamed I was walking through the hallway of a convent, and I stopped and glanced inside a nun's room. In my dream, I noticed one lone hook holding her simple dress on a single hanger. Something stirs deep within me as I recall my dream and wonder what it would be like to pare down my belongings to just a few items. And what would it be like for clothing not to be a factor in my life at all? Have you ever thought about the idea that the body is more than clothing? Have you ever contemplated flowers in the field or animals in their habitats and realized that they own nothing?

TRY: Before this week's gathering, ask each person in the circle to summon the courage to gather four boxes of items this week: one box of items to discard, one box to donate to charity, one box of items that need mending, and one box to give to someone else. You'll bring your box of items that need mending to next week's gathering. As you circle together tonight, make notes about any changes you'd like to make in your relationship with the things that you own or might own in the future.

MAKE: CEDARWOOD SACHETS

Do not store up for yourselves treasures on earth, where moth
and rust consume and where thieves break in and steal; but
store up for yourselves treasures in heaven, where neither moth
nor rust consumes and where thieves do not break in and steal.
For where your treasure is, there your heart will be also.

—MATTHEW 6:19

Cedar trees are beautiful, strong, tall, and wondrously fragrant. The oil
of cedar naturally repels moths and other pests. After you've cleaned
your closets (and cars, desks, cubbies, backpacks, sports bags, and so
on), make cedar sachets to keep everything fresh.

YIELD: 15 TO 20 SACHETS

INGREDIENTS
   6 cups cedarwood shavings
   2 cups dried lavender
   30 drops cedarwood oil
   20 drops lavender oil
   15 to 20 little muslin sachet bags (these can be purchased or sewn with
      a sewing machine or by hand)

DIRECTIONS
Combine the cedarwood shavings, lavender, and cedarwood and lavender oils in a large mixing bowl. Use a ladle or funnel to help you divide your mixture into the sachet bags. Cedarwood sachets are an easy
craft for kids, something fun to do with your hands while discussing
Jesus' cautionary words about how moths, rust, and thieves can consume those treasures we tend to store up on Earth.

MEND

Serve God, love me, and mend.
—WILLIAM SHAKESPEARE, *Much Ado About Nothing*, act 5, scene 2

Mending is an act that requires courage. To mend can be to repair a relationship, as described in the line above from Shakespeare's *Much Ado About Nothing*. In this splendid play, Benedick and Beatrice carry on what's often described as "a merry war" with each other, and toward the play's end, Benedick advises Beatrice to follow this pithy trifecta: Serve God, love him, and "mend" their fractured bond by forgiving. So this week, gather your courage and forgive someone. Or, you can take *mend* literally and make whole once again something from your recently cleaned closet: a sock, a torn shirt, or a beloved stuffed animal. My mom taught me how to sew when I was six or seven, and it's a skill I use regularly. Threading a needle, making a knot at the end, and letting strong fibers of thread hold a torn item back together: It feels like a little satisfying feat of magic.

Soon after Pope Francis was elected, the world learned of his affection for both a devotional practice and a baroque painting titled *Mary, Untier of Knots*. Painted by artist Johann Georg Melchior Schmidtner around 1700 in Augsburg, Germany, *Mary, Untier of Knots* shows Mary patiently untangling knots out of a long white ribbon. Smoothing out the knots, bringing some order to a small thing like a knotted ribbon or a torn sock: The small act of mending and untangling can give us a sense of resolve for the larger complexities and challenges.

WONDER: What are some little things you'd like to mend or untangle? Why haven't you yet? Wonder about this literally and figuratively.

TRY: Bring the box of items from your closet that needed to be mended to this week's gathering, along with needles, thread, and scissors. Everyone at the table can take one garment from someone else and mend it for them. If you don't yet know how to mend something, take heart and be of good courage, because there's no time like the present! Teach an older child how to thread a needle and make a stitch. To accompany your mending liturgy, listen to Mumford and Sons' song "Sigh No More," which derives from the lines in *Much Ado About Nothing*.

DISCOVER: THE COLLECT

Think of a prayer as a container that can hold deep feelings. The *collect* is a short prayer found in many liturgical traditions. The word *collect* derives from the Latin *collēcta,* which means "to gather everyone together." Collects follow a specific format, and thus are relatively simple and fun to compose. The format is as follows:

1. Name God.
2. Describe a divine attribute of God.
3. Name the request.
4. Give a reason for the request.
5. Conclude with praise.

I've annotated the following *Collect for Social Justice* (found in *The Book of Common Prayer*) so you can see how the format works. I've placed numbers in the collect that correspond to the format above:

Almighty God (1), who created us in your image (2): Grant us
grace fearlessly to contend against evil and to make no peace
with oppression (3); and, that we may reverently use our
freedom, help us to employ it in the maintenance of justice in
our communities and among the nations (4), to the glory of
your holy Name; through Jesus Christ our Lord, who lives and
reigns with you and the Holy Spirit, one God, now and for ever
(5). *Amen.*

Write a collect! Choose your topic, and use the format above to compose a collect together. Your collect can be appropriate to the liturgical season (e.g., A Collect for Easter Week), or for the season of the year (e.g., A Collect for the First Cool Breeze of Autumn), or for another feeling or occasion (e.g., A Collect for Mom's Fiftieth Birthday, A Collect for Peace in Our Time, A Collect for Rain, or A Collect for Housetraining the Family Dog). Think broadly, and get inspired by Terry J. Stokes, who wrote a fantastic book of collects, *Prayers for the People: Things We Didn't Know We Could Say to God.* A few of his witty, moving collects include "For a Relationship Quagmire" and "For Before Listening to Stevie Wonder," and "For Before Entering a Meeting That Could Have Been an Email."

ENDURE

God dwells in bodies that are not whole.
—HILDEGARD OF BINGEN

I t's mid-September—the heart of the green season that is Ordinary Time—and I'm sitting on a hundred-year-old stone bench looking out at the Cumberland Plateau. Before me, I see a patchwork of greens and browns—fields, treetops, rows of crops. I unfocus my eyes so all I see are the edges of colors bleeding into one another like oil dropped on the surface of water. The last time I was sitting here was in the springtime, five years ago at a writing retreat. It proved to be a productive and magical few days, during which I sat on this same bench for hours and drafted out the skeleton of a book I was writing on how walking can be a method for mindful awareness, exploration, creating, and connection. All weekend, I had been walking and stopping to write, testing out my methods and feeling quite proud of having something to say that felt useful. I published the book a year or so later.

About six weeks after my book about walking was published, I was hiking on an easy trail not too far from where I'm sitting today. My boys were with me that beautiful spring day, and I wanted to show them the wildflowers and other beauties of the trail, to show them that Mama wasn't just preaching walking, she was practicing it, too. And all of a sudden, I had one misstep on the trail. My heel collapsed in a hole, and my ankle twisted dramatically. I heard a pop as I fell hard onto the earth. The pain was agonizing. My ankle was dislocated from my leg, grotesquely hanging off to the right by what seemed to be a thread. I would later learn in the emergency room that my leg was broken in three places. The pain I felt was deeply physical, but as time and rehabilitation dragged on and on, I also felt deeply humbled. Honestly, I was embarrassed to be that woman who had written a book about walking and then promptly stumbled while walking with her children on a very easy mountain trail.

And now, a couple of years later, after the surgery and the metal placed in my leg, after so very much physical therapy, I'm walking much better, but I still have pain—truly, a bit of pain every time my right foot takes a step. But last night, here on that same mountain, a wondrous thing happened: I was able to walk myself home in the dark. I walked carefully over little rocks and roots under so many stars. I walked down a dirt trail all by myself using only my smartphone's flashlight to light my way. I walked past a pond where the moon and stars shimmered on the water like a mirror. I said a prayer of thanksgiving for enduring what felt like a long recovery. I am human, so I know that my body will falter again, but I vow to remember how good it felt to walk myself back home in the dark that September night.

WONDER: Bones break. Muscles ache. Thoughts blur. Our bodies are made to do wondrous things, but they are most certainly perishable! The human body falters from time to time, and our bodies won't last forever. When was the last time an injury or illness took you by surprise? When was the last time your body humbled you? When was the last time you endured?

TRY: Identify a caregiver, someone who cares for those who are enduring injury, pain, or illness. With your loved ones, plan something kind for a caregiver this week. Maybe you'll bake a cake, bring flowers, or write a note of thanks.

RECEIVE A STORY

Why does anybody tell a story? It does indeed have something to do with faith—faith that the universe has meaning, that our little human lives are not irrelevant, that what we choose or say or do matters, matters cosmically.

—MADELEINE L'ENGLE, *The Rock That Is Higher*

September and Ordinary Time was upon us, and my family was settling into a hard season. The previous month, Nana, my beloved grandmother, had endured two serious strokes and multiple pulmonary embolisms. As COVID-19 raged, the hospitals and ICUs filled up with unvaccinated patients, and so, because she was ninety-one, Nana was sent home. My mother dropped everything and moved eight hours away to care for her own mother with an extraordinary level of patience, calm, and devotion. Over the weeks, my sister, dad, and I started taking shifts driving hours to help with Nana's caregiving. As I was pulling out of the driveway to leave for one of my trips, I received a text message from my mother: "Would you please bring me an eyelash curler?"

I howled with laughter. Mom was so consumed with caregiving that she wasn't even leaving Nana's house to go to the drugstore. What was she thinking? No one would be paying much attention to the arc of her eyelashes! But by asking me to fetch her an eyelash curler at such a terrible time, my mom was giving me a story that I'd surely be telling for years to come. Sure, no one but Mom would know that she'd curled her eyelashes every morning, but that one little action would shore up her courage and give her some control, inner strength, and calm. Because of this moment, I now own and use an eyelash curler daily, and for the rest of my life, that strange little instrument will help me recall my mom's resilience and the superpower strength she summoned as she stood in the middle of an unfolding story whose outcome she could not predict.

WONDER: Jesus taught with stories, and storytelling—especially with and about the people we love—can build legacies of courage that we can draw on in hard times. Can you recall a story (about yourself or someone else) connected to a daily ritual that involves an everyday object that can be found around the house? If possible, go get the object and go around the table to tell your story.

TRY: As we tell stories, we dip into a wondrous well. Ordinary Time is an ideal season for storytelling and story-saving. In our family, we are so grateful that my husband used his iPad to record Nana telling family stories one Thanksgiving evening long before her strokes. Take some time to record the people you love telling their stories. Let children take the lead in forming interview questions. Be sure to give the storyteller *time* to respond to prompts and questions. Try not to interrupt, and be patient during inevitable silences or gaps in the telling. StoryCorps' website has excellent resources for initiating and sharing a meaningful, relaxed conversation.

MAKE: A FAMILY TIME CAPSULE

Receive a story in future days to come! Create a time capsule with your loved ones. A time capsule is a container of items that is sealed and then opened at a later date. The items in the time capsule represent a particular time and particular people.

First, decide where you're going to put your time capsule. If you want to bury it, you'll definitely need to get a stainless steel, waterproof capsule that will lock. If you're going to store it indoors—perhaps on a high closet shelf—you'll be okay with something like a shoebox. If you choose a box, decorate it with something like DO NOT OPEN UNTIL 2040—or whatever date you choose—on the outside. For example, you might choose to pick the year a child will graduate from high school as the time to open the time capsule.

What mementos, keepsakes, or representations of this time, this place, and these people should be included? This is a great topic for one of your weekly gatherings. Consider photos, artwork, and hand-prints. We have made lists of favorite foods, songs, sayings, and memorable quotations from family members.

Write a prayer for the future, or compose a letter to your future self. What would you like to say to God in the years to come? What are some thoughts or ideas you'd like to make sure your future self is aware of? Take time to compose your prayers and letters.

Seal up your capsule well, and put it in its hiding place for the next twenty years or so!

DISCOVER: A GREAT CLOUD OF WITNESSES

The Epistle to the Hebrews observes that "we are surrounded by so great a cloud of witnesses" (Hebrews 12:1). To me, this powerful image makes me think of a massive family album filled with portraits of imperfect human beings. They've departed from this life, and they have lived throughout space and time. I picture them encircling us, holding candles, and telling stories of how they tried—often clumsily or tragically—to love God and neighbor in a million different ways.

I have entered Catholic friends' homes to see portraits of John F. Kennedy, Frank Sinatra, and the pope on the wall. I've known African American friends whose homes displayed framed photographs of Dr. Martin Luther King, Jr. When Representative John Lewis died in 2020, I bought a small portrait of him to hang prominently on the wall in our home so my children would know that, in our family, we seek to follow his example of hope and optimism, and that we aren't afraid to "make some noise" and "get in good trouble" when called to stand up for ourselves and others.

As you sit around the table with the people you care for most in this world, contemplate names and images you'd like to add to your family's great cloud of witnesses. Consider the walls in your own home. Are there stories or even portraits you'd like to surround your loved ones with, literally or figuratively? To explore this question, peruse the calendar that teaches us about a different "witness" most days of the year in *A Great Cloud of Witnesses* (Church Publishing, 2016).

A few examples from the calendar include:

- February 20: Frederick Douglass escaped slavery to become a great voice for liberation.
- April 9: Dietrich Bonhoeffer, brilliant Lutheran pastor, professor, and theologian, fiercely and courageously opposed Nazism.
- May 13: Frances Perkins, human rights activist and first female member of the cabinet, was President Franklin Delano Roosevelt's secretary of labor.

* December 1: Nicholas Ferrar founded Little Gidding in 1626, an intentional community in England devoted to prayer and service.

Discovering a great cloud of witnesses is an enlightening way to learn together. You can write or recite your own prayers of commemoration and thanksgiving for the human beings throughout history who have been inspired to follow Christ's example of love and service.

Gather an offering from each member of the circle and share it at the table or place it on your family altar cloth (see page 152).

OCTOBER

LIGHT A FIRE

Make your lives like this fire.
A holy life that is seen.
A life of God that is seen.
A life that has no end.
A life that darkness does not overcome.
May this light of God in you grow.
Light a fire that is worthy of your children.
Light a fire that is worthy of your fathers.
Light a fire that is worthy of your mothers.
Light a fire that is worthy of God.

—MASAI, Tanzania. From Desmond Tutu's
An African Prayer Book

I love coming home with my hair and clothes smelling of a campfire. It's funny—even though I worked as a counselor and director at an Episcopal summer camp, and even though I grew up in a rural area where making fires in the woods was a teenage pastime, I've never had more opportunities to sit around a fire than I have during the COVID-19 pandemic. During this time, the primal human impulse to congregate in a circle outside around a fire emerged as a prudent way to gather with friends and loved ones.

One October evening during the pandemic, on a beach on a narrow, near-deserted cape in the Gulf of Mexico, we built a fire in the evening with the children. My husband, Ben, hauled wood out, and we made a bonfire right by the surf. We dragged out our chairs and the makings for s'mores. With a deep sense of gratitude and overflowing joy, we watched the tide come in under moonlight and starshine.

A couple of evenings later, I was back home in Tennessee. I had left the beach to come straight back home for a fire ceremony for my dearest friend Tallu, who had been diagnosed earlier that year with glioblastoma, an aggressive form of brain cancer. In addition to the traditional treatments—surgery, chemotherapy, radiation—she was meeting with a shamanic healer, a woman who herself was a survivor of brain cancer and who had offered to host a fire ceremony for Tallu and her close friends. In advance of the ritual, we were instructed to sit down and think about the roles we had held in our lives. My list was three crammed columns long on a sheet of paper torn out of my journal:

Daughter sister student employee wife friend mother professor administrator patient client consumer citizen homeowner writer author parishioner organizer chair-president volunteer donor caretaker cook granddaughter mentor mentee investor dancer swimmer singer fan dreamer leader follower planner helper partygoer researcher assistant counselor pet owner perfectionist helper achiever worrier crafter maker

Whew. Writing the list took a lot out of me, and I was surprised by how many roles I could quickly name for myself. At the fire ceremony, we took time to acknowledge the seasons; the elements; the east, the west, the north, and the south; and, most important, to acknowledge each other as we went one by one to the fire and burned our list of roles. We didn't talk about our lists. We didn't share them or comment on them. We simply knelt one by one before the fire that the shaman had made holy with herbs and water and prayer. We each took our time kneeling before the smoke. Awkwardly at first, we used our hands to move the smoke around our faces, to breathe it all in. I said a prayer for my friend Tallu: for her health, for her doctors, for her husband, for her children, for her parents, for her spirit. I said a prayer for myself. For whoever I had been in those roles. For who I might be in front of that fire. For who I might become after I stood up and emerged.

Later, we sat around the fire, and Tallu decided to go ahead and cut off her hair. The chemo had taken chunks out, and a new treatment would mean she'd need to shave it on a regular basis anyway. Someone went down to the house to get scissors, and someone else started cutting what was left of her gorgeous long blond hair, which she rightly proclaimed as "iconic" as we all sat around her. I took a clump and threw it in the fire with all of our old roles in the embers. The unmistakable smell of our friend's burning hair permeated the air. Our old roles smelled like burnt hair as they fused together in fire made holy by the shamanic healer.

Lighting a fire can be transformative, and Ordinary Time, the long season of growth, is an ideal time to light a fire and go inward to see what the light might reveal.

- ⬧ What does "lighting a fire" mean to you?
- ⬧ How do you and I cultivate an interior life in a world that constantly lures us outward?
- ⬧ How do we help others cultivate an interior life?

October Creation Care Challenge: Decide to stop buying disposable items and look around your home to see what can be used instead. As time goes on and you run out of paper napkins, you might decide to elevate mealtime by replacing paper napkins with cloth. Instead of buying a case of disposable water bottles, you might invest in a water bottle you can refill over and over.

CONSENT

There is in every person an inward sea, and in that sea there is an island and on that island there is an altar and standing guard before that altar is the "angel with the flaming sword." Nothing can get by that angel to be placed upon that altar unless it has the mark of your inner authority. Nothing passes "the angel with the flaming sword" to be placed upon your altar unless it be a part of "the fluid area of your consent." This is your crucial link with the Eternal.

—HOWARD THURMAN, *Meditations of the Heart*

All my life, I've heard people confess that they're going to the "Church of the Sacred Hike" or "Our Lady of the Holy Mattress" when on Sunday mornings they find themselves needing connection with our verdant natural world, or just a bit of exercise, or maybe just some plain old sleep instead of a church service. And I wish we would all freely admit that it's perfectly fine to do so because religion is so much bigger than the walls of a church. The birthplace of faith is wonder, marvel, and joy, and there are so many ways to encounter wonder, marvel, and joy as we exercise our bodies, sit for a spell beside a rushing mountain stream, or simply take a nap in the backyard hammock under a cathedral of clouds while the October breeze blows.

The words of Howard Thurman above capture the impulse to consent to the mysterious thing called "the Eternal" as well as any other words in the English language. We are manifestations of God's love through creation, and within each of us, there's an "inward sea" that we can always access through contemplation, through love, and through the quintessentially human impulse to "consent" or "say yes" to the angels and altars deep within our own souls. Saying "yes" can certainly mean joining an organized religion or attending services, but it doesn't have to.

WONDER: Contemplate Thurman's words above using *lectio divina* (page 53). What comes to you as you dwell especially on *altar, consent,* and *eternal*?

TRY: Go outside this week, and consent to the eternal by lying down on Earth or letting a park bench become your church pew. Make sure to include children: Perhaps you can give a child your smartphone so they can take photos or make videos of what they see—and thus give you a breather so you can "consent" on your own for a bit. What branches form the cathedral above your head? What do you hear from the choir of robins? What stained glass images can you find in the wings of the butterflies?

OCTOBER 4, BLESSING OF THE ANIMALS, ST. FRANCIS

As a friend of the poor who was loved by God's creatures, Saint Francis invited all of creation—animals, plants, natural forces, even Brother Sun and Sister Moon—to give honour and praise to the Lord. The poor man of Assisi gives us striking witness that when we are at peace with God we are better able to devote ourselves to building up that peace with all creation which is inseparable from peace among all peoples.

—POPE JOHN PAUL II, January 1, 1990

October 4 is the official day to honor Francis of Assisi, who we recall for his abiding desire to live like Jesus. Francis is known for his joy, his devotion to the Eucharist, and his love and connection to the natural world. Francis is the patron saint of animals and the environment, and it is said that the birds would gather around and listen when he was preaching. According to legend, once when a wolf was terrorizing a village, Francis was said to convince the wolf to leave the people of the village alone. Many churches and parishes offer a blessing of animals on October 4. Families bring dogs and cats, as well as hamsters, guinea pigs, fish, birds, and even horses to receive a blessing.

MAKE: "COOKIES" FOR THE BIRDS TO HONOR ST. FRANCIS[1]

YIELD: 12 "COOKIES"

INGREDIENTS AND EQUIPMENT

1 tablespoon unflavored gelatin

2 tablespoons cold water

⅓ cup boiling water

2 cups birdseed

12 cookie cutters

Needle and thread

DIRECTIONS

Combine the gelatin and cold water in a large bowl and let sit for 1 minute. After 1 minute, add the boiling water. Stir until the gelatin is dissolved. Add the birdseed and stir the mixture thoroughly to combine. Fill the cookie cutters with the seed mixture; press firmly to fill the mold completely. Refrigerate for 6 hours or overnight.

Let the "cookies" come to room temperature and gently remove them from the molds. Use a needle to pull the thread through the ornament, at least ½ inch from the edge, and tie a knot. Hang the ornaments from tree branches! Watch the birds as they gather around your creation, and imagine the birds gathering around Francis of Assisi to listen to him preach.

SCREAM

Anger is not inherently destructive. My anger can be a force for good. My anger can be creative and imaginative, seeing a better world that doesn't yet exist. It can fuel a righteous movement toward justice and freedom.

—Austin Channing Brown, *I'm Still Here: Black Dignity in a World Made for Whiteness*

The release of an angry scream was not something I fully let myself feel until I was a parent, mainly because out of the sheer exhaustion of new mothering, nursing, and lack of sleep, I simply became too tired to push my anger away any longer. Up until my mid-thirties, I allowed myself to tuck any emotions of anger away because I was so deeply formed by a culture that elevated positivity above authenticity. As a child, I desperately yearned for those yellow smiley-faced stickers that I saw on my teacher's desk. I tried to uplift myself and others with my pleasing, positive persona.

But when I became a parent, exhaustion truly wore me down for the first time in my life, and I had to start letting myself get angry enough to scream. My first child didn't sleep well, and I was so overcome with awe at his very existence that even when he finally was sleeping, I would just stare at him in astonishment when I probably should have been sleeping myself. Exhausted from not sleeping, from my own need to heal, and from my frustration at my new inability to keep the house as tidy as I liked it, I finally screamed at my husband. I screamed at myself, mostly, but I screamed if the countertops weren't clean. I screamed when heaps of tiny baby laundry sat wet in the washer.

Thank God I married a man who loved me and all my feelings. I didn't have to please Ben with Pollyanna-esque positivity to get him to love me; he even loved my tired self, and he even loved my mad self. He still loved me when I yelled at him that the countertops weren't clean or the laundry hadn't been moved. That I could be angry, that I could scream and fuss and let it all out when I was so tired and exhausted from mothering was truly liberating.

Though dirty countertops make me crazy, there's so much more to be angry about. All I have to do is take sixty seconds to look at the headlines to feel the injustice, to become furious at the abhorrence of racism, to recognize hypocrisy and never-ending stories of oppression, to be infuriated by the pillaging of creation, the toleration of preventable violence and willful ignorance. It's too much to bear, and I want to scream and rant at the top of my lungs until my anger convinces someone—anyone—to wake up and listen.

WONDER: What is something that really burns you up? Something that feels so unjust and wrong? Something that makes you so mad you can't stand it? Tell it out loud to your people at the table with you, and then go ahead and scream about it if you want.

Now that you have screamed and let your anger be known, can you imagine a way that this infuriating thing might light a fire inside you? Might your anger transform into a force for good? Might your anger help you articulate a healthy boundary?

TRY: Compose a blessing for righteous indignation. Everyone can write one line, and then you can put it all together. Here's a beautiful example you can use as a springboard:

May God bless you with discontent with easy answers, half-truths, and superficial relationships, so that you will live from deep within your heart.

May God bless you with anger at injustice, oppression, abuse, and exploitation of people, so that you will work for justice, equality, and peace.

May God bless you with tears to shed for those who suffer from pain, rejection, starvation, and war, so that you will reach out your hand to comfort them and to change their pain to joy.

May God bless you with the foolishness to think you can make a difference in this world, so that you will do the things which others tell you cannot be done.

—Sister Ruth Fox, Order of Saint Benedict

LAMENT

How long, Lord? Will you forget me forever?
How long will you hide your face from me?
How long must I wrestle with my thoughts
and day after day have sorrow in my heart?
—PSALMS 13:1–2 (NIV)

To lament is to rage, to cry, to grieve. To lament is an ancient way of being in the world, of responding to pain. As I write today in 2021, Afghanistan has fallen to the Taliban, and haunting videos show hundreds of human beings trying to cling to an American military plane as it takes off from Kabul. All the news is so hard, and I feel brokenhearted. This is the best way I know how to describe what's happening inside my body: These stories and images make my heart feel like a piece of meat being tenderized with a mallet.

"Blessed are those who mourn, for they shall be comforted," Jesus tells us in that greatest sermon of all, the Beatitudes. Mourning is necessary and holy. We must acknowledge those who are suffering and use our holy empathy to mourn alongside them. Just as God is present when we make budgets, clean our closets, or dream of a better future for our children, God surrounds us when we rant, scream, and lament.

WONDER: Look at a reputable news source together. Who around the world is mourning today? Call them by name, and extend compassion with your open heart. Invite any children to express something that makes them sad.

TRY: Read aloud some psalms of lament. You might read Psalm 10, Psalm 13, Psalm 38, and Psalms 42–43. Then, collaborate together to make a playlist of songs that express lament. A few to get you started include:

Leonard Cohen, "Hallelujah"
U2, "Pride (In the Name of Love)"
Patsy Cline, "I Fall to Pieces"
Lucinda Williams, "Sweet Old World"
Neil Young, "Only Love Can Break Your Heart"
Johnny Cash, "Hurt"
Al Green, "How Can You Mend a Broken Heart?"
Marvin Gaye, "Inner City Blues (Make Me Wanna Holler)"

MAKE: AN ICON OF A VULNERABLE OR ENDANGERED ANIMAL

[The ecological conversation we need to have] entails a loving awareness that we are not disconnected from the rest of creatures, but joined in a splendid universal communion.

—POPE FRANCIS, *Laudato Si'*

So many creatures are threatened or endangered because of human activity, loss of habitat, hunting, or viruses. Just a few of the many, many vulnerable or endangered animals include: Bornean orangutan, blue whale, Galápagos penguin, loggerhead turtle, red panda, black spider monkey, Arctic fox, barn owl, and honeybees.

Learn about an endangered animal and study its story. Why is it considered vulnerable or endangered? What efforts, if any, are under way to protect it? Then, follow in the example of artist Angela Manno and create a Byzantine-style icon of your chosen vulnerable or endangered animal. Spending time studying your creature is a way to become more enchanted, to know and even to love, and to sense your connection and communion with this animal. Display your icon in a prominent place, and write a prayer that this animal will survive and flourish.

CHANGE YOUR MIND

I was so much older then. I'm younger than that now.
—BOB DYLAN, "My Back Pages"

In the United States, the autumnal months mean election cycles. Especially in recent years, our public discourse is typically marked by foregone conclusions and postures of argument and defense. Rarely do we begin political conversations by assuming postures of openness and wonder. We tend to be hard, not soft; we tend to favor that which is unyielding over that which is tender.

Israeli poet Yehuda Amichai was born in 1924 in Germany, and his family fled to Palestine in 1936 to escape the Nazi regime. His experiences led him to become an advocate for reconciliation between Palestinians and Israelis. Amichai has a brief, vivid poem titled "The Place Where We Are Right." In it, he describes "the place where we are right" or the place where we are certain of our beliefs as a place marked by hard, unyielding ground, a place where "flowers will never grow in the spring." Our doubts and our loves, he writes, make the Earth soft and tender. Our doubts and loves can "dig up the world" like a mole or a plow and make for a more fertile, more wondrous, more lovely existence.

The Greek word *metanoia* literally means "change your mind" or "go beyond your mind," and many scholars have written about the extraordinary mistranslation of this word, which is found in the Gospels. Both Jesus and John the Baptist are said to have used the word, so it's critical to our understanding. In the fourth century, St. Jerome translated the word into Latin as *paenitentia* (to repent or do penance), which is a radically different idea than changing your mind. The difference in the two words is astounding and has had staggering consequences for the Christian tradition. *Metanoia* literally means "going into the larger mind, to go beyond the mind, to experience a shift in consciousness."

WONDER: When's the last time you reoriented in such a way that you assumed a posture of tenderness toward another's ideas—so much so that you changed your mind? Share a story about a new experience or new evidence that altered your way of thinking, being, or living. Make sure any children present hear their grown-ups talk about changing their minds; it's so important to model this action for them. Have you ever shared your "doubts and loves" and found that doing so opened a pathway for new growth and discovery? Have you ever thought about Jesus' teachings being about going into the "larger mind" or transforming your consciousness?

TRY: Read Amichai's poem "The Place Where We Are Right." Have everyone take out a sheet of paper and, at the top, write "I used to believe." Take twenty minutes or so to write about something you used to believe or think, and talk together about what it means to reconsider. Conclude with a final reading of Amichai's poem.

NOVEMBER

POINT TO LOVE

Love is what carries you, for it is always there, even in the dark, or most in the dark, but shining out at times like gold stitches in a piece of embroidery.

—WENDELL BERRY, *Hannah Coulter*

Welcome to November, a time when leaves fall from trees and fall bleeds into winter. In many cultures, the first week in November has been a time for festivals that mark the end of harvest and the beginning of winter. The first two days of the month, All Saints' Day and All Souls' Day, are a time to remember our connections—both cosmic connections and connections at the molecular level—to our ancestors and to those who are yet to be born. We have been carried by them, and we will carry those who come after us.

Many of us travel this month. We visit people who we share bonds with, people who are older and younger. Nurturing intergenerational relationships helps us remember how wisdom is passed down. Spending time with people who are of different ages is a constant reminder that the work we do during our lives on Earth may be nothing but scattering a seed or two. We may not live to see the crop grow or come to harvest.

November is an ideal time to point to the love that connects and carries us, a time to be grateful for the deeper mysteries. Pointing out Love helps us gasp in wonder at the astonishing value of our own lives, the lives of others—other beings, other creatures, the flora and fauna in creation. And the rainbows. For the past couple of years, my friends Marie, Jes, Wendy, Serena, Mary Claire, and I have pointed out more visions of rainbows to one another than you'd ever believe. We've sent each other pictures of rainbows we've spied on the way home from work or early in the morning. I've received a rainbow alert from one of them, dropped everything, and run outside while dinner burns on the stove just so I can see the same rainbow my friends are seeing. They have pointed me to love by helping me expand my creaturely vision.

I hope I'll always find myself surrounded by seekers and spiers of rainbows who will help me see these astonishments that I might not normally perceive if left to my own devices! One of my prayers is that we will develop "rainbow rituals" of our own that can bring us closer to the beloved community, a wondrous vision where swords and guns have been beaten into pruning hooks and shovels because there's no need to study war anymore. Religion can and should be a playbook for the lion lying down with the lamb and the leopard lying down with the goat and the little child leading us all.

During November, we can point to love by:

+ Connecting to people of different ages.
+ Looking to the legacies of loved ones and "saints" (official and un-official).
+ Gladdening the hearts of others by making imperfect offerings.

*   *   *

November Creation Care Challenge: Write a letter expressing your views on creation care and environmental justice to your representative. Find their names and contact information at www.house.gov or www.senate.gov.

DISCOVER: ALLHALLOWTIDE,
A TIME TO REMEMBER

October 31 (All Saints' Eve or Halloween), November 1 (All Saints' Day), and November 2 (All Souls' Day) comprise the season of Allhallowtide. During this brief but sacred period of time, the veil between this life and the next is especially gauzy and diaphanous. Allhallowtide provides an opportunity to reflect on the lives, stories, legacies, and even feel the ongoing *presence* of those who have died. All Hallows' Eve, All Saints' Day, and All Souls' Day have roots in Celtic traditions. If "thin spaces" are spaces in which the world beyond feels so close to Earth, then this three-day period can be thought of as a *thin time*—a period of time when we feel connected to the people who have died and gone beyond this world.

All Hallows' Eve or Halloween: October 31

This date is halfway between the autumnal equinox and the winter solstice, and Halloween has connections to the Celtic celebration of Samhain, which signifies summer's end or the beginning of winter in Gaelic. Bonfires, costumes, going door-to-door for treats, and having food and drink outside are all familiar rituals that were part of the annual Samhain festivals. Beltane or May Day is the Celtic celebration that is the equivalent halfway point between the spring equinox and the summer solstice.

All Saints' Day: November 1

All Saints' Day is a major feast day of the church, a time to honor the saints and martyrs, those who are known as saints and those saints who you know in your hearts. White linens, altar cloths, and vestments are brought out for this day to symbolize joy and purity. I think of All Saints' Day as a day for remembrance and inspiration—a time to acknowledge those who used their own lives to orient others toward The Way, the Divine, or Love.

All Souls' Day or All Faithful Departed: November 2

All Souls' Day is a more informal day on the liturgical calendar to commemorate those who have departed. In Mexico, Día de Muertos or Day of the Dead begins on November 1 and culminates the next day as a great celebration of storytelling, colorful flowers and costumes, special food, and creating altars (*ofrendas*) to commemorate those who have died. The first celebrations of Día de Muertos were recorded long before Mexico was colonized by the Spanish. Día de Muertos is rooted in Aztec tradition that has fused with the Christian calendar and commemorations over the years.

Allhallowtide reminds us that life and death are cyclical, not a straight line. Life and Death are not dualisms or binaries; they are the cycles of the seasons. Our ancestors are *with us* because we are made *by* them and *of* them.

Activities for your gatherings during Allhallowtide:

♦ Learn about a saint you aren't yet familiar with. *A Great Cloud of Witnesses,* published online by the Forward Movement, is an excellent and accessible free resource.

- ◆ Write funny epitaphs for people in the group, a Mexican tradition known as *calaveras literarias.*
- ◆ Watch *Coco,* the perfect film for audiences of all ages to reflect on the presence of those who have crossed over into the next world.

LOOK FOR MESSENGERS

God may be the source of love, but people are often the vessels.
—BISHOP MICHAEL CURRY, *Love Is the Way*

As part of our community's annual All Saints' Day ritual, members of the church bring framed photographs of their beloveds who have passed on: A Polaroid of a sister on her wedding day. A black-and-white image of a father holding a son on his shoulders. An image of a mother, smiling broadly with her arm around her son on graduation day. Each photograph bearer walks up to the front of the sanctuary to place the framed photograph around the altar. The space on and around the altar becomes filled with these wistful images of loved ones, those vessels of love known as human beings who meant something to those gathered for the feast. When I gaze upon them, I am always astonished at how tender I feel.

When I come up to the altar to receive the wine and bread of the Eucharist, I try to make an effort to study the lines and contours of their faces, to look closely at their eyes, to imagine what their voices sounded like. As we receive the bread and the wine, the faces on the photographs join the circle, and the body of Christ is palpable. The images are filled with people in various states of life. The faces of children who have passed are haunting and, for me as a parent, feel like a punch to the gut. Smiling faces of the old can't help but make me think of my own grandparents. The clothing worn by the various "saints" on the altar remind me that fashions come and go. Political battles are fought, are won, are lost, and are then forgotten. Buildings we design, create, and inhabit eventually come down and become dust again.

But love is the thing that lasts. Relationships we've nurtured endure through time and space. Tides keep coming in and going out, winds warm and cool us, stars form a womb overhead for the land and its creatures and flora. And these photographs we tuck into our bags and bring up to the altar on All Saints' Day are the messengers from beyond pointing us again and again to Love.

WONDER: Ask yourself: Is there a person or a group of people I have difficulty really *seeing*? Are there situations, phenomena, or elements of creation I tend to overlook? What would it mean to take a closer look? Who are some of the messengers in your life who have pointed you to the Way of Love? They can be messengers you've known personally or messengers who have provided powerful examples to you.

TRY: Make an *ofrenda* or altar together to commemorate loved ones who have passed on. Include their photos, flowers, candles, and favorite foods and drinks, and tell stories about their lives and the connections you have with them.

As an activity to train yourself and others to look closely, get a jeweler's loupe or magnifying glass to look more closely at some rocks, a blade of grass, or the veins of an autumnal leaf.

GLADDEN

Life is short, and we do not have much time to gladden the
hearts of those who are traveling the dark journey with us. Oh,
be swift to love, make haste to be kind.

—ATTRIBUTED TO HENRI-FRÉDÉRIC AMIEL

One autumn afternoon, a football team we root for in our household won a big game on a stunning last-second play. In the heat of the moment's glory, an acquaintance texted the coach to send his congratulations. Immediately, the coach wrote back, but in his message, he said nothing about the game, instead going on and on about how proud he was of the thanks he had received from the hotel staff in the small town where the game was held. The hotel staff told him every single room the players had occupied was all tidied up, and all the used towels had been placed in the sink rather than thrown on the floor. Apparently, the team's captains insisted that the players respect the service workers they will likely never meet in person by not making them bend over to pick up their used linens off the floor.[1] The team's captains are young college students no more than twenty-two years old, but they already seem to know that, during our short time on this spinning blue planet, we should all make haste to be kind. We should do what we can to gladden the hearts of others.

Furthermore, I love this story because it illustrates how a small community can make a simple, little choice to respect others, and that little choice can shape awareness in such a profound way that it ripples into the future. For example, that team's seemingly inconsequential choice to pick up their towels could inform how those players might eventually deal with an annoying colleague, regard public policy, or even teach their own children in the years to come.

Be swift to love. Make haste to be kind. Amiel's blessing, which is often used as a benediction at the end of church gatherings, distills it all down so well. Sometimes, at the end of a semester's worth of classes, I'll stand up at the very last moment of the very last class and offer these words as a blessing for my students: *Oh, my friends, life is so, so short . . . and during our hours, days, and years here, may we be in this glorious world in such a way that will gladden, heal, repair, and generally make lovelier the everyday existence of others.*

WONDER: What exactly is prayer? Does prayer have to be done with words? Can actions be prayers? Jesus taught ways of praying and worship that were done in secret ways—not public ways. To see what I mean, read Matthew 6:5–6. How might doing things to gladden the hearts of others or make their everyday existence a little lovelier be a form of prayer?

TRY: This week, offer this challenge to all adults and children alike: "Point to love" by doing something to gladden the heart of another. But it has to be secret; if they find out, do it again until you've truly *not* been recognized for your efforts.

OFFER

The gifts of God for the people of God.
—FROM THE LITURGY FOR THE BREAKING OF THE
BREAD, *The Book of Common Prayer*

One morning, I found a fully intact sand dollar in the surf. Full, white, and round, it reminded me of a large communion wafer, the kind a priest consecrates and holds up before the congregation during the Eucharistic prayer. The sun was high in the sky, and it felt like a magical discovery since I usually find shards and pieces of sand dollars—never the whole thing. Entranced, I held it up to the sky like the priest holds a communion wafer during the Eucharistic prayer. Alone on the beach, I pretended the line of ocean on the horizon was the endless cup of wine, and I held up my perfectly round sand dollar like a wafer to the sky and dipped it into the line of ocean on the horizon, saying out loud to no one in particular: "The gifts of God for the people of God."

Later that day, I found a safe place for my perfect, white sand dollar to dry out, and then I carefully wrapped it in bubble wrap and newspaper before packing it in my suitcase and bringing it back home on the plane. As I unpacked after returning home, I pulled out my perfect sand dollar and carefully unwrapped it to show the boys. Peter, who was four at the time, held out his little hands to touch it—just like a hungry boy at the altar rail who couldn't wait to taste the bread. He wanted to hold it, so he took it in his hands. Before I could even say the words "Be careful!" my darling child took that perfect sand dollar from my hands and snapped it in two—just like a priest would break the bread in front of the people as she blessed it.

Now that I have a few years of distance from that shocking moment when my sweet child snapped my perfect sand dollar in half, I can make a little sense of it. I suppose it's possible that he was doing what he had seen the priests in our church do as they consecrate the bread. But I think it's more likely that he just wanted to feel the essence of the sand dollar. His impulse to break it was rooted in a healthy impulse to wonder how he could connect with this little piece of creation his mama was so proud to show him. Because do you know what he did with it after he broke the perfect sand dollar? He smiled proudly, and he held out his little hands to offer the two broken pieces right back to me. And this is precisely what we do when we gather flour, salt, yeast, grapes, and sunlight and combine them together to make bread and wine. We make beautiful offerings, and then we break, sip, and share them together in the Eucharistic feast. The Eucharist is a process of gathering elements of creation together through the bread and wine, breaking them apart, and then offering them right back to Love.

WONDER: A Danish proverb claims, "Even crumbs are bread." What do you think crumbs represent? Why is it important to notice and cherish the so-called crumbs, to acknowledge them as sustenance and offer them to ourselves and to others? Why do they point to Love?

TRY: Identify something that seems humble or broken, and transform it into an offering to the group. Perhaps you'll rescue some day-old bread and turn it into zesty croutons for a salad. Or maybe you'll take a box of broken crayons and melt them into something bright and new.

ENCOUNTER

I thought when people got older they became more settled in
their ways. More conservative and careful. Less inclined to go
out searching for something new. But I seem to have become
the opposite. I am more of a spiritual nomad than ever, out
exploring the mysteries around me. I am sure I have a home in
the Spirit, but I cannot stop looking out the window. The night
sky looks like a roadmap, the first light of dawn like an
invitation. I see other seekers already heading for the unknown
and I long to be with them. We are a community old in
experience, but young in wonder.

—Steven Charleston[2]

As November progresses, the hours of sunlight wane, and the
church year approaches the conclusion of another cycle. Soon,
the green season's long season of growth and maturation will end, and
a new cycle will commence on the first Sunday of Advent. Always, we
begin again.

Through the liturgical cycle, we share a rhythm. We may not all
share a common list of beliefs, but by dwelling together in the cycle of
the seasons, we are in a kind of rhythm, moving together like a circle
of dancers. The dancers may not individually hold the same opinions
or set of beliefs, but they move together connected in their purpose,
with a shared sense of movement. Rather than remain endlessly grid-

locked over dogma and belief, we can agree that it's better to gather around the table, celebrate the liturgies, and honor the seasons and cycles.

Like Steven Charleston—a Choctaw elder and an Episcopal priest—I am finding that the more I age, the more I learn, and the more I experience, the more I want to know. The more light I encounter in other people, places, and practices, the less I am drawn to rigid structures. The more awe I feel in the presence of the flora and fauna of creation, the more I realize that I am not a god who has to know and understand everything. That awe and light sets me on a path that feels freer and freer to gather and celebrate alongside other seekers. Held by a common liturgy and the endless cycle of seasons, I am set on a path with other pilgrims heading out into the unknown.

WONDER: As fall temperatures drop, trees begin to lose their green (chlorophyll), and their fall foliage of vibrant red, yellow, and orange appears. Earlier in the year, maples have dropped seedpods (sometimes called helicopters, samaras, or whirligigs) that, remarkably, look like little angels. As maple leaves drop in fall, the seedpods have been preparing for new growth. And often near mid-November, goldenrod ginkgo leaves drop all at once! Like all deciduous trees, they have formed a scar between leaf and stem, but the first hard frost causes every ginkgo leaf to sever at once, forming a goldenrod aura on the ground. Encountering and pondering mysteries and wonders of trees make me contemplate intelligence. Can your group think of multiple ways to describe intelligence? As the green season of Ordinary Time comes to a close, can you ponder many different ways to describe wisdom? How do intelligence and wisdom differ? Can you name non-human ways of describing the two concepts? What might it mean to be old in experience but young in wonder?

*   *   *

TRY: Bring photos of your ancestors and share them around the table tonight. Imagine encountering them in this space. Tell stories about them, involving children as much as you can. What gems of wisdom and intelligence might your ancestors have contributed to the conversations you've had around the table this year?

DISCOVER: ORDINARY TIME ENDS, AND THE LITURGICAL YEAR BEGINS ANEW WITH THE FIRST SUNDAY OF ADVENT

Christ the King Sunday, the last Sunday of Ordinary Time, marks both an end and a beginning. As the liturgical cycle comes to a close, we begin again with Advent and reflect on all we have experienced through the seasons: In Advent, the first season of the church year, we have contemplated and waited for Love. And then Love has been made incarnate through the mysteries of Jesus' birth at Christmas and Epiphany. The Lenten season prepares us to immerse ourselves in the mystery of rebirth and renewal through death, resurrection, and ascension at Eastertime. At Pentecost, the spirit moves through fire and air, and the storytelling about God's love and mystery begins. Then through the weeks of Ordinary Time, we grow by contemplating and learning from Jesus' life. Ordinary Time, a long season to bask in the mysteries and wonders, culminates on the final Sunday of Ordinary Time, which is called Christ the King Sunday.

The first Sunday of Advent marks the beginning of a new year in the church. We have left the green of Ordinary Time behind, and it's time for purple vestments and altar linens, as well as Advent wreaths and Advent calendars (see page 262).

In a world of excess where Christmas decorations often start showing up in the stores in summertime, it takes some serious restraint not to begin decorating early for Christmas. I try to wait as long as possible to decorate, though it's tough to do so. There's an amusing internet meme of Lady Mary Crawley of *Downton Abbey* standing beneath the lights of the Christmas tree. Lady Mary insists: "The tree stays up until Epiphany. You'll get used to how things are done here. Properly."

Using the liturgical seasons as our guardrails, Christmas trees and decorations really should go up on Christmas Eve and come down on Epiphany, January 6. But that's admittedly tough, especially with excited children who are home from school and ready to celebrate. One compromise is to put the tree up on the second or third Sunday of Advent and decorate it and the rest of the house slowly. We have also tried to limit excessive spending, so many years ago, we tried to institute this guideline for buying gifts for the children: "something you want, something you need, something to wear, something to read" to keep the shopping and buying to a minimum.

DISCOVER: AN ADVENT WREATH
AND AN ADVENT CALENDAR

It's a chilly Sunday afternoon, and I'm eight years old and wandering through my backyard, gathering pine and cedar branches for our Advent wreath. My Sunday school teachers have just given us all a white circular Styrofoam form for the wreath, and having only recently learned the difference between evergreen and deciduous, I'm looking for the bright green leaves among the dusty branches that scatter the ground. My sister and I will stick the sharp ends of the branches into the Styrofoam form, and place four candles into the wreath with our mother's help. It will sit on top of a big plate in the middle of the dinner table; the plate is to prevent the sap and candle wax from getting on the dinner table. For the next four Sundays, our Advent wreath will fill the room with that evergreen fragrance I love to savor. The room will be lit up with Advent's promise of light and hope, and we will be excited and have a bit of our wild Christmas energy tamed by Advent's steady practices of preparation. Evergreen branches remind us that all is not lost in the dark and cold. The winter solstice is coming—right as Advent is about to end—December 21.

The Advent wreath uses three purple candles and one pink candle. The pink candle is for the third Sunday of Advent, Gaudete Sunday— and when you light the pink candle, you know that it's almost time for joy and celebration. A fifth white candle can be placed in the center of the wreath and lit on Christmas Eve.

Advent calendars are easy to find in stores and certainly add to feelings of expectation.

I quilted an Advent calendar wall hanging the winter I was pregnant with our first son, Henry. It's a wall hanging with a pocket for each day, and each of the days are arranged haphazardly, so the boys have to find the date. In each little pocket, we hide little chocolate treats and little poems and prayers on small pieces of paper in each pocket. Consider making your Advent calendar activity-based instead of (or in addition to) filled with treats. You can make up activities like "take a nighttime walk to look at Christmas lights," "have a dance party to Vince Guaraldi Trio's *A Charlie Brown Christmas*," "take canned goods to a food bank," or "watch a Christmas movie" (like *It's a Wonderful Life* or, my personal favorite, *Emmet Otter's Jug-Band Christmas*).

DECEMBER

LOOK FOR THE LIGHT

There is a quiet light that shines in every heart. It draws no attention to itself, though it is always secretly there. It is what illuminates our minds to see beauty, our desire to seek possibility, and our hearts to love life. Without this subtle quickening our days would be empty and wearisome, and no horizon would ever awaken our longing. Our passion for life is quietly sustained from somewhere in us that is welded to the energy and excitement of life. This shy inner light is what enables us to recognize and receive our very presence here as a blessing. We enter the world as strangers who all at once become heirs to a harvest of memory, spirit, and dream that has long preceded us and will now enfold, nourish, and sustain us.

—JOHN O'DONOHUE, *To Bless the Space Between Us*

December: The new liturgical year begins with the season of Advent, the light begins to return on the winter solstice, and we celebrate incarnation through the baby Jesus on Christmas Day. Advent begins four Sundays before Christmas, so the first day of Advent is sometime between November 27 and December 3. It's the perfect time to make an Advent wreath (see page 262) or start an Advent calendar. "Wait, wait, wait," I find myself saying more than usual since I became a mother: We don't need to put up the tree just yet, we don't need to wrap gifts and festoon everything with Christmas decorations. "Christmasing" becomes a part-time job for many as soon as the Thanksgiving dishes are washed, dried, and put away. Many put up their Christmas trees the weekend following Thanksgiving, and the activities, parties, decorating contests—and especially the relentless emails inviting me to buy things throughout Advent—ensue. Keeping Advent is countercultural, especially with excited children—and our culture tends to forget that "Christmas" begins on December 25, and the Christmas season actually continues for the next twelve days. But, of course, that calendar doesn't align with a capitalist model intent on profiting throughout Advent. Throughout the season of Advent, I receive emails tempting me to make purchases during erroneously named "twelve days of Christmas" promotions, and I want to call customer service and correct their manipulative error. I want to climb to the highest rooftops and shout "Wait, Wait, Wait!" "Subvert capitalistic Christmasing, and stop buying stuff!" and "Rebel!" I *need* Advent; I need a season that shows me how to wait and look for the light.

And yet, I can't help but give in: We put up our tree well before Christmas Eve, and I absolutely love creating, sending, receiving, and displaying holiday cards in particular. In early December 2020—that strangest and saddest of years—I needed to figure out what to do for our annual Christmas greeting card. One friend was making a card that looked like a Zoom screen filled with the faces of her husband, children, and pets. Later in the season, I'd chuckle when I received another that quipped "2020 is Hindsight." For our cards, I had always carefully considered the boys' outfits, planned for a seasonal setting, and, for better or worse, had tried to keep it *sort of* classy. I'd steer my family toward tasteful yard décor—a deer or some other sort of woodland animal festooned with a red velvet bow and lights. But in the last days of 2020, that year marked by death and disease and distancing, I could not wait to surprise my family with a five-foot inflatable Grogu holding a candy cane. Also known as "The Child" or "Baby Yoda," Grogu is a character in the *Star Wars* series *The Mandalorian,* and our seven- and nine-year-old sons were obsessed with the adorable character, who was from the same species as Grand Master Yoda, that most brilliant Jedi master of my own youth.

The giant "Baby Yoda" holding a big candy cane was looming and swaying in front of our home, and my people were happy. But what did it have to do with Advent or Christmas? I had no idea, but it made my children—who had been in and out of school and had not seen their grandparents since March—smile. So, I made the boys brush out their unruly hair, which had not been cut by anyone but me in months. They changed into their Christmas pajamas and came out into the yard to have their photo taken next to our brand-new giant inflatable Baby Yoda. I had no idea what language I would use on the card to send our pandemic greeting. In previous years, I'd quoted Kris Kristofferson's astonishingly good song "Jesus Was a Capricorn." One year I'd incorporated lines from Mark Strand's gorgeous Advent poem "The Coming of Light," and another, I'd included Madeleine L'Engle's wise words about the nature of Jesus' incarnation.

Not a superfan of *Star Wars,* I started googling, and I was stunned to come across wisdom that seemed to encapsulate lessons about the pandemic, as well as the mystery and very essence of what I believe it means to follow the Way of Jesus:

> Luminous beings are we. Not this crude matter.
>
> —MASTER YODA, as he gestures to Luke Skywalker's body,
> *The Empire Strikes Back* (1980)

Aha! I had found the language for my greeting! We beings are made up of flesh and bones and blood—crude matter. Vulnerable to sickness and disease, these bodies of ours eventually die. But there is this immortal, everlasting light within us, and, if we let it, it can enlighten our own paths and the paths of others.

When the cards I'd ordered arrived, I teared up, gazing at my children's bodies as they stood barefoot outside in the brown grass of a Tennessee December. In the midst of the pandemic, their mortality—and my own mortality—juxtaposed against the bright sweetness of a massive illuminated Baby Yoda on our lawn made me smile through my tears. Jesus of Nazareth, the Palestinian Jew born in a humble barn, shows us the Way of Love and the life beyond the "crude matter" of this body. We have been created in light, and we mirror God's light. There's luminosity within our beings, and we can use our light to illuminate the gifts of others and Love itself. Christmas is about light breaking into the world!

- ◆ What is the dream of God?
- ◆ How does the incarnational light of Jesus literally and figuratively enlighten the path?
- ◆ How can the seasons of Advent and Christmas deepen and unleash a radical way of caring for others?

*   *   *

December Creation Care Challenge: As you consider giving Christmas gifts this year, explore alternatives to pricey wrapping paper, which can only be used once. Reuse brown paper bags to wrap gifts, and decorate them yourself. Or use gift bags, which can be saved and reused over the years.

CARE

We are wired to be caring for the other and generous to one another. We shrivel when we are not able to interact. . . . We depend on the other in order for us to be fully who we are. . . . The concept of Ubuntu says: A person is a person through other persons.

—Archbishop Desmond Tutu, *The Book of Joy*
(co-authored with His Holiness the Dalai Lama)

More than fifteen years ago, I led a study abroad trip in South Africa and Botswana, and we learned together about the African concept of *ubuntu*, which essentially means, "I see you. You exist. I care for you. In fact, *I am* because *you are*. I am because *we* are."

Ubuntu is an extraordinary idea, one that doesn't translate well into English. My student Ashley, who was on the trip, immediately and deeply connected with the concept, and shortly after we returned to the United States, she had the word *ubuntu* tattooed on her body because it was something she wanted to remember for the rest of her life. *Ubuntu* was the gospel she wanted to preach with her own body and model with her life.

The season of Advent is a time to keep watch, take care, and realize the profound truth that I am my neighbor, and my neighbor is me. We are each other's keeper. When you tug on one thread, another is affected. The choices I make influence other lives.

* * *

WONDER: How does looking for the light in others connect to caring for them? Spend some time this week paying close attention to the light. Have you ever noticed the way light travels and changes in your own home? Can you find places where rainbows—the result of light shining through a prism—appear on the walls at certain times of day? Where is east (sunrise), and where is west (sunset)? Which of your rooms get morning light, and which spaces get evening light? Learn to connect with and care for a potted plant by learning what kind of light it needs, and orient your potted plant accordingly in your home. Furthermore, care and connect by contemplating the nature of a global pandemic, which surely makes our interconnectedness plainer than ever. What a myth individuality is, after all! What are some of the beliefs you've inherited that suggest that you and you alone are the author of your life story? How does the season of Advent disrupt and challenge those beliefs?

TRY: In your weekly gathering, make a specific plan to express care and love for your neighbors this week, and interpret the definitions of *care* and *neighbor* broadly. Maybe you'll help stock a local food pantry. Or maybe you'll offer to help a neighbor who lives alone by getting decorations out of the attic or putting up a wreath. Get creative, and try to make someone feel truly seen and acknowledged.

DISCOVER: A FESTIVAL OF LESSONS AND CAROLS

The first service of lessons and carols was held in England in the late nineteenth century on Christmas Eve. Generally, they're held now during late Advent and are opportunities for communities to gather, hear stories, and sing all sorts of seasonal songs in preparation for Christmas. Readings are followed by a carol (a song sung by the choir to the community) or a hymn (a song sung by both the choir and the community).

Here are some suggested readings:

Genesis 3:8–15
Genesis 22:15–18
Isaiah 9:2, 6–7
Isaiah 11:1–3a, 4a, 6–9
Luke 1:26–35, 38
Luke 2:1, 3–7
Luke 2:8–16
Matthew 2:1–12
John 1:1–14

A SELECTION OF SONGS FOR ADVENT

"O Come, O Come Emmanuel"
"Creator of the Stars of Night"
"Adam Lay Ybounden"
"The Holly and the Ivy"
"Lo, How a Rose E'er Blooming"
"I Look from Afar" (Giovanni da Palestrina)
"The Friendly Beasts"

REBEL

He came to a world which did not mesh,
To heal its tangles, shield its scorn.
In the mystery of the Word made Flesh
The Maker of the stars was born.
—MADELEINE L'ENGLE, "First Coming"

Even trees are lit up, animated, and illuminated by God's incarnate Love: That idea shaped the tradition of putting lights in Christmas trees. And in some stores, you can start purchasing artificial Christmas trees with lights already hardwired into them in *July*. Sometimes I can't understand how we got here: How did honoring the birth of a baby born in a barn end up being a time of frantic shopping and spending? I feel like Charlie Brown, who, in *A Charlie Brown Christmas*, rescues that one little live tree for the play. Exasperated after his friends fuss at him for picking such a sad little pine tree when he could have gotten one of the shiny, fluorescent aluminum ones, Charlie laments, "Isn't there anyone here who knows what Christmas is all about?"

In a season when everybody is trying to get me to spend money on Christmas, I want to observe countercultural movements like #OptOutside and head to the woods instead of the mall on Black Friday. Instead of picking up my credit card, I want to light a candle, pick up a book of poetry, and read in a quiet house.

* * *

WONDER: Listen to Jackson Browne and the Chieftains' song "The Rebel Jesus" on the latter's album titled *The Bells of Dublin*. What is a rebel, anyway? Have you ever thought of Jesus as a rebel? What was he rebelling against? Have you ever considered yourself a rebel? What are forces you've rebelled against?

TRY: Rebel against the chaos of consumerism by beginning a new Advent ritual: discovering the simple magic of a practice known as Poetry Teatime, a practice developed by home education expert and writer Julie Bogart.[1] Make your table "fancy" with candles and a tablecloth or homemade centerpiece, and prepare "tea"—a sweet treat and tea (or hot chocolate or lemonade) in a special teapot or pitcher. Gather a stack of poetry books from the public library or from your home shelves. Let everyone take turns flipping through the books and finding a poem to read out loud. There's no need to analyze, unpack the symbols, or do any of those things that make people fear poetry. Simply enjoy the poems, and savor good food and time at a lovely table together. You might even decide, as many others have, to make Poetry Teatime a weekly ritual.

Alternatively, create an Advent calendar with each day opening to a new poem you can read together at the close of day.

Some poems connected to the season of Advent include:

Christina Rossetti, "In the Bleak Midwinter"
Madeleine L'Engle, "First Coming"
Rowan Williams, "Advent Calendar"
Denise Levertov, "Annunciation"
Gjertrud Schnackenberg, "Advent Calendar"
Ted Kooser, "Christmas Mail"
Mark Strand, "The Coming of Light"

MAKE: HANDMADE GIFTS

Preparing gifts is an inevitable part of preparing for Christmas, and handmade gifts are such a thoughtful way to give something meaningful and personalized to the people on your list. I look forward to the day each December when my friends Scott and Mary Claire drop off their homemade eggnog (using Scott's beloved mother's recipe) at our door. When the recipient holds or sees the gift you made or knows the story behind it, they will think of *you* and the good, the joy, and the kindness you bring into this world.

You can prepare soup, bake sourdough bread, and make cookies or candy. And throughout the year, you've made candles (see page 33), a hiking stick (see page 39), a rosary (see page 72), a birdhouse (see page 129), a birdfeeder (see page 129), icons of saints and endangered animals (see pages 136 and 239), an altar cloth (see page 152), comfrey salve (see page 179), bath salts (see page 193), prayer cards (see page 202), and cedarwood sachets (see page 212). Perhaps you could make one or more of these again, and personalize them for those on your list. Personally, I'd rather spend my time in Advent making handmade gifts than wandering around a big box store or shopping mall with a huge list and a maxed-out credit card. Making gifts by hand feels like a more thoughtful, therapeutic, rejuvenating, delightful—and yes, even rebellious—way to spend my resources and my time.

REPRESENT

In the candlelight her face was all shiny with tears and she didn't even bother to wipe them away. She just sat there—awful old Imogene—in her crookedy veil, crying and crying and crying. Well. It was the best Christmas pageant we ever had.

—BARBARA ROBINSON, *The Best Christmas Pageant Ever*

In 1223, Francis of Assisi sought permission from Pope Honorius III to create the first nativity scene.[2] Francis wanted to inspire a kindling of wonder and devotion for the birth of Jesus. Up until that point, as author Richard Rohr points out, Easter—and thus resurrection—was the primary celebration for Christians. But Francis's desire for a nativity scene or a crèche would help Christmas become a celebration of God's incarnation—or embodiment—through human flesh, through God's willingness to become physical, to become human. Francis gathered a manger, hay, an ox, and a donkey and set them up in a cave in Greccio, Italy. He wanted to kindle his own imagination—and those of others as well—by contemplating the actual sight of a baby laid in the hay. According to reports from the scene, people gathered, bringing flowers and lit torches to the cave. Many supposedly recalled that the scene inspired the most joy they'd ever felt. The practice of enacting the nativity spread through Europe and, eventually, around the world. In 2019 at the original scene in Greccio, Pope Francis said that the crèche invites us to feel and touch the incarnate God so that we can serve "by showing mercy to those of our brothers and sisters in greatest need."[3]

People who don't ever come to church sign their kids up to be in our community's legendary Christmas pageant. Some kids who sign up to be an animal just end up wearing their Halloween costumes; many a time, a feathery chicken, a gleaming red lobster, a wiggly peacock, or even Captain Underpants has shown up alongside the more histori-cally appropriate camels, cows, and sheep. Sometimes even parents, exhausted from getting the kids in their costumes downstairs, decide at the last minute to put on one of the extra silver tinsel angel wings and join the scene themselves. All are welcome to come up to the altar to witness the humanity of that baby in the manger.

So often, Advent is synonymous with the word *wait,* which has al-ways puzzled me logically, because we aren't *waiting* for the baby Jesus to be born: The baby Jesus was born a long, long time ago in that man-ger in Bethlehem. It seems to me that what we are waiting for are those shocking moments of illumination, the recognition that the spirit is enfleshed, has taken on humanity, and is therefore reborn through life that goes on now. God is here, and we are waiting to bear witness to the miracle of incarnation over and over again, year after year, day after day, moment by moment: being by being.

* * *

WONDER: To *represent* is to stand in place of, or to provide a body for, someone who we can't see, feel, touch, or hear. How do you represent Jesus or God in your imagination? What are some rituals (like the pageant) that help you see, feel, touch, or hear God's presence?

TRY: Read about the Herdman family and their first encounter with a Christmas pageant in Barbara Robinson's *The Best Christmas Pageant Ever.* The book can be read aloud in one evening; pass it around the table, chapter by chapter.

For another activity, learn to sing "The Friendly Beasts," an often overlooked, wonderful song about the nativity from the perspective of the animals who were there at the scene. *Orientis partibus* originated in France for a festival to honor the donkey that helped the Holy Family flee to Egypt as Herod tried to have them killed. Amazingly, the music was written for that festival honoring the donkey around the same time Francis began the nativity tradition in Italy.

THE FRIENDLY BEASTS

Jesus our brother, kind and good
Was humbly born in a stable rude
And the friendly beasts around Him stood,
Jesus our brother, kind and good.

"I," said the donkey, shaggy and brown,
"I carried His mother up hill and down;
I carried her safely to Bethlehem town."
"I," said the donkey, shaggy and brown.

"I," said the cow all white and red
"I gave Him my manger for His bed;
I gave Him my hay to pillow his head."
"I," said the cow all white and red.

"I," said the sheep with curly horn,
"I gave Him my wool for His blanket warm;
He wore my coat on Christmas morn."
"I," said the sheep with curly horn.

"I," said the dove from the rafters high,
"I cooed Him to sleep so He would not cry;
We cooed Him to sleep, my mate and I."
"I," said the dove from the rafters high.

Thus every beast by some good spell,
In the stable dark was glad to tell

Of the gift he gave Immanuel,
The gift he gave Immanuel.

"I," was glad to tell
Of the gift he gave Immanuel,
The gift he gave Immanuel.
Jesus our brother, kind and good.

—*Traditional English*[4]

UNLEASH

When the song of the angels is stilled,
When the star in the sky is gone,
When the kings and princes are back home,
When the shepherds are back with their flock,
The work of Christmas begins:
To find the lost,
To heal the broken,
To feed the hungry,
To release the prisoner,
To rebuild the nations,
To bring peace among brothers,
To make music in the heart.
—HOWARD THURMAN, "The Work of Christmas"[5]

I grew up in a small southern town with a really great arts council. One year in the early 1980s, the arts council brought a folk singer named John McCutcheon to town, and I went to see him with my family in the junior high school auditorium. What was unforgettable about that performance was hearing him sing his song "Christmas in the Trenches," which imagines the true story of a series of unofficial cease-fires that took place during World War I.

On Christmas of 1914, soldiers came out of the trenches where they had been battling each other for five months in one of the most brutal wars the world had ever seen and started talking, sharing food, exchanging little gifts, and singing carols. They helped each other bury their dead. Possibly, they even played a little soccer in no-man's-land, the blood-soaked area between the trenches. Within a few days, they went down into their respective trenches and started battling again, and the war went on until 1918. But for a brief time, Love's dream came to life, and Christmas cast a spell: Annihilation transformed into creativity, and hatred morphed into tenderness.

WONDER: What really *is* the work of Christmas? Read Howard Thurman's poem on the previous page. How does it inform the prophet Isaiah's vision of what the world could be?

> . . . they shall beat their swords into plowshares,
> and their spears into pruninghooks;
> nation shall not lift up sword against nation,
> neither shall they learn war any more.
>
> —ISAIAH 2:4

Imagine, what could *this particular Christmas* unleash in you? In the world?

TRY: You've come together weekly for a while now, so you should know each other pretty well. Gather colorful markers or brush pens and thick sheets of paper. Your task is to write a word or two about something wonderful each person at the table might unleash in the world. Spend some time in silence doing this, and then share your vision for each person. Take it a step further by imagining a rock, mineral, plant, animal, microorganism, or other element of nonhuman life that symbolizes each person at the gathering.

DISCOVER: BLUE CHRISTMAS

I said to my soul, be still, and wait without hope
For hope would be hope for the wrong thing; wait without love,
For love would be love of the wrong thing; there is yet faith
But the faith and the love and the hope are all in the waiting.
                    —T. S. Eliot, "East Coker"

Many communities acknowledge that the season can be overwhelming for those who are grieving or struggling with painful memories, darkness, addiction, or depression. Blue Christmas (or sometimes called The Longest Night) observances can be held on or around the longest night of the year, December 21. These services can offer a place to acknowledge the hardness of a season adorned with tinsel and filled with parties and gatherings. The Feast of St. Thomas is also observed on December 21, which seems fitting since Thomas is often known for his holy doubts.

- ◆ Light the Advent candle wreath.
- ◆ Mark Blue Christmas by giving each other time and space to name and even write your grief and sadness.
- ◆ Offer anointing with your special oil, as you acknowledge each other's suffering and pray for peace and healing.
- ◆ Use the loving-kindness meditation on page 167.
- ◆ Pray for compassion, kindness, illumination, and healing.
- ◆ Consider a special offering and intentional prayers for an organization in your community that addresses addiction.

DISCOVER: CHRISTMAS DAY
(DECEMBER 25, NATIVITY OF JESUS)

Once in royal David's city
Stood a lowly cattle shed,
Where a mother laid her baby
In a manger for his bed;
Mary was the Mother mild,
Jesus Christ her little child.

—CECIL FRANCES ALEXANDER[6]

A joyful day of celebration, Christmas is one of the principal feasts of the church. On Christmas, we send greeting cards, decorate with greenery, give gifts, gather, go caroling, feast, light candles, and burn yule logs. The word *Christmas* derives from the Old English *Cristes maesse* (Christ's Mass), and the date of December 25 has no historical foundation and was probably chosen in the fourth century to oppose *Dies natalis solis invicti*, a Roman feast that was in celebration of Saturn.[7]

Christmas Day is wildly, obscenely overcommercialized, and the emotional expectations we set for ourselves to have "a perfect Christmas" are so very far from the "lowly cattle shed" where Jesus was born. Some meaningful rituals you might begin this Christmas to rebel against the commercialization of Christmas and connect to the deeper meaning of the day include:

- Host a Christmas Day Poetry Teatime (see page 275).
- Make and share a playlist of Christmas music.
- If you live in a city or neighborhood, build a fire in the front yard, prepare some hot cocoa, and see who drops by.
- Take a Christmas hike among the evergreens, symbols of the day.

- Volunteer to work in a shelter or food kitchen on Christmas Day.
- Invite someone who is alone or grieving to share your Christmas feast.
- Record loved ones telling stories about what their Christmases were like growing up.

DISCOVER: THE SEASON OF CHRISTMAS

The word *incarnate* comes from the Latin "in carne" or "in flesh" or enfleshed. Beginning at midnight on Christmas Eve, we celebrate the season of Christmas, the incarnation, God's decision to fuse with humanity, and Mary's *yes* to carrying and birthing Love. The Christmas season lasts for twelve days, beginning at midnight on December 24, which is often why Midnight Masses are held—and concluding on January 5, the day before Epiphany.

January 1, the eighth day of Christmas, is the Feast of the Holy Name, which commemorates the circumcision and naming of the baby Jesus. The first day of the calendar year often overshadows this commemoration, but it's an important day to remember Jesus' Way of Love, a way of being in the world that honors life, liberation, and creation.

FOUR SPECIAL WEEKS
IN THE LIVES
OF LOVED ONES

SAVOR

CELEBRATING A BIRTHDAY

From wonder into wonder existence opens.

—LAO-TZU

Aging is an honor and a privilege; a birthday symbolizes a threshold moment from the past into the future. How will we celebrate and mark this threshold? Stores have entire aisles devoted to mass-produced, throwaway items we can buy and consume to celebrate birthdays. But we can develop meaningful family traditions and rituals in which we savor birthdays in eternal ways by reflecting on what has happened so far in life, noticing what is happening in the present, and contemplating what may be yet to come. As you mark a birthday, try to:

REVEAL THE PAST

Recall stories and gather pictures from important years of your life.
Share baby pictures, family photos, and important moments.
Who have been the most important people in your life?
What ideas and relationships have shaped your consciousness?
What are the greatest gifts you've ever received?

SAVOR THE PRESENT

Notice and reflect on the astonishing fact of existing.

Show gratitude to those who join you in this celebration.

Reflect on your role in creation—am I caring for my neighbor, for
   the Earth, for the creatures and plants on it?

CONTEMPLATE THE FUTURE

Consider the year to come.

What do you long for?

Name some of the hopes and dreams you have.

What gifts would you still like to offer others?

Pray the beautiful birthday prayer from *The Book of Common Prayer*
that begins "Watch over thy child, O Lord, as *her* days increase . . ."
   Or, you can pray:

We gather together to give thanks for this life, for this being's
remarkable and delightful existence on Earth. In _____, we see
a child of God. There is no one else quite like him/her/them. We
are grateful for the ways this life is woven into ours,
especially_____. May _____'s sense of marvel
increase day by day, and may _____ know how much we
love, celebrate, honor her/him/them.

RESTORE

HEALING FROM AN INJURY OR SICKNESS

For this brief pause, for this reminder of my own weakness and
of my dependence on you, I thank you, O Lord.
—Douglas McKelvey, "A Liturgy for a Sick Day"

When we are ill, everything else falls away—especially pride.
When we are injured or sick, we can't do it all alone; we have to
lean on others. A time of illness tends to strip relationships down to
nothing but love.

ACKNOWLEDGE SUFFERING

Nothing reminds us of our impermanence like an illness or injury;
health is a precious gift. Acknowledge our bodies with a sense of wonder, for they possess not just the capacity to suffer and feel pain but
also the wisdom to endure, to heal, and to recover.

Feeling uncertain is a form of suffering; we pray for patience, for
healing takes time.

EXTEND COMPASSION

Extend compassion to the pains and aches within our own bodies. Extend compassion to those family members, friends, medical profes-
sionals, and other caregivers who are helping us through this time.
Extend compassion to those who have studied and trained to develop

vaccines, medicines, and devices that help develop immunity and diagnose and heal our ailments. Extend compassion to those beings around the world who are suffering in body, mind, or spirit.

CONTEMPLATE WELL-BEING

We can't assume good health. May we be grateful for our health and for the limited days we have to live on this Earth. May we find delight in relationships and in these bodies we have been given. May we use our health to care for creation, to love our neighbors, to love ourselves.

As you are recovering, close your eyes, and pray with the rosary; make your own prayers in which you acknowledge suffering, extend compassion, and contemplate well-being.

RETREAT

TAKING A JOURNEY TOGETHER

From the moon, the Earth is so small and so fragile and such a precious little spot in that vast universe that you can block it out with your thumb, and you realize that on that small spot, that little blue and white thing, is everything that means everything to you—all of history and music and poetry and art and death and birth and love, tears, joy, games—all of it on that little spot out there and you can cover it with your thumb. And you realize that from that perspective you've changed, that there's something new there, that the relationship is no longer what it was.

—RUSTY SCHWEICKART, Apollo 9 astronaut

TO CONTEMPLATE UPON DEPARTURE

Oh, God, there's still so much to do at home and at work. Let it be.
May we not overpack.
May we resolve to share the load.
May we be patient as we encounter the inevitable delays to come.
May we be kind to those workers in airports and rest stops and gas
    stations who are just doing their best.
May we be safe.

TO CONTEMPLATE UPON ARRIVAL

God, we need this time together to explore, time to be pilgrims on
    the road.

We need to encounter new people and places, to shift our
    perspectives.

We need time to laugh, time to play games, time to walk hand in
    hand as we go nowhere in particular.

Let there be joy and surprises along the way as we sightsee.

Let us resolve to take a little longer than usual at meals.

May we experience different cultures with a sense of wonder and
    humility.

May we see more starlight than crowds.

May we encounter more blossoms and branches and fewer buttons
    and screens.

May we be kind to the strangers we encounter, and may we be open
    to kindling new connections and friendships.

Help us remember that nature is not merely scenery or a backdrop
    for photos—nature is *us,* and nature is you, O God.

TO CONTEMPLATE UPON RETURNING BACK HOME

May we reflect on the insights we gained from being in this place.

May we resolve to record and preserve stories, moments, and in-
    sights for the future with photos and writing.

Help us to remember those moments that surprised us.

May our sense of wonder about the people, places, and phenomena
    we encountered grow now that we have returned home and have
    time to research and reflect.

God, thank you for the gift of adventure with those we love, and
    thank you for bringing us safely back to this sanctuary we call
    home.

ENCIRCLE

BLESSING A HOME

The desire to go home is a desire to be whole, to know where
you are, to be the point of intersection of all the lines drawn
through all the stars, to be the constellation-maker and the
center of the world, that center called love. To awaken from
sleep, to rest from awakening, to tame the animal, to let the soul
go wild, to shelter in darkness and blaze with light, to cease to
speak and be perfectly understood.

—Rebecca Solnit, *Storming the Gates of Paradise*

Jesus began his life encircled by love in a stable—not in a palace or
even a well-appointed house. Much of his ministry played out in
ordinary homes. May our homes be sanctuaries of safety and shelter.
May our homes be known as places of hospitality. May our homes be
places of care, renewal, and, above all, love.

Blessing a home with intentionality is at once simple and momen-
tous. Gather at the entryway with a candle, a bouquet of flowers, a loaf
of bread, a bottle of wine, a box of salt, a throw, or some other simple,
meaningful embodiment of home. Adapt the blessings below as you'd
like.

* * *

At the entryway: Loving God, we pause here to pray that this home will always be a place where we come in to share our joys, sorrows, and all that makes up our everyday lives. May this home be a place where we bring our tears, our laughter, our groceries, our books, our family albums, our toys, and our clothing—as well as our doubts, our questions, and our stories. May our guests feel truly at home here. May this space be a sanctuary where we can be authentically ourselves. May this threshold be a place where we say hello and goodbye with sincerity. May we leave nothing unsaid.

In the kitchen: May this kitchen be an alchemical place of possibility, a place to feed one another's bodies and souls. May we bring our imaginations and our family recipes as we measure, chop, stir, mix, salt, heat, and preserve in this holy space. May we delight in the smell of bread baking here. May we clean up after ourselves so that this space is always ready for the next meal.

At the table: May this table be a surface on which we rest our forearms and clasp our hands in gratitude for the food and drink we share. May this table be a place where we linger to tell stories from our day. May this table offer a legacy of gratefulness, authenticity, and hospitality to all who encircle it in the days and years to come.

In the living room: May we gather in this space to relax and find refuge. May we nurture creativity in ourselves and appreciate the creativity of others here. May there be a soft blanket or two to warm us on cold nights so we can linger a little bit longer in the company of those we love.

*   *   *

At the threshold of the bathroom: May this room be a place where we find relief and where we nurture a sense of health and well-being. May we cleanse and rejuvenate ourselves here. As we rinse off particles of dirt and bathe, refresh, and purify ourselves, may the bathtub or shower be a place where we do some of our finest contemplating.

In the bedroom: In this space, we rise up when we wake and we lie down to go to sleep. May the pillows cradle our heads, may the linens be soft and warm, and may the soothing aroma of lavender perfume the air just a bit. May a spirit of quietude permeate this space to help us sleep, love, and read bedtime stories.

In the outdoor space or garden: May we breathe in the atmosphere of this place and be grateful for a connection to the outdoors. May the air be clean and safe. May the soil be rich and fertile. May this earth beneath our feet (or the soil in the pots on this terrace) be devoted to honoring, protecting, and nurturing bees, butterflies, birds, squirrels, bunnies, vegetables, and flowers. May this space kindle our imaginations and be a place where we can be joyful and lighthearted.

CONCLUDING PRAYER

May the Spirit of Love permeate all the cracks and crevices of this
   home.
May this home be a haven where we have meaningful conversations,
   laugh, and tell stories.
May this home be a sanctuary where we know others, where we
   know ourselves.
May we be grateful for this home and the shelter, hospitality, and refuge it brings.

BENEDICTION

MAY WONDERS NEVER CEASE

Love all of God's creation, both the whole of it and every grain of sand. Love every leaf, every ray of God's light. Love animals, love plants, love each thing. If you love each thing, you will perceive the mystery of God in things. Once you have perceived it, you will begin tirelessly to perceive more and more of it every day. And you will come at last to love the whole world with an entire, universal love.

—FYODOR DOSTOEVSKY, *The Brothers Karamazov*

Early one morning while it was still dark and I was writing quietly at the dining room table, my son Henry came down in his *Star Wars* pajamas and asked me, "What is your book about, Mama?" I told him I hoped it would be about how being a spiritual person was not about being certain about everything. I told him that I hoped it would help people be amazed, pay attention, and be delighted by that which was good and enchanting. I showed him how I had organized it around fifty-two actions—one action verb for each week of the year—and told him that, in my opinion, each action amounted to a kind of a superpower. I said I hoped that each week could help us think about how what we *do, learn,* and *be* connects to awe, surprise, and wonder—and how awe, surprise, and wonder bring us close to the Holy Spirit.

What I didn't say to my child that morning is that I wanted to write this book because I don't relish the idea of a future in which we mainly know of religion in terms of authority, orthodoxy, and certainty. At its heart, *Seasons of Wonder* is a plea to view and know the Divine not in terms of certitude but as a vast unfolding, unknowable mystery.

As time goes on, I yearn to put myself in a posture of learning, seeking, and being open to God as a Surprise. We can look for signs, symbols, and words of God's as Surprise any time and any place. We don't have to wait to be told where God is by institutions or their leaders. Though institutions can certainly be places that edify, teach, and sustain, God is certainly not confined to institutions! Lately, I have been encountering the Holy Spirit as I dance in the kitchen and contemplate Brandi Carlile's exquisite lyrics. In spring, I've deeply felt the presence of Love when I watched my ten-year-old son gasp in wonder as he watches the crocus bulb he planted in the fall emerge on a cold spring morning. The day after Christmas this year, I went to see my close friend who has terminal brain cancer. I wanted to bring her a gift, but what could I bring? She didn't need jewelry or clothes or food. So I poured some oil into a little glass vessel and added twenty drops of frankincense and lavender, and took it to her bedside. She could barely put words together anymore, so we just lay together, told each other we loved each other, and I rubbed frankincense oil on her wrists and her feet. God was right there with us as Surprise, as Holy Spirit present in the fragrant oils from the earth.

Earth is our home—a dwelling that teems with wonder, delight, and glory—a place to be contemplated, beheld, loved, protected, and cherished. There's light, energy, and an evergreen-ness in all beings, all creatures, all flora, and I hope *Seasons of Wonder* offers concrete ways to love, enjoy, and care for our common home and one another through the seasons.

Recently, Bishop Michael Curry expressed a yearning that the church would not be formed in "the way of the world" but would be formed in "the way of Jesus and his love." Bishop Curry employed the narthex, the space between a sanctuary and the world, as the symbolic space for this vision. At the narthex, he said, we can find

> a community of small gatherings and congregations of all
> stripes and types, a human tapestry, God's wondrous variety, the
> Kingdom, the reign of God, the beloved community, no longer
> centered on empire or establishment, no longer fixated on the
> preservation of institution, no longer propping up white
> supremacy or in collusion with anything that hurts or harms
> any child of God or God's creation—by God's grace, a church
> that looks and acts and lives like Jesus.[1]

As we vow to recognize and honor our wondrous variety, may we be good company for one another, year after year, cycle after cycle, season after season.

May we never forget that Jesus is a teacher who encourages us to transform the world and to transform our consciousnesses.

May our prayers, liturgies, and rituals become containers for our big feelings, for our gladness and joy, as well as our anger and our lament.

May our light never be contained, and may we be beacons for others throughout our lives and beyond as our ancestors have been beacons for us.

May we meet the light of the incarnate God in ourselves, in one another, and through creation.

May our prayers be occasions to use language and words but, maybe more often, occasions to listen and feel embraced by the Divine.

May we value and nurture imagination, intuition, and intelligence in ourselves and in others.

May we come to know our own vastness and *creatureliness* infinitely more deeply than we know our own capacities for productivity.

May we return to wonder again and again—wonder for God, wonder for other people, wonder for other creatures, and wonder for our kin on this planet again and again.

May we steadfastly return to wonder even when it means we have to pry the door open and light a homemade candle to see the path— because wonder brings us to the liberating Way of Love.

ACKNOWLEDGMENTS

A friend is a loved one who awakens your life in order to free
the wild possibilities within you.
　　—John O'Donohue, *Anam Cara: A Book of Celtic Wisdom*

The idea for and shape of this book emerged over a few precious
November days in 2020. Tallu Quinn and I had escaped to a farmhouse in White Bluff, Tennessee, to write together for a few days, four
short months following her terminal diagnosis of glioblastoma, a dev-
astating brain cancer. During those days, Tallu diligently worked on a
luminous series of essays that would become *What We Wish Were
True*. While she worked so very hard while she still could, I made us
tea, transcribed her ideas, painted, read, and wrote out some of my
own rough essays and half-baked ideas. As we talked about the various
unorthodox ways we had experienced God's calling throughout our
lives, Tallu pulled a piece of paper out of her bag and sketched out an
ingenious circle detailing a renewal cycle that correlated to the seasons. Almost immediately, I knew I wanted to write about how the liturgical seasons orient me to wonder. I will forever be grateful to Tallu
for her Circle (both the circle she made on the paper and The Circle
she made of her friends as soon as she was diagnosed) . . . as well as her
brilliance, her lifelong commitment to depth over shallowness, her
simple and perfect ways of cooking and sharing, and her uproarious
laughter. Love never dies.

To my clergy friends Serena Sides, Claire Brown, Scott Owings, Becca Stevens, Lissa Smith, Frances Hall Kieschnick, and Jeff Markay: Thank you for your insightful feedback and occasional reassurances that it was okay for a mere lay person like me to write a book like this.

To Ann & Ken King and Katy Varney & Dave Goetz: Thank you for sharing your quiet, well-lit homes so this working mama could escape to write.

To Dr. Ellen Wright: Thank you for allowing me to relay your poignant words and insights about how wondrous it can feel to drown out your own voice during common prayer.

To Professor Derek Nelson, a theologian and historian at Wabash College: I am grateful you allowed me to retell your eloquent social media post about the Wabash football coach, who showed such pride in his team's efforts to show respect both on and off the field.

To the Femme de Valeur & the Second Sunday Book Club: I don't think I would be standing upright if not for our appointments, traditions, laughs, text chains, and soul-nourishing friendships.

To Fidelity 204 and my wonderful colleagues at Belmont: You have encouraged, sustained, and supported me in a truckload of ways, and I am so very fortunate to be part of your team.

To Becky Nesbitt, Ashley Hong, Leita Williams, Nancy Delia, Alisse Goldsmith-Wissman, and Rachel Tockstein: Your editorial feedback, vision, and wisdom improved this book in more ways that I could ever begin to calculate. Even as I work on the final draft, I still cannot believe I am fortunate enough to work with you and the rest of the team at Convergent. What a dream come to life!

To my dear Anna Knutson Geller: Your generosity, curiosity, kindness, friendship, intelligence, good humor, seemingly infinite well of ideas, and savvy guidance have set me on paths I never imagined I could go. Working with you is a gift.

To Mom/Honey and Dad/Bud: Thank you for always encouraging your daughters to ask the hard, unanswerable questions about faith. Thank you for taking us to church but also showing us how the mountains, trails, and sunsets were church, too.

To Ben: Thank you for absolutely everything—the morning coffee, the Bonvoy points so I could run off to hotels and write for twenty-four hours, the extraordinary meals you make, the dancing in the kitchen at the end of the day, and your boundless love. You are my favorite husband, and I love living life with you more and more every day, every week, every season.

To Henry and Peter, my beloved children of God: This book is all for you. Thank you for being so patient while I wrote and revised it, and thank you for sharing your incredible ideas with me; they made it a better book. Mamalove loves you beyond all measure. May you grow in love and compassion, and may you never forget those words on Charlotte's web "that proved human beings must always be on the lookout for the presence of wonder" (E. B. White, *Charlotte's Web*).

And finally, to my remarkable sister, Kelly: You are a wonder. Thank you for marrying Derek so we will never stop laughing. Thank you for sharing Rufus with us. And above all, thank you for reading this manuscript at various stages and offering your wise, pointed, and indispensable feedback. You are the finest writer, editor, friend, and sissy in the cosmos.

SOURCES

Ackerman, Diane. *The Rarest of the Rare: Vanishing Animals, Timeless Worlds.* New York: Random House, 1995.

Amichai, Yehuda. "The Place Where We Are Right." In *The Selected Poetry of Yehuda Amichai*, 34. Berkeley: University of California Press, 2013.

Angelou, Maya. "Interview with Oprah Winfrey." Oprah Winfrey Network: *Super Soul Sunday.* May 12, 2013. https://www.youtube.com/watch?v=Irs5tJgokys.

Attenborough, David. *A Life on Our Planet: My Witness Statement and a Vision for the Future.* Attitude Film Entertainment, 2020.

Augustine of Hippo and Henry Bettenson. *City of God.* New York: Penguin Classics, 2004.

Bahnson, Fred. *Soil and Sacrament: A Spiritual Memoir of Food and Faith.* New York: Simon and Schuster, 2013.

Bailey, Maggie Blake. *Visitation.* Red Wing, Minn.: Tinderbox Editions, 2020.

Bernardi, L., et al. "Effect of Rosary Prayer and Yoga Mantras on Autonomic Cardiovascular Rhythms: Comparative Study." *BMJ* 323 (2001): 1446–49. doi:10.1136/bmj.323.7327.1446.

Berry, Thomas. *The Christian Future and the Fate of Earth.* Maryknoll, N.Y.: Orbis Books, 2009.

Berry, Wendell. *Hannah Coulter.* New York: Shoemaker and Hoard, 2004.

———. "Manifesto: The Mad Farmer Liberation Front." In *The Country of Marriage*, 16–17. New York: Harcourt Brace Jovanovich, 1973.

———. "The Peace of Wild Things." In *Collected Poems, 1957–1982*, 69. New York: North Point Press, 1987.

Bessey, Sarah. *Jesus Feminist: An Invitation to Revisit the Bible's View of Women.* Brentwood, Tenn.: Howard Books, 2013.

Bogart, Julie. *The Brave Learner: Finding Everyday Magic in Homeschool, Learning, and Life.* New York: TarcherPerigee, 2019.

The Book of Common Prayer and Administration of the Sacraments and Other Rites and Ceremonies of the Church. New York: Seabury Press, 1979.

Bourgeault, Cynthia. *The Wisdom Jesus: Transforming Heart and Mind—a New Perspective on Christ and His Message.* Boston: Shambhala, 2008.

Brown, Austin Channing. *I'm Still Here: Black Dignity in a World Made for Whiteness.* New York: Convergent Books, 2018.

Brown, Claire, and Anita Peebles. *New Directions for Holy Questions: Progressive Christian Theology for Families.* New York: Morehouse Publishing, 2022.

Buechner, Frederick. *Wishful Thinking: A Seeker's ABC.* San Francisco: HarperSanFrancisco, 1993.

Carson, Rachel. *The Sense of Wonder.* New York: HarperCollins, 2017.

Carter, Sydney. *Green Print for Song.* London: Stainer & Bell, 1974.

Chacour, Elias. *We Belong to the Land: The Story of a Palestinian Israeli Who Lives for Peace and Reconciliation.* South Bend, Ind.: University of Notre Dame Press, 2001.

Charleston, Steven. *Ladder of the Light: An Indigenous Elder's Meditations on Hope and Courage.* Minneapolis: Broadleaf Books, 2021.

The Chieftains with Jackson Browne. "The Rebel Jesus." *The Bells of Dublin.* RCA Victor, 1991.

Chödrön, Pema. "How to Practice Tonglen." *Lion's Roar.* December 21, 2021. https://www.lionsroar.com/how-to-practice-tonglen/.

Clinton, Hillary, host. "Believe in Yourself" with Brandi Carlile. *You and Me Both.* February 1, 2022.

Crossan, John Dominic. *How to Read the Bible and Still Be a Christian: Struggling with Divine Violence from Genesis Through Revelation.* New York: HarperOne, 2015.

Crossan, John Dominic, and Sarah Sexton Crossan. *Resurrecting Easter: How the West Lost and the East Kept the Original Easter Vision.* New York: HarperOne, 2018.

Curry, Bishop Michael. *Love Is the Way: Holding on to Hope in Troubling Times.* New York: Avery, 2020.

Dillard, Annie. *Pilgrim at Tinker Creek.* New York: HarperPerennial, 2013.

Dostoevsky, Fyodor. *The Brothers Karamazov.* Translated by Richard Pevear. New York: Everyman's Library, 1992.

Dozier, Verna. *The Dream of God: A Call to Return.* New York: Seabury Books, 2006.

Dozier, Verna, with Celia A. Hahn. *The Authority of the Laity.* Washington, D.C.: The Alban Institute, 1982.

Dubliners. "Lord of the Dance." *Now.* Polydor Records, 1975.

Evans, Rachel Held. *Wholehearted Faith.* New York: HarperCollins, 2021.

Francis, Pope. *"Laudato Si': On Care for Our Common Home."* The Holy See. 2015. https://www.vatican.va/content/francesco/en/encyclicals/documents/papa-francesco_20150524_enciclica-laudato-si.html.

Gordon, Mary. "Mysteriously Woman: A Feminist View of the Rosary." *The Furrow* 55, no. 5 (May 2004): 259–72.

A Great Cloud of Witnesses: A Calendar of Commemoration. New York: Church Publishing, 2016. https://extranet.generalconvention.org/staff/files/download/19349.

Griffin, Patty. "Mary." *Flaming Red.* A&M Records, 1998.

The Highwomen. "Crowded Table." *The Highwomen.* Elektra Records, 2019.

Hildegard of Bingen, *Symphonia.* Edited by Barbara Newman. Ithaca, N.Y.: Cornell University Press, 1988.

Holmes, Barbara A. *Joy Unspeakable: Contemplative Practices of the Black Church*. Minneapolis: Fortress Press, 2004.

Hummon, Marcus. "Life Is a Church." *The Sound of One Fan Clapping*. Velvet Armadillo Records, 1997.

Johnson, James Weldon, and J. Rosamund Johnson. "Lift Every Voice and Sing." 1900.

Julian of Norwich. *Showings*. Translated by Edmund Walsh and James Walsh. Mahwah, N.J.: Paulist Press, 1978.

Keating, Thomas. *Open Mind, Open Heart: The Contemplative Dimension of the Gospel*. New York: Continuum, 1999.

Kershner, Irvin, and George Lucas. *The Empire Strikes Back*. Twentieth Century-Fox Film Corporation, 1980.

Kidd, Sue Monk. *When the Heart Waits: Spiritual Direction for Life's Sacred Questions*. New York: HarperOne, 2016.

Kimmerer, Robin Wall. *Braiding Sweetgrass: Indigenous Wisdom, Scientific Knowledge, and the Teachings of Plants*. Minneapolis: Milkweed Editions, 2015.

———. "Nature Needs a New Pronoun: To Stop the Age of Extinction, Let's Start by Ditching 'It.'" *Yes!*, March 30, 2015. https://www.yesmagazine.org/issue/together-earth/2015/03/30/alternative-grammar-a-new-language-of-kinship.

Kristofferson, Kris. "Jesus Was a Capricorn." *Jesus Was a Capricorn*. Monument Records, 1972.

Lawrence, Brother. *The Practice of the Presence of God*. Eastford, Conn.: Martino Fine Books, 2016; reprint of 1895 edition.

L'Engle, Madeleine. *The Irrational Season*. New York: HarperOne, 1984.

———. *The Rock That Is Higher: Story as Truth*. New York: Convergent Books, 2018.

———. *Walking on Water: Reflections on Faith and Art*. New York: Convergent Books, 2016.

Levertov, Denise. "Annunciation." In *The Collected Poems of Denise Levertov*, 836–37. New York: New Directions, 2013.

Linn, Dennis, Sheila Fabricant Linn, and Matthew Linn. *Sleeping with Bread: Holding What Gives You Life*. Mahwah, N.J.: Paulist Press, 1995.

Mayfield, Curtis. "People Get Ready." Chicago: Universal Recording, 1964.

McCutcheon, John. "Christmas in the Trenches." *Winter Solstice*. Rounder, 1984.

McFague, Sallie. *The Body of God: An Ecological Theology*. Minneapolis: Augsburg Fortress Press, 1993.

McKelvey, Douglas. *Every Moment Holy*. Volume 1. Nashville: Rabbit Room Press, 2020.

Mendelson, Lee, Charles M. Schulz, Bill Melendez, et al. *A Charlie Brown Christmas*. Burbank, Calif.: Warner Home Video, 2008.

Merton, Thomas. *Conjectures of a Guilty Bystander*. New York: Doubleday, 1966.

———. *New Seeds of Contemplation*. New York: New Directions, 1972.

Morissette, Alanis. "Ablaze." *Such Pretty Forks in the Road*. RCA, 2020.

Nhat Hanh, Thich. *Living Buddha, Living Christ*. New York: Riverhead Books, 1995.

Nouwen, Henri. *The Return of the Prodigal Son: A Story of Homecoming*. New York: Deckle Edge, 1995.

O'Donohue, John. *Anam Cara: A Book of Celtic Wisdom*. New York: HarperPerennial, 1997.

———. *To Bless the Space Between Us: A Book of Blessings*. New York: Convergent Books, 2008.

Oliver, Mary. "I Worried." In *Swan: Poems and Prose Poems*, 39. Boston: Beacon Press, 2012.

———. *Upstream: Selected Essays.* New York: Penguin Books, 2013.

———. "Wild Geese." In *Owls and Other Fantasies: Poems and Essays,* 1. Boston: Beacon Press, 2003.

Ó Tuama, Pádraig, *Daily Prayer with the Corrymeela Community.* London: Canterbury Press Norwich, 2017.

Pasolini, Pier Paolo, and Luis Bacalov. *Il Vangelo Secondo Matteo.* Milan, Italy: Garzanti, 1964.

Pecinovsky, Teresa Kim. *Mother God.* Minneapolis: Beaming Books, 2022.

Pelagius. *The Letters of Pelagius: Celtic Soul Friend.* Edited by Robert Van de Weyer. Berkhamsted, England: Arthur James, 1995.

Ponticus, Evagrius. *The Praktikos, Chapters on Prayer.* Collegedale, Minn.: Cistercian Press, 1972.

Prine, John. "Boundless Love." *The Tree of Forgiveness.* RCA Studio A, 2018.

Quinn, Tallu Schuyler. *What We Wish Were True: Reflections on Nurturing Life and Facing Death.* New York: Convergent, 2022.

Renkl, Margaret. "This 'Shazam' for Birds Could Help Save Them." *New York Times,* July 26, 2021.

Revised Common Lectionary. Vanderbilt Divinity Library. https://lectionary.library .vanderbilt.edu.

Robinson, Barbara. *The Best Christmas Pageant Ever.* New York: HarperCollins, 2005.

Rohr, Richard. *Eager to Love: The Alternative Way of Francis of Assisi.* Cincinnati: Franciscan Media, 2016.

———. *The Naked Now: Learning to See as the Mystics See.* New York: Crossroad, 2009.

———. *The Universal Christ: How a Forgotten Reality Can Change Everything We See, Hope For, and Believe.* New York: Convergent, 2019.

Rohr, Richard, with Mike Morrell. *The Divine Dance: The Trinity and Your Transformation.* New Kensington, Penn.: Whitaker House, 2016.

Russell, Bertrand. *In Praise of Idleness and Other Essays.* London: Routledge, 2004.

Simon & Garfunkel. "Blessed." *Sounds of Silence.* Columbia, 1966.

Solnit, Rebecca. *Storming the Gates of Paradise.* Berkeley: University of California Press, 2007.

Starr, Mirabai. *Wild Mercy: Living the Fierce and Tender Wisdom of the Women Mystics.* Boulder, Colo.: Sounds True, 2019.

Stevens, Cat. "Morning Has Broken." *Teaser and the Firecat.* Island Records, 1971.

Strand, Clark, and Perdita Finn. *The Way of the Rose.* New York: Random House, 2019.

Stokes, Terry J. *Prayers for the People: Things We Didn't Know We Could Say to God.* New York: Convergent, 2021.

Teilhard de Chardin, Pierre. *Hymn of the Universe.* New York: HarperCollins, 1969.

Teresa of Avila. *The Interior Castle.* Translated by Mirabai Starr. New York: Riverhead, 2004.

Thurman, Howard. *Jesus and the Disinherited.* Boston: Beacon Press, 1996.

———. *Meditations of the Heart.* Boston: Beacon Press, 1999.

———. "The Work of Christmas." In *The Mood of Christmas and Other Celebrations,* 23. Richmond, Ind.: Friends United Press, 1985.

Tutu, Desmond. *An African Prayer Book.* New York: Doubleday, 2006.

Wings of Life. Disney Nature, 2015.

Wood, James. "God Talk: The Book of Common Prayer at Three Hundred and Fifty." *The New Yorker,* October 15, 2012.

NOTES

INTRODUCTION

1. In *Seasons of Wonder,* as in the Episcopal tradition, the season of Epiphany is January 6 (the Feast of the Epiphany) through the Tuesday before Ash Wednesday. On the Roman Catholic calendar, the time between the Monday after the feast of Jesus' baptism and the Tuesday before Ash Wednesday is generally designated as Spring Ordinary Time.
2. Steven Charleston, *Ladder to the Light* (Minneapolis: Broadleaf Books, 2021), 96.
3. James Wood, "God Talk: The Book of Common Prayer at Three Hundred and Fifty," *The New Yorker,* October 22, 2012.
4. www.episcopalchurch.org.

JANUARY: TRANSCEND DUALITIES

1. This King Cake recipe is closely based on a recipe published by Bobby Hebert's Cajun Cannon on their Facebook page.
2. Based on a tutorial found on the YouTube channel of Katrinaosity.
3. Rachel Held Evans, *Wholehearted Faith* (New York: HarperCollins, 2021), 20.

FEBRUARY: DISCOVER CONTEMPLATION

1. Based on an activity found here: https://scoutlife.org/hobbies-projects/projects/1108/take-a-hike/.
2. This is our family's riff on a Williams Sonoma pancake recipe that can be found here: https://www.williams-sonoma.com/recipe/buttermilk-pancakes.html.

MARCH: EMBRACE MYSTERY

1. See https://www.churchofengland.org/prayer-and-worship/worship-texts-and
-resources/common-worship/churchs-year/holy-week-and-easter-1.
2. L. Bernardi, et al. "Effect of Rosary Prayer and Yoga Mantras on Autonomic Cardiovascular Rhythms: Comparative Study." *BMJ* (Clinical research ed.), vol. 323,7327
(2001): 1446–9. doi:10.1136/bmj.323.7327.1446.
3. https://www.ssje.org/2017/07/31/altar-bread/.
4. *The Book of Common Prayer,* Eucharistic Prayer C.

APRIL: WELCOME INCARNATION

1. Pelagius, *The Letters of Pelagius: Celtic Soul Friend,* edited by Robert Van de Weyer
(Berkhamsted, England: Arthur James, 1995).
2. Richard Rohr, *The Universal Christ: How a Forgotten Reality Can Change Everything We See, Hope For, and Believe* (New York: Convergent, 2019), 14–15, 18.
3. Wendell Berry, "Manifesto: The Mad Farmer Liberation front," in *The Country of
Marriage* (New York: Harcourt Brace Jovanovich, 1973), 16–17.
4. For an illuminating treatment of Francis, see Richard Rohr, *Eager to Love: The Alternative Way of Francis of Assisi* (Cincinnati, Ohio: Franciscan Media, 2014).
5. From Sydney Carter, *Green Print for Song* (London: Stainer & Bell, 1974).

MAY: ADORE CREATION

1. Thomas Berry, "The Meadow Across the Creek," in *The Great Work: Our Way into
the Future* (New York: Bell Tower, 1999), 17.
2. From the "Believe in Yourself" episode of the podcast *You and Me Both* with Hillary Clinton, February 1, 2022.

JUNE: COME ALIVE

1. Summarized from the catechism found in *The Book of Common Prayer.*

JULY: CULTIVATE RESILIENCE

1. Interview with Charlie Rose, May 27, 1993.
2. Pema Chödrön, "How to Practice Tonglen," *Lion's Roar,* January 14, 2022. https://
www.lionsroar.com/how-to-practice-tonglen/.

AUGUST: CHERISH THE HOLY PAUSE

1. I am exceedingly grateful to my friend Dr. Ellen Wright for letting me paraphrase
her beautiful retelling of this experience, which she detailed to me in an email.
2. See https://extranet.generalconvention.org/staff/files/download/19349.

SEPTEMBER: GATHER COURAGE

1. From the Library of Congress National Recording Registry, found at https://www .loc.gov/static/programs/national-recording-preservation-board/documents /PeopleGetReady.pdf.
2. Daily email, *Brother, Give Us a Word*, October 28, 2021.
3. Bureau of Labor Statistics, U.S. Department of Labor, "Number of Jobs, Labor Market Experience, Marital Status, and Health: Results from a National Longitudional Survey," accessed October 28, 2021, https://www.bls.gov/news.release/pdf/nlsoy .pdf.
4. See Luke 12:27–28.

OCTOBER: LIGHT A FIRE

1. Recipe based on "Bird Seed Ornaments" from Audubon.org.

NOVEMBER: POINT TO LOVE

1. Thank you to Professor Derek Nelson, a theologian at Wabash College, for letting me share this story.
2. From Steven Charleston's daily Facebook post following his morning prayers, October 18, 2021.

DECEMBER: LOOK FOR THE LIGHT

1. Poetry Teatime ritual adapted from *The Brave Learner* by Julie Bogart (New York: TarcherPerigee, 2019), 130–31.
2. Much of our understanding of Francis's life comes from the thirteenth-century theologian St. Bonaventure's *Life of St. Francis.*
3. Gerard O'Connell, "Pope Francis, at Site of First Nativity Scene, Issues Letter on the Importance of the Crèche," *America: The Jesuit Review,* December 1, 2019.
4. From *The Coming of the Prince of Peace* found at https://books.google.com/books ?id=0atGAQAAMAAJ&printsec=frontcover&source=gbs_ge_summary_r&cad=0 #v=onepage&q&f=false.
5. The poem "The Work of Christmas" is excerpted from Howard Thurman's *The Mood of Christmas and Other Celebrations* and is used by permission of Friends United Press. All rights reserved. https://bookstore.friendsunitedmeeting.org /collections/howard-thurman/products/mood-of-christmas-and-other-celebrations -the.
6. Cecil Frances Alexander, "Once in Royal David's City," in *Hymns for Little Children,* 25th ed. (London: J. Masters, 1848).
7. "Christmas," in *An Episcopal Dictionary of the Church,* edited by Don Armentrout and Robert Boak Slocum (New York: Church Publishing, 1999).]

BENEDICTION: MAY WONDERS NEVER CEASE

1. https://www.episcopalnewsservice.org/2021/09/21/presiding-bishop-calls-for-church -reformation-in-the-way-of-jesus-at-house-of-bishops-meeting/.

PRAYERS,
MEMORIES & NOTES

ABOUT THE AUTHOR

BONNIE SMITH WHITEHOUSE, PhD, is a writer and professor who studies storytelling, creativity, contemplation, and wonder. She is the author of Nautilus Award–winner *Afoot and Lighthearted: A Journal for Mindful Walking* and *Kickstart Creativity: 50 Prompted Cards to Spark Inspiration*. A lifelong Episcopalian, she has spent the last twenty years as a lay leader of St. Augustine's Episcopal Chapel at Vanderbilt University. Bonnie is professor of English and director of the honors program at Belmont University, and she lives in Nashville with her family.